Hope & GLORY

Hope & GLORY

Rugby League in Thatcher's Britain

Anthony Broxton

pitch

First published by Pitch Publishing, 2023

Pitch Publishing
A2 Yeoman Gate
Yeoman Way
Worthing
Sussex
BN13 3QZ
www.pitchpublishing.co.uk
info@pitchpublishing.co.uk

A CIP catalogue record is available for this book from the British Library.

ISBN 978 1 80150 455 3

Typesetting and origination by Pitch Publishing

Printed and bound in Great Britain by TJ Books, Padstow

Contents

For my Grandad, who taught me how to document the greatest game.

BRITISH RUGBY LEAGUE in the 1970s. A northern game watched by northern people. A sport where the top players had been to the same school, did the same jobs and drank in the same pubs as their spectators. No fixed salaries, no contracts and no security. A sport that prided itself on economic equality where the star half-back earned as much as the forwards who did the 'donkey work'. An honest game respected around the country for its toughness, where players would break a leg and try and play the ball rather than turn over possession. The sport of Eddie Waring, the 'national treasure' who introduced the coal miners of the north to the housewives of Surbiton. An insiders' game run by committees and traditions where the power brokers had earned their stripes doing the hard yards on the pitch themselves. A rebellious sport chained to its geography in the north, where clubs were the physical embodiment of the industries that had grown up around it. A sport that was discriminated against and banned in the armed forces, where playing for just one minute could have you banned from playing the other code for life. A place where women were seen on the terraces but not heard in boardrooms or changing rooms. Television coverage that usually amounted to showing the second-half highlights of a match on *Grandstand* a few times a year. A game misunderstood by outsiders, described by comedians on television as a remarkably 'stupid game' played by a 'muddied lot of half-drunk idiots'. A place where Australians were banned from playing and ideas of 'British exceptionalism' still ruled. No shirt sponsorship, no national advertising, no presence outside the areas where it had been forged after the Industrial Revolution. A newspaper world that still printed northern and southern editions of papers and rarely put rugby league in either. A sport which seemed unprepared for the competition and demands of the new decade that Thatcherism promised to bring.

Introduction
From Thatcher to Brexit

AS BRITAIN went to the polls in the 2019 general election, Boris Johnson knew he needed to do something remarkable to 'Get Brexit Done'. In the past, the great election winners have won big by reaching out to people who are not their natural supporters. In 1945, Clement Attlee reassured Conservative voters in the Home Counties that he was not a revolutionary figure. In the 1980s, Margaret Thatcher tapped into the working-class aspirations of 'Essex Man', while Tony Blair reached out to middle England's 'Mondeo Man' to pave his path to victory in 1997. But while those winners all looked to the south for new support, Boris Johnson decided to go north. And to the surprise of many, he turned to the last people on Earth expected to determine the outcome of general elections: rugby league supporters.

When the Brexit vote occurred in 2016, there were many commentators and politicians who were shocked to find that they no longer understood the country they lived in. In the aftermath of the referendum, there was much discussion about the people who lived in the rugby league towns and what had happened to those areas since the end of the Thatcher Years. In the intervening years there has been much written about who these people are and where they fit into the nation's story. But perhaps the clearest lesson to draw is that we still don't fully understand what happened in the north in the 1980s. And while people are naturally drawn to the idea of things being done to people during the Thatcher Years that were beyond their control, the story of rugby league shows there is a richer, more nuanced and complex tale to tell.

Hope and Glory is the story of the profound change that came over rugby league in the 1980s and early 90s that was as wide-ranging and disorientating as any in the game's history. Thatcher's Britain embodies the moment when the working class of the old industrial world crumbled under the weight of global competition and the free market. The levels of unemployment that followed, the highest since the 1930s, impacted rugby league towns as hard as any recession in any part of western Europe.

The people who were once the bedrock of plans to build a new Britain – the miners, the steelworkers, the glassmakers, the carmakers, the dockers – were advised to 'get on their bike' and look for different jobs. The changes in trade union legislation dramatically reduced their ability to fight back and an old way of life slowly vanished. The central tenets of the post-war working-class life – the council estate, the Labour club, the seaside holiday resort – were in rapid decline. It seemed inevitable that the rugby league clubs that had surrounded them would join them as a monument to a lost golden age.

Yet far from accelerating the decline, the 1980s was the decade when rugby league fought back. Long before the advent of football's Premier League, clubs turned fans into consumers, managers into coaches and part-time players into superstar professionals. The Australian influence advanced the British game at such lightning speed, attracting more spectators, more sponsors and more money, that watching a match in 1980 and 1995 was like watching games from different planets. As the sport increasingly crossed over into the realms of entertainment, the business conditions switched decisively in favour of the risk-takers at the expense of the traditional collectivised way of running things.

This book does not detail the matches, the statistics and the league tables that made up rugby league in the 80s and 90s. Instead, this is the story about the idea of rugby league in the hearts and minds of the people that loved it and those that never watched a game in their life. It is the story of a decade where ideas mattered, where, despite the apparent success of Thatcherite ideas and politics, nothing appeared set in stone. It is the story of a country that was coming to terms with a profound industrial change and was uncertain about where the future lay.

It is the story of ideas of the editors, the journalists, the referees and the administrators who believed that another future was possible. It was a battle of ideas that raged across the game, not just in the boardrooms and changing rooms of each club, but in newspaper offices, Labour clubs and advertising agencies. It is about the physical reshaping of rugby league's image, from how the pundits talked about it and how the cameras filmed it, to how the creative industries made posters about it. It is the story of the people who challenged the traditional hierarchies to create a new game that was more open and more accessible to all.

As rugby league remains the subject of much intense debate in the public imagination, *Hope and Glory* revisits the same issues that took hold of another generation of working-class men and women a generation ago. Like all historical accounts of the 1980s, there are winners and losers from a decade that split the nation in two. Forty years on, rugby league is still coming to terms with the consequences of Thatcher's Britain whether we like it or not.

Above all it is the story of ambition, and of ambitious players who began to think of themselves as brands and adopted phrases that would have been, just a few years prior, more familiar in a FTSE 100 board meeting than a changing room. It's about a realisation that players could be sold to the mass public at a time of rising celebrity culture, that meant by the 1990s you were more likely to find a rugby league player in the VIP section of the Hacienda than in a working men's club. It is a story about hope, hope that rugby league could replace football as the national game. But also a hope that one day communities that had lost everything could be at the centre of industrial and economic life once again.

It is a snapshot of a period where people genuinely believed that rugby league was, as Martin Offiah put it, in 'the big time'. It was a brief period when anything seemed possible and, more often than not, probable. Such moments in time do not appear too often in a sport that is so used to being the underdog.

Anthony Broxton
May 2023

PART ONE: ILLUSIONS

Chapter 1

Decline

AS BRITAIN approached the end of the 1970s, there was much talk about the managed decline of a once-great powerhouse. Debts had spiralled out of control and as the creditors came knocking at the door, people wondered just how far and how fast things had fallen. In the pubs and clubs of the North West, people traded stories of former glories and wondered just how they had become the 'sick man' of English rugby. And then, in April 1980, the inevitable finally happened. Wigan RL were relegated to the Second Division.

Wigan's descent from Cup Kings of the 1960s to the minnows of the sport made an appealing story for journalists seeking symbols of British decline. In the post-war years, Wigan had prided themselves on scouring all corners of the globe to bring the best and most talented athletes to Central Park. Over nine months in the 1940s, it was calculated that over one million people had watched the cherry and whites play across the country as they established themselves as the dominant force in the game. In one month alone in the 1950s the club played three home games to crowds of over 40,000. It put them on a par with the great northern football teams such as Manchester United, Liverpool and Everton.

By the late 1970s, the club didn't often feature in the national news pages. But the story of their relegation was different. London editors at *The Observer* sent special news reporters up north to unpick the story of the club's decline. The slide towards the bottom had been slow and painful. Attendances dropped and the superstars that had once packed out the terraces, such as Billy Boston and Eric Ashton, were replaced by mere mortals. Over time the better players from the local area were signed up by Widnes, Warrington and St Helens. The blame for the loss of talent was aimed squarely at the directors who seemed powerless to stem the flow.

'They began to lose credibility. They began to lose friends,' argued the *Wigan Observer* editor Jack Winstanley. And it was the little things that the club got wrong, beginning with their failed relationship with the media, that soon added to the big things: 'The club does not appreciate the value of free publicity.' Winstanley noted 'the dearth of national press coverage being especially noticeable' over the 70s. With a decline in standards came a retreat into themselves. Isolationist, the club had lost its grip on the game and the game was all the worse for it.

Within the town itself there was a mixture of shock and sadness at the turning of events. 'Badly sickening' was the verdict of the club's head groundsman Billy Mitchell who, after 29 years looking after the pitch, had taken the relegation harder than anyone else. Mitchell was 'reckoned to be the finest groundsman in rugby league'. He took his craft seriously and held 16 diplomas in various aspects of agriculture. Such was his reputation that the ground staff at Wembley Stadium once asked his advice to help them with the famous pitch.

And in the days following the result, locals came up to him everywhere he went, asking him for pieces of the turf as souvenirs. 'I can't go to a pub or a club, even the church and they're all asking me when we're selling off the ground,' he told *The Observer*. In the Royal Oak pub, journalists found fans congregated to drown their sorrows, where a 'combative middle-aged blonde' reflected on the club's decline: 'We've flogged good lads, and then they've bought trash. Some of them couldn't catch a bus.' Lodged between their coverage of the Iranian Embassy crisis and a diplomatic fight over lamb quotas in Europe, a photographer for *The Observer* captured the disconsolate-looking Wigan captain George Fairbairn on the banks of the 'infamous' Wigan Pier. The story captured the mood: 'If a town's well-being is related to the success of its sporting heroes, Wigan is in deep trouble.'

* * *

Wigan rugby's decline appeared to mirror wider changes in both the working class and the political landscape in the late 1970s. At some point in the decade, the words 'decline' and 'declinism' had become central to the debates about Britain's place in the world. To those on the political right, these described the loss of power and influence since the retreat of the Empire after the Second World War. To the left, it was the inability to maintain levels of full employment and deliver on the promises of a more affluent and equal society.

At the 1979 general election, the Conservative leader Margaret Thatcher tapped into the feeling of decline by arguing that it was the sign of a post-war consensus that's time had come to an end. 'Travel round our towns and cities and see the shabby scars of Labour Britain, open and unhealing,' she said in one speech. The eagerness for change in the country was enough to give her a landslide election victory on the biggest swing since 1945. Privately, a leaked memo from the British ambassador to Washington captured the loss of hope in the corridors of power: 'You only have to move around western Europe nowadays to realise how poor and unproud the British have become in relation to their neighbours. It shows in the look of our towns.'

Wigan was thought to be one of the towns that had been left behind by Britain's decline in the post-war years. For journalists, writers, commentators, politicians and historians, Wigan has often been the place where people go to try and tell the story about the state of the British nation. As some historians have argued, it is 'less a place' and more a 'state of mind in the British psyche'. When the travel writer H.V. Morton visited the town in the 1920s for his book *In Search of England*, he observed how the music-hall joke about 'Wigan Pier' was enough to make the audience laugh: 'Wigan, to millions of people, who have never seen and never will see the town, represents the apex of the world's pyramid of gloom.'

'Wigan has been picked on as a symbol of the ugliness of the industrial areas,' said George Orwell after he spent a few weeks in the town for his book *The Road to Wigan Pier.* Orwell could have found a similar story in London, the North East or Yorkshire, but he chose Wigan because of its emotive connotations with the public. The success of his book, within intellectual circles, made Wigan the symbol of the 1930s, of the social deprivation, poverty and slum housing that came with it.

The success of the rugby league club in the 1950s and 60s was gradually able to chip away at those attitudes, usually formed by outsiders, who had little affinity with the town. One of the media organisations that heard about the team was the popular photography magazine *Picture Post.* At its peak the magazine used photography to communicate a range of social issues to one in three of the British population each week. And in 1950 they found themselves running a special feature on Wigan as the 'powerhouse' of British sport: 'Synonymous in most people's minds with supremacy in the world of Rugby League football.'

Wigan's success in the rugby league world had coincided with the post-war boom in employment and leisure that made live sport the favourite pastime of the working people. In the immediate post-war years, sports like rugby league had grown because they were catering for a population with full employment and money to spend at the weekend. The total crowds for rugby league matches reached almost seven million in the 1949/50 season, which marked a post-war high. The nationalisation of the coal industry had brought jobs back to many rugby league towns, while the development of housing and the welfare state gave people the freedom to enjoy their time at the weekends.

But by the 1970s the much-mythologised golden age was fast becoming a distant dream. The securities of employment disappeared, and Wigan was hit particularly hard by the coal cuts enacted under Harold Wilson's government. Unemployment reached levels not seen since the 1930s and when people talked about British decline, they found themselves back in Wigan to try and understand what had happened to the working class in the post-war years. For left-wing writers such as Jeremy Seabrook, Wigan was the embodiment of what had gone wrong in the 1970s. The loss of the coal industry had seen the population struggling to find a purpose and identity. He lamented how the new jobs in factories and manufacturing had left people feeling alienated. Wigan had been built on the physical strength of its population but, suddenly, that strength was no longer required or desired. It had no outlet. 'The sense of loss,' Seabrook concluded, 'was overwhelming.'

It was a theme that the popular American travel writer Paul Theroux returned to when he visited the town at the beginning of the 80s. He wrote of a 'lifeless' town centre where fear of working down the mines had been replaced by a different fear: 'Not the blackened factory chimneys and the smoke and the slag-heaps and the racket of the machines; it was the empty chimneys and the clear air and the grass growing on slag-heaps and the great silence.' Everybody who appeared to have a view on the decline of Britain placed Wigan as a central part of that story. It seemed inevitable that when their rugby league side was relegated, they would be the next to disappear.

* * *

Wigan rugby's decline did not just mirror the changes in the industrial working class in the 1970s. It also symbolised the problems that every rugby league town faced. In the beginning there had been just one code of rugby. But in 1895 representatives from the northern clubs met at the George Hotel in Huddersfield and broke from the Rugby Football Union (RFU) to form a northern game. Later to become known as rugby league, the rebel clubs had wanted to be able to compensate players who took time off work to play for their club (known as 'broken time') or who became injured through playing the game.

After the split, league created a sport that mirrored the heavy industries that emerged from the time of the Industrial Revolution. League became part of a working-class culture that was intrinsically Labour – played out across the coalfields of Lancashire and Yorkshire, in the weapon and shipbuilding plants of Cumbria, by the docks in Hull, and the heavy industries of Warrington, Widnes and St Helens. The sort of towns where the people often said 'a monkey in a red rosette could win here'.

The game firmly established itself in those areas as a competitive rival to football and cricket as the leisure pursuit of the manual worker. But as the author Geoffrey Nicholson identified in his book *The Professionals*, rugby league remained wedded to its communities in a way that other sports did not. Clubs often belonged to the town with most of the team working alongside the supporters in the workplaces, drinking in the same pubs and sending their children to the same schools: 'Rugby league doesn't lift a man out of his environment as soccer does.'

In the *Picture Post* feature on Wigan in the 1950s, the journalists examined how the players and the fans were united by their class: 'The Saturday afternoon stars are ordinary workmen in the week.' Players were workers by day and heroes by night. In the neighbouring town of St Helens, players such as Vince Karalius admitted that it was sometimes difficult to separate the two roles: 'If you talk to the blokes the boss thinks you're idle, and if you don't talk to them he thinks you're big-headed,' he told the *Sunday Times*.

Pride in the local side as an extension of your class was something that Richard Hoggart referred to in his hugely influential book on working-class life *The Uses of Literacy*. Hoggart had been one of the 'crowds of lads' who took to the streets of Hunslet after they had won the Challenge Cup in 1934. He watched the players return with the cup on 'top of a charabanc', following them from pub to pub and 'staying out hours after their bedtime for the excitement of seeing their local champions'. When the scene was recounted some decades later, rugby league was identified as the most 'important element in the group life' of the town – as important to the daily conversation as sex or the royal family. It was part of a working-class culture that was intrinsically local, from the local butchers and grocers to the bakers and scrap merchants. But by the 1970s, Hoggart was among the many who questioned whether the ties that bound working-class people would survive.

As early as 1964, there were already outsiders writing about the decline of rugby league. Arthur Hopcroft was a sports writer who would become well known for TV play adaptations of *Tinker Tailor Soldier Spy* and *Bleak House*. As a football writer, he had written one of the definitive books on the game in the 60s, *The Football Man*, which looked thoughtfully at the culture of the football manager. And when he was tasked with looking at rugby league for a major *Sunday Times* magazine feature, he had found it to be a sport of the past: 'Rugby league men give the impression that they know they are tethered somewhere back in the social evolution.' Hopcroft concluded that rugby league was played on grounds 'bounded by the heyday of heavy industry; a railway line on one side, the eyeless wall of some tired-out old mill, the colour of dried blood'.

While Hopcroft angered some within the game with his stereotyped view, the economic changes were real and the decline in people watching the sport emphasised what had been lost. Overall the game lost over one and a half million spectators from 1959 to 1964 and those running the sport struggled to find a solution to turn it around.

One of the first clubs that became the symbol of the decline was Bradford Northern. Bradford had been one of the founding members of the game and the first team to appear in three successive Challenge Cup finals, in the 1940s. In the 50s, their Odsal Stadium had been dubbed the 'Wembley of the North' after it hosted the best-attended game in the sport's history. Officially there were 102,569 packed in to see a monumental Warrington win, but there were a lot more as gates had been opened to avoid a crush outside.

However, just nine years later the support for the game in the area had fallen off a cliff. Nobody living in Bradford talked about rugby league. In one fixture in November 1963, just 324 diehards braved torrential rain and wind to watch Northern play a match against Barrow. The decline had profound cash implications for the club, which was running a deficit and was soon forced to disband because it could no longer afford to put players on the pitch. In the battle for leisure time, it was clear that rugby league was losing ground. A few days after Bradford reached their lowest ebb, there was a symbol of the shift right on their doorstep. In December 1963 the city was gripped by the arrival of The Beatles at the Gaumont Cinema where they were performing on their UK tour. As the new generation of consumers turned towards different leisure pursuits from their parents, rugby league wondered how it could win them back.

Many arguments were put forward to explain rugby league's declining crowd numbers. As the BBC commentator Eddie Waring acknowledged in the *Rugby League Yearbook*, the culture shift resulting from changes in technology, and consumer goods meant they were probably never coming back. In the immediate post-war period, 'Everything was on ration, so sport was the only free outlet,' he argued. 'Now there are 17 million cars in England, every electrical appliance imaginable, holidays abroad, new houses, changing fashions in clothes, people eating out and so many other things that have attired the pattern of life.' Others stretched to even more dramatic conclusions. Some blamed the advent of central heating – one of the arguments doing the rounds at Bradford was that people had only come to watch in the 1950s because it was cheaper and warmer to visit Odsal with the packed crowds than it was to heat the house.

One Doncaster fan wrote to the *Rugby Leaguer,* the sport's most prominent weekly newspaper, to urge the game to join the 'jet-set' age and modernise the offer to supporters: 'It is like stepping back 40 years, with corrugated metal fences, patched up wooden stands, broken down terracing and a general look which has varied little since the Second World War.' By the end of the 1960s, there was still a sense that the game's leadership was managing a decline into irrelevance. Writers in the *Rugby Leaguer* talked about how Britain had moved into a new age and left the sport behind: 'This is the age of the cabaret club, the discotheque, colour television and the sports car.' League administrators, by contrast, offered 'a pint under the bar and a warmed-up meat pie' to entice people in.

Wigan were one of the clubs that had resisted the idea that you needed to offer something else to supporters beyond the events on the pitch. At a shareholders' meeting, one director scoffed at the idea that 'bingo and the like' would be able to save the game. By the early 70s, the *Rugby Leaguer* had decided to act by launching a study into what had gone wrong with the sport over the period. First, in a dramatic front-page editorial, the paper called for a 'halt to the massive slide' after they calculated that the game had lost over 200,000 more spectators in just a few months. Then, in block capitals, they called on the game to act: 'IN THE PAST THREE SEASONS, MORE THAN HALF A MILLION FANS HAVE BEEN LOST TO THE GAME – AND THAT'S ONLY IN LEAGUE MATCHES – THE SLIDE MUST BE STOPPED'.

* * *

Those at the top of the RFL admitted that they no longer had the answers. 'We try hard,' said long-serving secretary Bill Fallowfield. 'But your guess is as good as mine as to why the bloody public doesn't come.' After a decade of decline in the 1960s, administrators were increasingly desperate to find a solution to their problems. One suggestion had been to bring in management consultants to try and identify potential solutions to the decline. Consultancy had become a buzzword across British industry after US management consultants had followed leading US companies into Europe. The expansion of McKinsey across British industry was well known, after they did work for firms such as Cadbury, Tate & Lyle and Rolls-Royce. In the public sector, British Rail, the Bank of England and the Post Office employed McKinsey for advice about restructuring.

Rugby league couldn't afford McKinsey. Instead, they turned to a local Manchester firm to advise on how they could reimagine the sport for the 1980s. John Caine Associates of Manchester agreed to a £3,000-a-year consultancy to equip the game for the demands of the new age. They began by surveying club owners to gather their opinions and there was great anticipation about what Caine could deliver. The *Rugby Leaguer* threw its weight behind the researchers, urging them to imagine selling the game like a loaf of bread. The modern supporter was affluent, owned a car and had 'the wife nagging him to go shopping' each weekend. Therefore, the sport had to offer 'more than a splinter-ridden seat and a clinker terrace to draw him to the match'.

Quickly dubbed the 'Manchester Wizkid' by his supporters in the media, Caine was soon frustrated by the 'inexplicable reluctance' of Bill Fallowfield to answer letters on the 'important matters'. Without guidance from the top, Caine had free rein to develop a set of radical proposals to change the face of the sport. And when he presented the findings to the RL Council – the game's ruling body – he refused to hold back his criticisms of the failure of leadership. Caine began by unpicking the dwindling media profile, which he blamed on the leadership's lack of resources and urgency: 'It is not sufficient for the press and others to be told that they were too busy to answer telephone calls.' The sport had little support from friends at the BBC either: 'The direction of the cameras and overall style of the programme' promoted a sense of 'slag heap and drizzle' every time a viewer tuned in.

Caine recommended that the clubs streamline, create a smaller governing body and appoint an outside chairman to manage the game's affairs. The report recommended creating a new two-division structure and converting rugby league to a Sunday sport to differentiate it from football. To reverse the slow-paced nature of the game, he proposed reducing the number of players on the pitch to 11 to promote attacking play. Caine concluded that the 'single-minded, loyal supporter' was 'rapidly disappearing' and that the only way the game could survive into the 1980s would be to appeal to the 'better-off, more mobile, more sophisticated and consequently more discriminating generation'.

The Caine Report was meant to set the sport up for the demands of a changing working class with different demands on leisure time. But it proved to be too controversial to implement. Embroiled in a debate about the role of commentator Eddie Waring at the BBC, Fallowfield quickly engineered a confidence vote in his leadership before Caine could deliver a follow-up report and a plan to enact the changes. While the sport did move to two divisions, the more radical aspects around the coverage and presentation of the game were ignored. Caine found that the clubs and the administrators were unwilling to support him, particularly in his battle with the BBC. Finally, in April 1972, the RL Council decided it no longer wanted the consultancy involved in the game and ended the contract. The RFL, it seemed, was powerless to address the problems that its own research had identified.

* * *

Nowhere had the shift in youth culture been more apparent than in Wigan. Young people had packed the terraces at Central Park in the 1950s and 60s, making its famous 'hen pen' a magnet for children and teenagers to watch their idols play each week. But by the 70s, the young people in the ground had all but vanished and many of them were using their pocket money elsewhere. In 1973, the first all-night session of Northern Soul took place at Wigan Casino where it would go on to become a magnet for young people across the country. The term Northern Soul was coined by writer Dave Godin, when he noticed northern football fans in his London record shop asking for stuff nobody had heard of.

And the casino drew a very different crowd than the ones who had gone to pubs and rugby league matches in the 1950s. For young people such as Paul Mason, it was about creating a space where people could be liberated from the day-to-day realities of industrial work. It had, he recalled, 'athletic dance, sleek fashion and illegal stimulants' that gave people the opportunity to express themselves. While workers had previously used their weekends to stand in unison on the open terraces of the rugby grounds, the casino allowed them to dance in unison in the darkness of the nightclub. The emergence of a counter-culture was captured by an infamous Granada documentary which intercut imagery of the town's industrial past with the energy and dynamism of the scene.

Wigan rugby league didn't even try and win over those young people in the 1970s. The club had long resisted the idea that it should offer entertainment on top of the action on the pitch to attract supporters. But their outdated image could be summed up by how they rebuilt the team's post-match social club. Jack Winstanley, who had covered the club for decades in the *Wigan Observer*, was angry at their feeble attempts to build a new bar within the ground: 'Instead of equipping the finest ground in the game with the finest facilities in the game, they built a glorified "working men's club",' he wrote. And while some teams such as Salford and Warrington had built highly profitable social clubs that overlooked the ground, 'The only window in the Wigan club overlooking the pitch is in the gent's toilet.'

Wigan lived off its historic reputation for much of the 70s, but just as Bradford had found the decade before, there was always going to be a financial reckoning. Wigan's relegation in 1980 had economic consequences for the club as well as emotional ones. As the club's debt teetered towards £100,000, rumours began to spread throughout the town that Central Park would be sold off to the football side, Wigan Athletic. Fearing the worst, two club directors quit citing 'business reasons' as their motivation for leaving. Harry Gostelow, the Wigan chairman who had presided over the club's decline, was tasked with finding new investors to join the board.

Gostelow had become a much-maligned figure in the town. A self-employed builder, he had his own problems to deal with in early 1980 when his firm was accused of installing faulty gas fires that were 'in a highly dangerous condition when a gas board official made an inspection'. The *Wigan Observer* reported how Gostelow admitted to six offences relating to faulty installations at three houses in the town. There was little chance of local businesses coming on board with the club in the Second Division. The great sell-off of the club's assets seemed inevitable.

But when Gostelow was looking for new investors to join the board, people kept telling him to approach a small business owner by the name of Maurice Lindsay. Lindsay had been one of the many young people who had travelled to Wigan from Bolton in the 1950s to stand in the 'hen pen'. Each fortnight he would return to Wigan and look at the impact on the people around him of a successful rugby league team. He knew that if Wigan won, more coal would be produced, more baked bean tins would be made in the Heinz factory, and more money would be put in the tills of the pubs. It impacted the pride of the town and the way that people went about their work.

As a teenager, Lindsay was so desperate to find a way to watch Wigan in the Challenge Cup Final that he took a job as a porter with British Rail. The magic of Wembley and the romance of it had never left Lindsay, but after a spate of defeats in the 60s, Wigan's trips to the twin towers dried up. Lindsay instead focused on building a business and setting up links with rugby league clubs across the North West. He popped up everywhere in rugby league circles in the 70s. A self-made entrepreneur who made a fortune hiring out construction equipment, Lindsay often used rugby league to promote his business ends. In an era when shirt sponsorship of league clubs was still forbidden, he found a way around it by plastering 'Transkabin' – the name of his firm – all over the shirts oflocal amateur club Wigan St Patricks instead.

In a sport with few rich benefactors, he was soon in demand, sponsoring man-of-the-match prizes at Salford and Warrington. There, he got to know the St Helens great Alex Murphy, and the pair could often be found putting the world to rights in saunas and hotel bars across the North West. But by the time Lindsay watched Wigan matches from the executive boxes in the late 1970s, the spirit he had witnessed on the terraces as a child had vanished.

What frustrated Lindsay was that the club had accepted its decline. After each defeat, he watched as the ageing businessmen poured the whisky and champagne for each other. Downstairs, tucked away in a tea room, the players made do with warm beer. The players were not treated as stars and there was no appetite to find a solution. Above all, the board had stopped communicating with the fans. In desperate need of some cash, Gostelow made Lindsay an offer to come on the board of directors. Lindsay was advised by his friends not to bother sinking money into a club that was beyond repair. But while Lindsay was a ruthless businessman with little sympathy for lame ducks, he was also, to his very fingertips, a gambler.

As a child on the Central Park terraces, he had been as amazed by the hustlers and the bookmakers – who he called the 'spivs' – as he had been by the players. Lindsay became an on-course bookmaker himself. As part of the mythology he created around himself, he framed himself as the small-time bookmaker fighting it out with Ladbrokes, the Tote and William Hill each week. But there was also a subtle truth to it. To be successful, he had to quickly master the art of making calculations in an instant, a trait that was all too rare in rugby league circles. At that moment, just days before Wigan were relegated to the Second Division, he decided that Wigan was still worth a punt.

Within hours of his appointment, he was already working with the media and framing a new narrative in his direction. The *Wigan*

Observer put his picture on the front page and ran an interview where he promised to put the pride back in the shirt. 'Any effort I can make to improve the club's fortunes will be made,' he revealed. 'I am not afraid of a struggle.' He even appeared to embrace the dreaded relegation that had long been feared by everyone else in the town: 'If Wigan go down it is not the end of the world and if it means hard work to get back up then let's get to it.'

* * *

The decline of Wigan was part of a wider trend in which the bigger clubs had felt that they had lost control and power over the decision-making in the sport. But the consequence of this was that the 1970s became one of the most equal and highly contested decades in the sport's history. Rugby league culture was dominated more than anything by its supporters' addiction and obsession with cup tournaments. Cups had been at the heart of British sporting life in the post-war years. 'Instant death,' argued Ray French in *Simply the Best*, is what appealed to supporters. 'They like to go to a match where it is all or nothing.'

In the 70s the rugby league season could be broken up into four different distinct phases to ensure that every team had something to play for at any given time. The season kicked off with the Yorkshire and Lancashire Cup, which was soon followed by the John Player Special (JPS) Trophy that ran through the autumn, leading to a final in January to kick off the New Year. Both were seen as important precursors to the main event of the season which was the Challenge Cup. This ran from January to May and drew in most of the media attention, and the prospect of playing at Wembley was the dream of every player who ever picked up a rugby ball.

Then after the climax of the Challenge Cup, the top eight sides competed for the Premiership trophy to round off the season.

And in between all the knock-out fixtures was a 30-game league season to determine who the champions were. It meant that if you were fortunate enough to play in every round of every competition, you could be involved in over 50 matches each season. More cup games suited everybody. The clubs had opportunities to make extra gate revenue while the administrators had the opportunity to sell each one to a different sponsor.

And for all the talk of decline and the reduced national profile, the sport had never been as competitive and equal in sharing out the trophies amongst its clubs. Over that decade, if you supported Castleford, Leigh, St Helens, Featherstone, Warrington, Widnes or Leeds, you saw your side lift the Challenge Cup. If you supported Dewsbury, Salford or Hull KR, you watched as your team lifted the Championship title. Bradford fans enjoyed a Premiership win, while strugglers Wigan and Workington could point to victories in the Lancashire Cup. Halifax fans saw their side win a JPS Trophy. Even Bramley enjoyed a rare moment in the spotlight when they lifted the BBC Floodlit Trophy, before it was axed. And while all those clubs tasted some success, other smaller clubs came very close to doing so. Swinton, Blackpool, Rochdale and York participated in a major final in the decade.

But when Maurice Lindsay looked around the game for a side that he could model a potential Wigan revival on, he was inevitably drawn to Humberside. Just as Wigan had grown on the back of coal nationalisation after 1945, Hull's fishing industry had been pinpointed as an area for expansion to ship fish exports to Britain and the rest of the world. At one point in the 1960s, there had been over 8,000 trawlermen working out of Hull, with economists calculating that three times that figure earned a living off the back of the fishing industry. Hull was one of the world's biggest fishing harbours and by 1970 its people landed 197,000 tonnes of fish a year.

Fishing was integral to both the economy and the identity of the local population. Deep-sea trawling was respected as one of the most dangerous jobs in the world. Locals used to argue they were much tougher than the mythologised coal miners in Yorkshire and Lancashire. On Humberside, workers would say that four fishermen died at sea for every miner killed in an accident. It is estimated that more than 6,000 trawlermen from Hull alone died between 1835 and 1980.

The area was also famous for its rugby league team. Hessle Road, where Hull's trawlermen and families lived, was where Hull FC developed a club that became one of the biggest names in the sport. The workers around the area would spend weeks away at sea and, upon their return, fill the pubs and restaurants with their bulging pay packets. They would then head straight for Hull's notorious home ground, the Boulevard. Johnny Whiteley was a Hull legend who had been central to the team's success in the 1950s. He recalled how fans 'would come down the North Sea, flat out, to catch the tide for the match singing "Old Faithful"', which was the club's anthem.

In the 1960s, one of the most famous residents of Hessle Road was Lillian Bilocca, who led a women's movement known as the 'headscarf revolutionaries', to improve safety at sea after a tragic accident had killed local workers. The 70s would, however, change debates around fishing from issues of safety to issues of survival. Just as the coal industry had begun to decline in areas like Wigan, the fishing industry was hammered in Hull by Britain's entry into the European Economic Community (EEC) in 1973. This had flooded the market with cheap frozen fish. The much-reviled policy had been the subject of considerable debate in Britain in the 1970s. But it had been put together before Britain entered and gave the country very little control over its fishing quotas.

In the mid-1970s, the public had been gripped by a diplomatic stand-off between Britain and Iceland over the so-called 'Cod Wars'. The Labour government, led by Jim Callaghan, tasked the Royal Navy with protecting British trawlers against the Icelandic boats who wanted to fish in the same waters. As a result, tensions between the two countries began to rise. But when the Icelandic government threatened to withdraw from NATO as a retaliation, the British government had little option but to compromise.

The trade-off was not a hugely significant one for the British economy as it accepted the inevitable decline of the fishing industry. But in places like Hull, Grimsby and Peterhead, it was a seismic blow to their industries and their identity. And the debate over fish and the fortunes of Hull as a fishing port symbolised Britain's decline in some quarters. Journalists, commentators and politicians soon started talking about the great betrayal of Humberside. For the *Daily Mail*, the fish workers had been 'sold down the river', the innocent victims of 'the most abjectly disgraceful surrender of traditional rights in our island's seafaring history'.

The blame was squared at the EEC 'bureaucrats' who had told them 'where and when they can fish, and how much they can catch even in British waters'. Within the space of a decade, exports had been massively reduced. By 1980, just 15,000 tonnes of fish came from Hull. As the industry declined, a young photographer called Alec Gill captured the changing fortunes of working-class people on Hessle Road as the community was slowly broken up. As people left the squalor of housing that had been left to rot, the community spread out across new housing estates with the offer of inside toilets and hot running water.

Hull FC was not expected to survive those wider economic changes. In the mid-1970s, they had become a symbol for the game's ills when they infamously drew in a crowd of just 721 people for a match against Huyton. They too were relegated to the Second

Division towards the end of the 70s. Yet somehow the club had been able to defy the logic of managed decline and revitalise their fortunes both on and off the pitch. A new coach in Arthur Bunting proved to be the spark that reignited the city's passion for the black and whites when he brought in some old heads, such as Steve Norton, to play alongside players Vince Farrar, Charlie Stone, Sammy Lloyd and Paul Prendiville. Despite languishing in the Second Division, the club managed to reconnect with its supporters by playing attractive rugby league. When promotion to the First Division was secured in front of 12,000 people, the club sensed that it was on the cusp of a revival.

The supporters stuck around for the next few years as Hull assembled a Championship-winning side that took the league by storm. By the early 1980s, their turnaround was evident in the sheer number of people who wanted to watch them play. While historic clubs around the game struggled, Hull had become the talk of the city again. Within just 12 games of the 1979/80 season, almost 120,000 people had passed through their turnstiles, which was the highest attendance of the decade.

Hull's revival was boosted by their rivalry with their city neighbours Hull Kingston Rovers. KR had long lived in the shadow of their neighbours, waiting until the 1960s before appearing at Wembley for the first time. Formed in 1882 by a group of boilermakers, they played on a ground west of the city. Like their rivals, they had been relegated in the 1970s, and it proved the catalyst for a revival. The directors responded to the setback by signing several experienced players, including rugby league greats Neil Fox and Clive Sullivan. By the beginning of the new decade, the Humberside derby was the number-one fixture in the game. When *The Observer* football journalist Phil Shaw visited the city in 1980, he discovered that 'the youth are drawn to rugby league like wasps to a picnic'.

In the 60s, the sport had longed to see the giants of Lancashire, Wigan and St Helens battle it out in the Challenge Cup Final at Wembley. The pair met twice; once in 1961 and again in 1966, when Prime Minister Harold Wilson joined a record crowd inside the stadium to watch the heavyweight rivals Alex Murphy and Billy Boston face off against each other. There were more people in the ground in April 1966 to watch Wigan v St Helens than there were at the World Cup Final between England and West Germany a few months later. But by 1980 there was little doubt that the Humberside derby had now replaced it as the top rivalry in the sport. Those running the game dreamed of an all-Hull derby to generate the same kind of impact. And in 1980 it finally happened.

'Humberside is gripped by Wembley fever,' declared the *Rugby Leaguer* as supporters across the city queued in the middle of the night to buy the first train tickets when they went on sale. In the build-up, the *Hull Daily Mail* found that few people could speak of anything else in the pubs. One landlord found a way to cash in on the hype by painting two large arrows (one in black and white, one in red and white) pointing to two separate areas of the bar. A local hair salon offered supporters the option of coloured dye in their team's colours. 'It started off with people wanting either squares or stripes in their hair,' said the owner.

With Hull the subject of much debate in the 1970s as a symbol of British decline, the interest in the 1980 Challenge Cup Final went far beyond the sports pages. The *Daily Mirror* sent a special investigator to the area to capture the mood on the ground. They found that the players would face a rather 'gloomier homecoming' than usual with 'One in ten out of work' and 'Its unemployment record is among the worst in Britain.' Most significantly, reporters highlighted how nearly four-fifths of the local fishing industry had been wiped out: 'Empty docks and factories, shuttered shops and boarded-up stores stand as silent witnesses to a sad slump.'

At the same time, the success of the two rugby sides had given people a sense of pride and optimism for the future. One trawlerman, who had spent 21 years at sea, said the final was the catalyst to begin a new chapter of his life – 'I decided there was no way I could miss it' – so he spent his last pay packet on seven tickets for him, his wife and his children. Another supporter revealed how he had saved up all his earnings as a part-time barman to pay for a ticket. The BBC ran a special feature on the packed trains as they arrived at Euston station. 'Will the last person to leave,' a banner draped over a bridge on the A63 asked, 'please turn out the lights?' In front of the Queen Mother, who was the guest of honour, Hull KR lifted the trophy. But the organisers were the big winners. 'The attendance could easily have topped 100,000 had we been allowed,' admitted an RFL spokesperson.

The challenge for the 1980s was to foster the spirit of Humberside and spread it across the league. Over in Wigan, Maurice Lindsay studied Hull and wondered whether Wigan would ever make it back to Wembley at all. A few weeks into life as a director at the club, he was finding out how difficult it would be to enact any actual change. Initially, Lindsay found that his wealth didn't actually buy him any influence or power in the world of rugby league. Joining an unruly board of 12, alongside another young and ambitious businessman, Jack Robinson, the pair found the club still run by tradition, the 'rulebook' and hierarchies. Decisions were made collectively and often kicked into the long grass, meaning the lines of accountability were blurred. At his first board meeting, Lindsay began to propose some solutions to the problems they faced when he was interrupted mid-sentence and informed that his job as the most junior member was simply to pour the tea for the others.

Chapter 2

Image Problems

ONE FEBRUARY afternoon in 1978, the BBC *Grandstand* cameras were going to Yorkshire to cover an eagerly anticipated Challenge Cup tie between York and Warrington. The cup remained the jewel in the BBC's rugby league coverage and guaranteed the best audience figures. Since first taking to the air in October 1958, *Grandstand* had become a staple of the sports watchers' weekend, delivering everything from football results to gymnastics to horse racing, boxing and golf. Rugby league was often allocated a 50-minute slot in the packed four-hour broadcast and was its rare window into connecting with viewers outside its core audience.

But as the producers headed towards York, they heard the news that the game was off due to a frozen pitch. With Headingley in Leeds one of the only grounds in Britain fitted with undersoil heating, the BBC cameras decided to cover their match with Halifax instead. With an entire round of fixtures postponed due to frozen pitches, those wanting their rugby league fix tuned in to *Grandstand* for the afternoon. But as they did, something unusual happened. As the game kicked off, viewers noticed that the players were distracted. A collie dog had broken loose from its owner and ended up on the field of play. The game did not stop, and the dog was central to the viewers' eye. It ran alongside attackers who were attacking and came into the defensive line when others were defending. At one stage, the dog stood patiently at the side of a goal kicker as a crucial conversion was taken.

With the referee failing to halt the game, *Grandstand* producers knew they needed to address the issue for the viewers. One producer suggested that they have a bit of fun with it all. The word went up that they should zoom in the cameras on the dog and give him his own name and number. As the cup tie reached a dramatic conclusion, the words K. NINE appeared on the screen, in reference to the popular *Dr Who* character. The next day, the *Daily Mirror* ran a picture of K. Nine in action, declaring him the star of the show: 'The sport-loving pooch was the pick of the pack. His dogged display of dazzling runs had thousands of TV viewers howling with delight.'

The press managed to track down the owner, a local security guard who lived just a few yards away from Headingley. Like millions of others he had spotted the dog whilst watching the game: 'Hey, that's my Mac!' he shouted at the television. Only then was the story revealed: the owner had let him out for a walk and assumed he was playing in the street, until he switched the game on. The story proved popular with the tabloids, and within a few days, Mac was asked on to *Blue Peter*, the flagship teatime children's show where the story was retold to millions of viewers across the country. Mac was described as 'The collie dog who found instant fame when Eddie Waring gave him just as many mentions as the two-legged players.' In the aftermath of the events Waring briefed the press that it was the first time he had ever witnessed something like that at a game: 'He certainly knew when to keep onside.'

The story achieved cut-through on a national scale and was a feel-good story for a few weeks. But nobody at rugby league HQ was laughing. For those who were worried about the image of the game, they believed that it symbolised everything that had gone wrong with it in the 1970s. Nobody in the ground that day was able to take control of the situation, and nobody worried about what impact it would have on the spectators who had paid their hard-earned money. People within the game had long argued that the BBC treated the sport as a joke compared to its football, cricket and rugby union coverage and now they had the evidence. A spokesman for the RFL warned that the incident might well have 'set the game back years' in terms of credibility. And when people looked at who was to blame for making light of the situation, they turned to the person responsible for selling it to the world.

* * *

By the late 1970s, Eddie Waring had been on television for so long that he had become part of the very fabric of British cultural life. Emerging as the top rugby league columnist in the 1940s, Waring became the voice of sport when the BBC first began to show it regularly on television. Redefining the art of sports commentary, Waring's Dewsbury accent was a novelty in an era that predated *Coronation Street* and the kitchen-sink dramas of the 1960s. His catchphrases – such as 'he's off for an early bath' and 'the up and under' – soon became part of the national vocabulary. To the TV presenter Stuart Hall, Waring was the man who had taken the sport into the nation's living room: 'Waring sold rugby league in areas where it should never really have transgressed. He sold it to madams in Surbiton and High Court judges in Basingstoke.'

The RFL had not made Eddie Waring's job easy. In the 1950s, several clubs campaigned against cameras being used for fear of declining attendance. As the game lamented the loss of its golden age, television was the key factor in breaking up the traditional supporter bases. The television actor, and rugby league supporter, Colin Welland once argued that television was responsible for people no longer turning up to matches in person. In the 60s, Wigan had campaigned hard to prevent television cameras appearing at the ground. One member of the board, when arguing his case to a shareholder meeting in 1965, compared the club to a 'dumb animal' for eventually allowing the cameras in: 'Wigan's action is tantamount to selling one's soul to the devil for little or no gain at all.'

The game wasn't helped by how it physically looked on television either. The grounds built in the late 19th century were not set up for television. Some clubs had impacted the view by installing floodlights in front of stands. Other clubs refused to put cameras in front of the VIP spectators in the main stand, meaning that coverage was tilted from above. Others simply didn't have the money to build floodlights. One of the popular arguments of the time was why didn't the game have coverage like Twickenham had? But for the BBC, all their difficulties negotiating deals were offset by their personable and profitable relationship with Waring.

Waring was a key asset to the BBC beyond their rugby league coverage. As the commentator/referee/presenter on *It's a Knockout* – which regularly drew in audiences of 17 million – he acquired national treasure status. 'Uncle Eddie's' popularity enabled him to transcend the boundary between sport and light entertainment for much of the 1970s. He made guest appearances on *The Goodies* sketch show while impressionists such as Mike Yarwood knew that he was a reliable figure to satirise to guarantee a laugh each week. *Monty Python's Flying Circus* ridiculed him as a newsreader recounting famous historical battles, while the Warrington club comic Nicky Martyn even recorded his own tribute song: 'His accent's glaring … That's Eddie Waring!' Waring understood celebrity in a way that players he commentated on did not. The TV agency Bagenal Harvey represented some of the sports stars of the day, such as Denis Compton, Jimmy Greaves and Bobby Charlton. But the only rugby league person they had on their books was Waring.

The true sign of Waring's popularity within the country was the decision to feature him in the 1977 *Morecambe and Wise* Christmas show. The show was the programme that 'stopped the nation', and Waring slotted in alongside Barry Norman and Frank Bough for a remake of the cabaret song *There Is Nothing Like a Dame.* He was a cult figure with students, many of whom had never watched a rugby league game in person. Waring appreciation societies popped up in university towns, and he was even asked to speak at the Oxford Union. References to Waring cut across the popular culture of the country. In 1980, when the comedic duo Little and Large made a guest appearance presenting *Top of the Pops*, they joked that Eddie Waring would be the perfect person to do a cover of The Police's hit single 'De Do Do'.

Waring often divided opinion in rugby league circles, but his profile as a comedic figure led people to wonder where the boundaries between rugby league and *It's a Knockout* were drawn. In the mid-1970s, one rugby league supporter decided that the game had to do something radical to alter perceptions that it was a joke. The St Helens fan Michael Hevey launched a petition to express supporters' dismay at 'the manner in which rugby league is abused, exploited and misrepresented by the BBC'. Acquiring over 10,000 signatures, he aimed his anger at Waring, who was accused of turning the sport into a 'music hall joke'. Hevey believed that southerners would think, 'we go around wearing cloth caps and muffers' because of him.

The Waring debate often showed up in the most unusual places. One night, on the *Parkinson* chat show, a discussion between Michael Parkinson, the comedian Peter Cook and the footballer Danny Blanchflower turned to a wider discussion about sports.

Cook, renowned for his 'anti-establishment' approach to comedy, launched into a tirade about his hatred for rugby league, which he found to be a 'remarkably stupid game' played by a 'muddied lot of half-drunk idiots'. This was despite his love for Eddie Waring, who he greatly 'worshipped and admired'. Parkinson put it down to Cook's public school education. But in reality, the view that Waring was more popular than the sport was ingrained in the BBC.

When Caine Associates studied rugby league in the 70s, they concluded that Waring was responsible for the image problem. Buried in their 30-page report was a controversial half-page criticism which would draw worldwide media attention and scupper Caine's plans to revolutionise the game. The report said that Waring was holding the game back and was judged to have 'little credibility as a serious interpreter of the game'. While he may be 'immensely entertaining and amusing', the 'laughter is patronising'. Waring did not take too kindly to the attack. The day after publication, the BBC and Eddie Waring called a press conference in Manchester where he defended himself and threatened to take legal action against the game. 'I tell the truth about a particular image. I am using the language of the north of England,' he said. A media storm ensued, with newspapers debating whether Waring should be replaced. In his *Sunday Times* column, Michael Parkinson launched a defence of a game which is 'played in some of our unloveliest northern industrial towns'. He concluded that the consultants didn't understand the game and could have learned more about the league by having a pint with him in Barnsley instead.

The BBC had no intention of removing Waring, and it was made clear to the sport that there would be little chance of a new contract without him. Those running the game had hoped to present the game in a different light but found obstacles across the media. In 1976 the RFL had dined the top sports writers and editors at the Garrick Club to sell them the game's virtues. Ian Wooldridge was emerging as one of the key voices for sport at the *Daily Mail.* But when he heard of the plans to move away from Eddie Waring, he was 'staggered' that they found him embarrassing: 'Slagheaps, Tetley's ale, black pudding, Lowry paintings, busted noses, huge white thighs and players who talk precisely as he talks, which is bluff and blunt and volubly.' This, Wooldridge told his readers, was rugby league's image too. 'And the day it becomes a sophisticated art form is the day they might as well drive their Northern wagons into a circle and play some private game instead.'

Beyond Eddie Waring, the sport's image remained fixed by the impression it had created for itself in the immediate post-war years. The idea of rugby league as tough and uncompromising was proving difficult to shake off. In the 1960s, the toughness of the play was celebrated in the film adaptation of David Storey's novel *This Sporting Life*, which had secured Oscar nominations for Richard Harris and supporting actress Rachel Roberts. But while the critics marvelled at the dynamic action shots of Harris playing the game, there was little doubt that the film tapped into the stereotype of working-class life. In the *Daily Mail* the cinema critic Cecil Wilson viewed the central character as 'an arrogant, inarticulate muscle-brained ape'.

By the 1970s, the 'tough and uncompromising' image had more pressing consequences. The decade was a more hostile environment for the working class than the immediate post-war years, as newspapers increasingly wrote of a moral panic of violence, muggings and a breakdown in law and order. Films such as *A Clockwork Orange* had prompted debates about the moral corruption of society and the impact of violence on television. And rugby league was not immune from that debate. In 1970, after an explosive World Cup Final – dominated by punch-ups, kicking and spitting – was broadcast to millions of afternoon viewers on the BBC, the

Daily Mail launched a campaign to ban it from television. 'Get these savages off our TV screen', ran one headline. 'This was pure, bloody mayhem paraded as sport. And it happens most weeks,' concluded the sports editorial. Even the political cartoonists joked that the players were lucky not to be in prison for their behaviour.

The game was linked to the image of the 'traditional' working-class male that was becoming outdated as the 1970s progressed. It was an observation not lost on the comedy writers Dick Clement and Ian La Frenais when they turned to write an episode of their hit 1970s sitcom *Whatever Happened to the Likely Lads?* The show dealt with the division between working-class Terry Collier and aspiring middle-class Bob Ferris at a time of rapid social change. In one episode, the division is highlighted by Bob wanting to go out shopping for the weekend while Terry intends to stay in and watch the rugby league on *Grandstand* instead. The punchline was clear: rugby league was seen as a sport for the manual workers and not the upwardly mobile Bob Ferrises of the world.

* * *

One of the issues facing the sport in the early 1980s was the changes in newspaper coverage and the lack of journalists with profile to write about it. In the 1950s, rugby league had benefited from the huge number of newspapers that operated out of Manchester that produced northern editions of national newspapers. In addition to titles such as the *Manchester Guardian*, there was a range of major regional titles, such as the *Lancashire Evening Post* and the *Yorkshire Post*, which had dedicated rugby league writers. By the early 1980s, the number of dedicated journalists covering the game had declined. And those that did cover it had little opportunity to present the game beyond the scorelines, transfer rumours and novelty stories about dogs. There needed to be more outlets to discuss what the sport could become.

One afternoon in the mid-1970s, a young student was sitting in his Oxford University common room waiting for *Grandstand* to come on. Harry Edgar was born in Whitehaven and had followed rugby league in Cumbria as a child. His first experience of the Challenge Cup was in 1964 when his school's headmaster had organised a trip down to the twin towers. Edgar had always sensed that people saw rugby league as a joke, but in the cocooned environment of a rugby league heartland it was much harder to identify. Whilst sitting in the communal television room one afternoon, he had invited some friends to watch a Test match between Great Britain and New Zealand. But they quickly laughed at the suggestion.

Edgar enjoyed writing and creating his own magazines as a child and wondered why there wasn't a rugby league publication for young writers and supporters. Newspapers such as the *Rugby League Gazette* and the *Rugby Leaguer* emerged as dedicated papers to run alongside the local coverage to cover the sport in the 1950s and 60s. But these newspapers were part of the establishment, and those that did want to challenge the way things were done would be met by restrictions on space and access to sources.

Beyond rugby league, however, there was a movement for young people to create their own media. The year 1976 was the year that punk music cut through to the popular imagination. Boosted by developments in printing technology that made photocopying cheaper, the punk scene developed around fanzines such as *Sniffin' Glue*. The spirit of punk music was about access to it: anybody could create their own product and put their point across. Fanzines could be photocopied for 3p a time, and the speed and cheapness of the format – A4 pages photocopied and stapled together – allowed for instant reporting. Most importantly, there were no advertisers or editors to stifle creativity or promote agendas.

In the summer of 1976, as the Sex Pistols moved from the fanzines to the front pages of the tabloids, Harry Edgar decided that rugby league needed a voice of its own. In the spirit of the punk movement, he created a fanzine that wouldn't 'follow the party line' or represent the game negatively as the mass media did. In his mission statement, Edgar declared that the game suffered from smear campaigns from 'a few sick-minded patrons of a rival rugby code' and its inability 'to promote its own assets'. Edgar believed it was 'a great injustice' that the game had not created the profile the players deserved and that the lack of good writers was partly responsible: 'Our aim is to provide intelligent reading for all people who care about rugby.'

The *Rugby Leaguer* was the main trade paper of the time, but it was often criticised because it operated a closed shop for writers. To submit an article, you had to be a member of the journalists' trade union, which meant that only those working in the media could contribute. If a club wanted their team to feature more in the *Rugby Leaguer*, it required either a member of staff or a local journalist to supply them with a story. Edgar called his fanzine *Open Rugby* because he wanted the debate and the ideas to be as open about the sport as possible. He put together a four-page news sheet and printed 270 copies to sell for 10p each. The early issues included features on the French game and diaries from players that would struggle to get a hearing otherwise. He wanted to appeal to people who were in their early 20s and write about the aspects of the game that young people would be interested in.

Edgar soon found that people wanted to hear what he had to say and copies were being shared outside grounds across the country. He quickly sensed a real appetite amongst the supporters for something new. But in April 1979, just as Mrs Thatcher was about to come to power, Edgar was ready to give it all up. Operating a rugby league fanzine from Oxford had its challenges. It wasn't just the writing but the whole process of putting it together. 'All the work involved in distributing the copies; trying (not always successfully) to collect the cash; and trying to keep correspondence up has just got TOO much,' he wrote in what was intended to be his farewell issue. Historically, other rugby league publications had been forced to close because of a lack of demand. But Edgar was closing his because he did not have the resources to keep up with support.

He realised that he had to step up if he wanted to change the game and that killing *Open Rugby* because it was too popular would prove how parochial the rugby league media was. Instead he decided to keep it going. *Open Rugby* stage two was going to be different from the first one. After 18 issues of the fanzine, Edgar now wanted it to compete on the shelves with the football and the music magazines. Edgar declared that the supporters of the game deserved a high-quality magazine that reflected the appetite of its supporters, 'not newspapers with pictures of dogs on the front or programmes giving half the visiting team's names mis-spelt and containing wrong information'.

The key factor underpinning the magazine was the visual impact. Edgar wanted it to showcase the best photography and capture the players dynamically. He obsessed with finding the best layout to convey the information and keep the readers excited. Most of all, Edgar wanted his new magazine to collaborate with all the people with ideas on the fringes of the game who wouldn't find a voice otherwise. He put out a statement that declared that the whole venture would live or die 'on the faith of RL people'. And to make it happen, he took a bold personal step to signal to the readers that he was serious about changing the debate within the game. He packed up his things, quit his day job and moved from Oxford to the north.

* * *

By the end of the 1970s, rugby league had virtually no profile in the south of England. Apart from Cumbria, the rest of the clubs remained effectively contained by the boundaries of the newly built M62 motorway – where they had congregated since 1895. Widnes and Doncaster were as south as it was possible to go and watch a top-level game. The sport struggled with expansion, even in areas where the game was already popular. In the 1950s, there had been a push for a team in Blackpool to tap into its location as a holiday spot for northerners. The rationale was that people would combine holidays with a game of rugby when their team played away. For a short while, it was successful. When Blackpool drew Leigh in a Challenge Cup tie in 1957, they packed over 20,000 people into the stands. But it proved to be a rare high point. By the early 1980s, the club was drawing in crowds of 500 each week, and they were rooted to the bottom of the lower divisions. Between Blackpool's arrival in 1955 and 1980, no new professional club was set up.

Journalists had often urged the game to push beyond its boundaries in the north. After one spectacular Challenge Cup Final, the writer J.L. Manning pleaded with the sport to move south of its 'artificial' frontier: 'The trouble with rugby league is that it has an inferiority complex and a regional resignation to its unimportance,' but the offer was rarely taken up. When the Australian Kangaroos arrived in 1973 and demanded one of their matches be played at Wembley, the sport had yet to get the first idea about promoting the game to locals. The Aussies had anticipated a crowd of 30,000 or more, but there was huge embarrassment for the British organisers when just 13,000 people turned up. The Australian manager, Charlie Gibson, was so angry that the English game had been unable to drum up support that he promised never to come back to the city: 'I don't think it will be worth playing in London on future tours if that is all we can get,' he told the *Sunday Telegraph*. On the BBC's Saturday afternoon broadcast, the sight of empty terraces spooked those running the game into retreat.

Harold Genders was a former Warrington player and director who believed it was time to address the game's southern discomfort. After the 1979 Challenge Cup Final, he was shocked to find that there was no coverage of the match in the southern editions of the newspapers. Not only did Genders think the game needed more column inches, he also sensed that the sport had an opportunity to actively challenge the football market. In the late 1970s, football was arguably in a graver situation than rugby league. With millions of people lost to the terraces since the 50s, barely a week passed without a tabloid story on crowd violence and hooliganism.

Over the summer of 1980, Margaret Thatcher was forced to condemn the actions of England supporters in Turin after bottles were hurled on the pitch and riot police fought back with batons and tear gas. When, a few weeks later, Oldham v Sheffield Wednesday was abandoned for 30 minutes due to a terrace 'riot', a national panic ensued. A spokesman for the FA admitted that the tensions between supporters were now a primary concern: 'We should actively discourage travel to away games,' he announced. 'By the end of the eighties,' predicted a *Daily Mail* special report, 'TV could be dubbing crowd sound effects on to film of matches played for the benefit of their cameras in otherwise virtually deserted grounds.'

Rugby league expansionists believed there was an opportunity to frame itself as the family game for the 1980s. Fulham was identified as a possible area to develop a team after Harold Genders convinced the owner of the football club, Ernie Clay, that it would bring in extra revenue. It would be more difficult to convince the other rugby league clubs that it was worth investing in the south. In a sport fighting for every penny, there would be inevitable questions about sharing sponsorship deals and paying travel costs. Rumours began circulating in the media that clubs would vote down any attempt to spread the resources to London. Fearing that the venture would be thwarted before it had even begun, the two men appealed to the man at the very top of the sport: David Oxley.

* * *

David Oxley was a rugby league 'outsider'. An Oxford graduate with a degree in English literature, he seemed destined for a career as a leading educator in Britain's public schools. Although he was originally from Hull and had maintained an interest in the game's fortunes, he had played rugby union at university and had virtually no contacts within the sport. In the 1970s, rugby league didn't take too kindly to outsiders because, while there was lots of talk about change, the clubs were still run by ex-players and local businessmen who had been around the game their entire lives. The Salford chairman Brian Snape, who also chaired the Rugby League Council, alluded to the game's problems when he declared it was now 'an old game' with 'too many old men in it'. So when he was tasked with finding a new chief executive for the sport, he stipulated that any candidate had to be under 45. One morning, David Oxley saw the advert hidden away at the bottom of the *Daily Telegraph* jobs page. 'More out of curiosity than anything, I applied,' he later recalled.

The smart money for the role was on the former Leeds player Bev Risman, whose father Gus had been a legend in the sport in the 1920s. But when the 36-year-old Oxley arrived for his interview, he impressed upon the selection panel the stark realities of the game's image outside of the north. He presented a two-page briefing note and outlined the ten steps he would instigate to save the sport. His communication style triggered something in the club chairmen, who were tasked with deciding the appointment. In the end, Oxley saw off Risman by one vote.

Oxley arrived at Red Hall the same day as Brian Clough arrived at Leeds United. Legend has it that Brian Clough sought to shake things up overnight by telling the Leeds United players to grab all their medals and throw them in the bin. Oxley didn't have the space to instigate overnight change. Nor would he have wanted to. In contrast to Clough he was not confrontational and preferred to bring people together rather than develop creative tension. But even he was taken aback by what he found when he walked into the game's headquarters. 'I don't know why you have taken this job because we won't have jobs in a year or so,' remarked one colleague.

Oxley soon signalled that he would change the feel of the game: 'No game can live on memories alone. Whilst honouring the past, we must consolidate the present, plan for an imaginative future and, above all, learn to be ourselves once more.' Recognising that the game had not equipped itself for the demands of the new media age, he approached David Howes about becoming the sport's first public relations officer and, together, they would set out the agenda for the game in the late 1970s.

The first step the two Davids took was to go out and sell the game to its existing supporters again. They both undertook a tour of the heartlands, accepting any invitation that came their way and hijacking supporter events wherever they could. The mood on the ground was bleak. The pair didn't have much cash in the early days but had passion. When Oxley first heard about the plans, he warned that 'the financial implications for a professional southern rugby league club are enormous' but that 'every problem can be surmounted'. Oxley persuaded the clubs that it would boost revenue into the game. In the summer of 1980, the clubs agreed to endorse the plan, and rugby league had its first new club for a quarter of a century.

There was no template for setting up a new club, and no sooner had the venture been announced than residents began a protest against another sporting club being opened in the area. 'Threat to rugby,' reported the *Fulham Chronicle* a few days later. Objections to the club came from religious groups, such as the Lord's Day Observance Society, who didn't believe sport should be played on a Sunday, and a local residents' group concerned about parking and hooliganism.

In the early 1980s, there were still huge restrictions on what people could do on Sundays. One angry resident claimed it was against the Sunday Observance Act of 1780 to play rugby and charge admission to the ground. While playing their home games on Sunday was not a problem, the law did restrict the club from selling advance tickets, which meant that they had no idea how well they would do. Other journalists wondered whether it could take off. 'I'll eat Eddie Waring's trilby,' argued the *Daily Mirror* writer Mike Bowen, 'if London fans ever unravel League's code.'

At the same time, the fact that there was no template for developing a new club meant that Fulham could experiment in innovative ways. The organisers understood that the media would be the most important aspect of gaining free advertising and communication of the club to the public. One tactic was to recruit the Fulham football manager, Malcolm Macdonald, to spearhead the publicity drive. A cult figure at Newcastle United and Arsenal in the 70s, Macdonald was tasked with helping communicate the new joint venture in the media. 'We are getting good luck telegrams and letters from Fulham soccer fans, applications for jobs and requests for season tickets,' he told *The Times*. Macdonald proved to be a hit with the southern football writers interested in how the Fulham team would work.

At the same time, the club knew they needed someone who could connect with rugby league fans across the country. Colin Welland, along with Eddie Waring, was perhaps the most famous person associated with the sport in the 70s. Welland had gained fame as an actor in the hit police drama *Z Cars*, a show which had been widely praised for ushering in a new era of domestic, soap-style storytelling. He followed it up with a star turn in the 1969 classic *Kes,* which told the tragic story of a working-class boy subjected to abuse at school and home.

What made Welland unique was how he advocated for more working-class stories to be told on television. He wrote his own dramas for *Play for Today* in the 1970s, which captured the new demand for social realism. His most famous work was *Leeds United!*, a play about a strike in the clothing industry where workers, mostly women, came out on strike and were undermined by their own union. Most importantly, he was a huge rugby league fan: 'It surrounded us – Wigan to the north, Warrington south, the Saints to the west, and Leigh to the east. Rugby engulfed us, devoured every minute we could spare it,' he once wrote in his column in *The Observer.*

Traditionally, leadership roles had gone to club legends or people in local businesses. But Fulham were doing things without a rulebook. 'I jumped at the chance. I want a say, to play a part in presenting a piece of my old home culture on my new home patch,' he revealed in a *Guardian* column a few days later. His appointment to the board of directors opened the chance to sell the game to the public in the broadsheets that had long ignored the game. Julie Welch had been Fleet Street's first female football reporter in the 70s. On the eve of the new season, she was tasked with determining whether the venture would succeed. She reported that a meeting with Welland had convinced her that it was going to be a success. She challenged the doubters, coming away from a behind-the-scenes training session believing that 'the decision to experiment with rugby league might be the best thing they've ever done'.

In contrast to the moral panic around football segregation, Fulham encouraged as many away supporters as possible to come down and witness their debut match. Supporters could be trusted to handle their drink too. Fans travelling down were urged to go for a pre-match pint at the Boileau Arms in Barnes, run by the former Huddersfield and Kiwi player Dave McManus.

Everything about the event had been planned to mirror a cup final, from a parade of former stars pre-match to the slow walk out of the players side by side from the tunnel. Welland also reached into his address book to invite celebrities interested in the game. Former Manchester United manager Tommy Docherty, the actor Windsor Davies from *It Ain't Half Hot Mum*, the ex-Wales rugby union coach Carwyn James and the football referee Clive Thomas were among the crowd's big names.

It turned out to be the biggest media event in the game's history. The club had calculated that around 600 spectators were needed to break even. The official attendance of 9,500 was more than double the best football attendance at Craven Cottage that year and one of the biggest crowds seen in the history of the Second Division. The group of national sports writers who had been sent to cover the game were left spellbound by the whole event and the performance of Fulham, who added to Wigan's woes with a shock victory.

Immediate success could be measured by how the southern media engaged with it. *The Sun* placed the match on the back page under the heading, 'Oh, what a knees up and under'. Over at the *Daily Mirror*, the sports editor had sent Christine Garbutt, a popular and well-known personality in London, to report on her first game of rugby league. She had arrived at the ground with hard images of Eddie Waring, Richard Harris and the 'man's world' of rugby league in her head. She left having loved 'every minute of it': 'It was sport in the raw without the rudeness.'

The most important image that the journalists drew was the contrast with football. 'Carnival spirit as Fulham launches into rugby league' was Roger Heywood's take in *The Telegraph* where 'The family atmosphere contrasted with the hooliganism and rowdyism of soccer in recent weeks.' Others noted how the police that had attended could interact with the fans, talk with them and soak up the atmosphere. The *Evening Standard* picked up on the same theme by publishing a photograph of a family sitting on the terraces watching the game: 'FUN for all the family? A rare sight on the Fulham terraces.'

* * *

The immediate burst of publicity and excitement at Fulham drew attention from the owners of football clubs around the country who wondered whether they might be missing out on a potential gold mine. Events were given a prominent space on *Grandstand* the following Saturday, where Bob Wilson introduced an in-depth feature on Fulham. 'With the football side of Fulham losing a quarter of a million pounds a year, these rugby league posts could signal a remarkable road to salvation.' For the football clubs that were losing money every week, a sharp contrast was drawn between the £8,000-a-week wage bill for the footballers and just £900 for the rugby league players. In the immediate aftermath of the Fulham game, there was a scramble to find the next football club to do the same.

After 30 years without a new club entering the game, the RFL was flooded with enquiries from other owners. Clubs such as Luton Town, Notts County, Charlton Athletic, Crystal Palace, Bolton Wanderers, Portsmouth and Glasgow Rangers enquired about how they could form their own side. John Deacon at Portsmouth talked about forming a side and copying the Fulham model of signing players. 'I feel certain we will go ahead. Rugby league is subsidising soccer at Fulham, and we feel it will go down well at Fratton Park.' The Crystal Palace chairman claimed he was also a huge fan of the game. 'We think the sport would catch on; it is more exciting than Rugby Union,' he revealed in *The Telegraph*.

For years, the expansionists had argued that they had the right product but needed the means and the resources to sell it nationally. The example of Fulham proved how it could be done. After just five rounds, Fulham were heading for a record attendance for the Second Division and well on course for promotion. Over beers in a pub in Barnes, Colin Welland told journalists that rugby league's time had finally arrived: 'We have climbed the hills, and now all I see is the green valley of the Thames, and London and the south – all there for the taking by rugby league.'

Rugby league had never had media coverage as positive and as diverse across Fleet Street, and the editors of the southern newspapers soon found ways to generate more stories about the players and personalities in the Fulham squad. Throughout the 1980/81 season, the player who was most talked about was a Welsh winger called Adrian Cambriani. Cambriani had been picked up by Fulham from rugby union in the summer and had been responsible for the first-ever try for the club in the match against Wigan.

Most importantly, he didn't look like a rugby league player for the tabloids. The club programme noted how he had 'made an impression on the supporters, particularly the women in the crowd'. The *Daily Mirror* asked him to pose topless for the newspaper and wrote about how he had 'pulled in the fans' with his physique. One feature outlined how he spent eight hours a week in his local YMCA, 'building up the muscles which have already wowed the girls at Craven Cottage'. The club even reworked the words 'Don't Cry for Me Argentina' to 'Don't Cry for Me Cambriani' and handed the lyrics out to generate some publicity around him. Cambriani had emerged as one of the new marketable stars in the game and the support of the London media was integral to that rise. 'This would never have happened had he signed for Wigan,' concluded one former player. 'London will be the way for rugby players to become nationally known in the 1980s.'

Fulham secured promotion to the First Division alongside York and Wigan in 1981 to the excitement of everyone in the game. Harry Edgar declared them the most important thing to happen to the game in years: 'For sheer, unadulterated entertainment value, enthusiasm and a general shot in the arm for the game of rugby league, nothing can touch Fulham.' And just as the season was ending, the game was set for another dramatic image change.

* * *

Five years after the fans launched a petition to have him sacked, Eddie Waring finally announced his retirement from the commentary box. The departure of Waring was a truly national media event with the newspapers paying homage to 'the man in a league of his own'. *The Times* ran the story on its front page while everyone from sports writers to TV critics wrote about his impact on the nation. Most writers believed that Waring had elevated rugby league to a position well beyond where it should actually have been.

In *The Guardian*, the TV critic Nancy Banks-Smith announced that she would miss him greatly: 'He brought warmth if not light to the ancient ritual of rugby league.' Over at the *Sunday Times*, one features writer who profiled Waring's career concluded that he had propelled 'rugby league from a grim and barely understood northern ritual into a television spectacular'. The BBC quickly commissioned a profile, 'A Salute to Eddie', an hour-long documentary to be shown ahead of his final commentary, as appreciation societies at Liverpool and Manchester Universities paid their tribute.

The reaction within rugby league circles was significantly different. For those that wanted the game to change its image as it moved into the 1980s, the departure of Eddie Waring was seen as a great opportunity. The *Rugby Leaguer* noted that it was an important moment: 'It's not It's a Knockout with an oval ball. It's a professional sport with a long and colourful heritage, a fast and skilful game played by men who train hard and play hard, men with a fierce pride in their sport.'

At *Open Rugby*, anger was aimed at the BBC and the newspapers for enabling and encouraging a 'jokey image for the game' through Waring. Most importantly, the success of Fulham offered an alternative vision for the sport. In London, Colin Welland had seen how people had come and watched rugby league for the first time. They told him they couldn't believe how different it was in real life compared to television. 'The blunt truth of the matter is that rugby league has evolved beyond him, passed him by,' he argued.

There was no natural successor to Eddie Waring. Various names were put forward in the letters pages of newspapers and magazines about the kind of person the game wanted. Some suggested another larger-than-life character in Alex Murphy. Others suggested that the game go for Stuart Hall from *It's a Knockout* to maintain the Waring legacy. But few had thought about the St Helens schoolteacher Ray French. French had played union and league and thought deeply about both codes since retiring in the 60s, having written a manual on rugby tactics and studying for a BA in English. He had virtually no broadcast experience in the game. But when the BBC ran commentary tests, they believed he had the communication style to take the sport in a new direction.

French was clear that he had no intention of following Eddie's style. 'The problem is to present the sport to the public as an entertainment and at the same time to have enough expertise to please the pundits,' he revealed. Before he had even picked up a microphone, journalists were keen to differentiate him from what had come before. *The Guardian* described him as 'a smooth-talking English graduate and accomplished after-dinner speaker', while the *Daily Mail* observed the huge differences between the two men:

'There couldn't be a greater difference in style between him and Eddie Waring if Les Dawson were invited to take over the Chair in English at Oxford.'

The departure of Eddie Waring and the arrival of rugby league in London marked the end of one era and the beginning of a new one. Fulham had provided the shot in the arm that the game had needed to kick off the new decade. The *Rugby Leaguer* newspaper signed off 1980 by confidently asserting, 'Rugby league is spiralling skywards into the eighties on a shooting star of success.' Over at *Open Rugby*, Harry Edgar could not believe the transformation before him: '1980-81 will go down as one of the most significant seasons in the history of British rugby league.' And when the FA finally changed their rules to allow Sunday matches for football clubs, Fulham admitted that rugby league was now a top priority instead. Fulham had lobbied for Sunday football but now sensed that league was a more profitable venture. 'We get a different audience at rugby. It's a family audience. Football, on the other hand, will take a long time to remove the stigma of hooliganism,' argued Ernie Clay.

Chapter 3

Windrush

THE YEAR 1981 began with a tragedy. Hundreds of miles away from the heartlands of rugby league, a group of young people had come together to celebrate a birthday party in New Cross, London. As the night unfolded, a fire engulfed the flat, killing 13 people and injuring lots more. All of those who died were black, and there was an immediate suspicion within the local community that it had been a racially motivated attack. Over the next few weeks, the media, the police and the politicians failed to address their concerns as protests and rallies called for change. And when tensions spilt over into Brixton – after the Metropolitan Police began 'Operation Swamp 81', using century-old laws to stop and search thousands of black residents – Britain was hit by a series of city riots across the country.

In the wake of Brixton, old arguments about what should be done about 'young West Indian men' returned to the political arena. The late 1970s had been a difficult time to be young, British and black. In the 1950s people had arrived in Britain from Caribbean countries to work as builders, cleaners, drivers and nurses in the newly established NHS. Yet by the 1970s, attitudes were becoming more hostile to immigration. As Leader of the Opposition, Margaret Thatcher warned that Britain was in danger of being 'swamped' by people from other cultures due to the rise in immigration from Windrush and then from the Commonwealth. And within her first few years in office, tensions rose between the black population and the police as unemployment reached critical levels.

Despite the evidence that black people were at a substantial disadvantage on every social indicator – unemployment, overcrowded housing and educational attainment – the debate after Brixton turned into one about culture. As Stuart Hall outlined in *Policing the Crisis,* the media had turned concern about street robberies in the 1970s into a moral panic about 'muggings' by young black men. The Britain of the early 1980s was a place where jokes about black people were still common within the wider culture. The Manchester comedian Bernard Manning opened his set in an episode of the show *Over the Top* with a joke about a man who walked into a sex shop to buy a blow-up doll to find that they only had black ones left: 'He got it home, he blew it up and it mugged him.'

The tensions between the black community and the police gave space for political figures such as Enoch Powell to return to the centre stage of politics, declaring Britain to be on the verge of racial violence 'which can only adequately be described as a civil war'. In a speech to the Young Conservatives in Ashton-under-Lyne he argued that the only practical solution was repatriation: 'Voluntary, orderly, humane, even generous, no doubt, but repatriation.' Political commentators agreed that it was time to have a 'serious and detailed argument' about voluntary assisted repatriation to reflect the feelings of 'ordinary people' who thought that Windrush immigration had been wrong.

The Conservative Party began to talk about a new repatriation policy for people who were the children of the Windrush generation. Mrs Thatcher ruled out the repatriation policy, instead urging the black community to recognise their opportunities. But there was increasing pressure within her party to reverse the stance. The notoriously hard-right Monday Club, led by chairman Harvey Proctor, proposed a 'multi-million-pound programme to repatriate 100,000 coloured people a year from Britain' ahead of the 1981 Conservative Party conference. *The Times* reported how 'the offer would be open to all coloured people', including those whose parents or grandparents were born in Britain. One of the recurring political arguments of the time was about how the children of Windrush had no affinity with the nation. At one speech in London, Enoch Powell had articulated a widely held view that the 'West Indian or the Asian does not, by being born in England, become an Englishman.'

* * *

Just as those debates were taking hold of the media and the Conservative Party, rugby league was benefiting from the decision of families to move to Britain in the 1950s. Historically, league had always prided itself on advancing black players long before other sports had caught up. Forty years before Viv Anderson became the first black player to represent the England football side, Jimmy Cumberbatch made history when he was selected to play for England against France. Others soon followed, such as Roy Francis, who played for Wigan in the 1930s and went on to represent Great Britain after the war.

The biggest advantage it gave the game was its ability to attract players from Wales and rugby union. In the early 1950s, players like Phil Delargo, Billy Douglas and David Jones all moved north. And in the post-war years, few stars shined as brightly as Billy Boston. Of the dreams of two children on the impoverished streets of Cardiff's Tiger Bay docklands, Boston's was the more unlikely. While Shirley Bassey dreamed of breaking out of poverty to become an international star, Boston dreamed of representing his country at Arms Park. Boston scored hundreds of tries while playing in the army but the knock on the door never came. Instead, it was Wigan who promised to turn him into a superstar.

Boston proved to be an immediate sensation in rugby league, and he quickly worked his way into the Great Britain side after just a handful of games for Wigan. The opportunity to travel to Australia opened his eyes to a new world. As the *Maryborough Chronicle* in Queensland reported as he arrived, the hot weather, the rich steaks and the exotic fruits made him ill at the beginning of the tour. But he was soon the most-talked-about player on the tour because of his try-scoring ability. There were reports of locals queuing up at 10pm the day before the game to get a glimpse of him in action.

Billy Boston helped sustain the boom in Wigan's attendances in the 1950s when he regularly played before up to 50,000 people. 'Once again,' opened the club programme in March 1954, 'the immense popularity of the rugby league game in and around Wigan has been proved.' Boston was box office, and everywhere he went to play the attendances increased. But not every country was as accommodating. In 1957 Great Britain played several matches in South Africa where the apartheid system would have meant he could not stay in the same hotel as the rest of the squad or play in any of the games. Boston encouraged the team to go on and play without him.

A writer in the *Rugby League Gazette* made it clear that the players were wrong for carrying on: 'We have no colour bar; we judge a man to be a man irrespective of colour, and anyone good enough is eligible to play for the country of his birth. That is as it should be, and anyone who tinkers about with this to "fit in" with South African standards is dealing a death blow at every civilised concept of sportsmanship.'

Boston was pushing the boundaries as one of Britain's most prominent black sportsmen when there were no black politicians or major leaders in industry. Politically the 50s was a time when there was still a deep antagonism towards black people in Britain. The experience of Dr David Pitt, who stood as a Labour candidate at that time, was evidence of where politics and sport diverged. Pitt – who came to Britain from Grenada to study medicine in the 1930s – was a prominent champion of immigration and minority ethnic rights at a time of dangerous hostility to the cause. Pitt went toe to toe with Oswald Mosley and the White Defence League in Notting Hill, demanding legislation make 'incitement to racial hatred illegal'. He espoused radical solutions to avert tensions – such as police forces recruiting more black officers.

Pitt believed that Parliament was the best route to achieve social change but found that his attempts to become an MP were met with fierce resistance. In 1959 he made history – as the first person of African descent to stand for Parliament since universal suffrage – for Labour in Hampstead. Mosley supporters disrupted meetings and heckled him with their slogan 'Keep Britain White'. Fights broke out, and Pitt was forced to seek police support after death threats and a barrage of abusive 'go home n****r' phone calls were made. He subsequently failed to take the seat.

When he stood again in 1970, he had been expected to win and become the only black MP in the Commons. He suffered a major swing against him of 10.2%, double that of neighbouring constituencies and the national average. In the days following the result, a leaflet was unearthed by the *South London Press*, which had been sent to 'electors who have coloured families as neighbours', by an unknown protest group. It was reprinted in full, reading, 'If you want a coloured for a neighbour, vote Labour. If you're already burdened with one, vote Conservative'. Underneath, it urged voters to support the Tories to bring up to date the 'Ministry of Repatriation'.

In the same year, as the National Front grew ever more popular, Great Britain appointed Clive Sullivan as captain of their rugby league side. Born in Splott in Cardiff in 1943 to parents of Antiguan and Jamaican heritage, Sullivan followed Billy Boston's path from rugby union to rugby league in the belief that he would probably never get the chance to play for Wales. Sullivan went on to become one of the game's best wingers, scoring over 350 tries in his career. Remarkably, he bridged the divide between the two Hull clubs, winning a Challenge Cup with each one.

It seemed a natural step for him to take on the captaincy of the Great Britain side. But the most remarkable aspect was how little acknowledgement there was even within the sport of his historic achievement. When Sullivan was announced as captain of the side, the story did not reach the desk of any southern newspaper editions. Even *The Guardian*, printed in Manchester, thought that story was worthy of only a single line. Lodged between the horse-racing selections at Newbury and Catterick Bridge, the paper announced that 'Clive Sullivan, the Hull winger, will become the first coloured player to captain a Great Britain team.' Sullivan proved to be a successful captain when he brought home the World Cup trophy a few months later but the country had missed the whole thing. When Sullivan returned home, no press or fanfare was awaiting the team. Even the *Hull Daily Mail* didn't report the story of Sullivan's match-winning try. And when he returned to the Hull side, just over 2,000 spectators were at the Boulevard to watch his homecoming game against Oldham.

* * *

The lack of recognition for Clive Sullivan emphasised how commonplace it was for black players to reach the very top of the sport. But it also pointed to a deeper problem that showed just how far rugby league had fallen down the pecking order in terms of national profile in the early 70s. Rugby league had often prided itself on not really having 'stars'. In the film adaption of *This Sporting Life*, Richard Harris's character explains to the chairman's wife why rugby league is different. 'We don't have stars in this game, Mrs Weaver, that's soccer.' 'Well, what do you have then?' she replies. 'People like me.' But the lack of stars was becoming a problem in a media climate that was increasingly interested in individual players.

In the late 1970s, Granada commissioned a television drama centred around a rugby league player coming towards the end of his career. Like *This Sporting Life* a few years earlier, *Fallen Hero* centred around a player, Gareth Hopkins, who had retired with no money and little to show for his efforts. When the doctors declare that he'll never play again, he remarks that it could have been worse: 'I could have been Kevin Keegan with £100,000 a year at stake.' As the series progressed, he began to lament how little he had actually made from his time playing the sport. In one confrontational scene with the chairman of the club he accuses him of signing him on the cheap: 'There's not much money to be made in the game, is there? Not after tax!'

Fallen Hero tried to convey the idea that the life of a rugby league player was not glamorous nor a solid foundation to build a career around. Hopkins was written as a former Great Britain centre who had wowed the nation down under when playing for his country against Australia. But while he may have been a star on the pitch, he had been unable to build a meaningful life off it. He soon finds himself unemployed when, after an injury, he loses his job as a groundsman at the club.

The story of Hopkins was a fictional account, but it symbolised where the game was in the popular culture of the time. The sport wasn't interested in generating individual stars in the 70s and early 80s and was beginning to pay the price in terms of national profile.

Ahead of the 1981 Challenge Cup Final between Widnes and Hull KR, David Howes secured a major national profile for the *Daily Mirror* with the up-and-coming journalist Anne Robinson. Yet devoid of superstars to focus on, she interviewed a player called Eric Prescott instead.

Prescott had been an integral part of the Salford side that dominated the league in the 70s. But few people knew who he was. When Robinson profiled him she was drawn to the humble nature of the game and the lack of glamour. 'He shows genuine astonishment that you should want to interview him,' observed Robinson, who outlined how Prescott had been given a week off as a painter and decorator to train. 'Unlike top soccer heroes the rugby league lads do not own sets of Carmen rollers, huge motor cars, houses with swimming pools or have half shares in local fashion boutiques.'

The fact that rugby league players were humble and respected for their working-class roots was integral to its identity. But, at the same time, it was clear that other sports were fast moving beyond this world. Snooker had embraced the idea that television could help it replace football as the leisure pursuit of the working class. Snooker generated stars and marketed them to the public as characters with rivalries and egos. The journalist Gordon Burn captured the 'boom' of the game in the early 1980s and travelled across the country for his book *Pocket Money*. He found that marketing, public relations and television had turned snooker from 'a marginal activity, capable of supporting no more than a handful of professionals, into part of the fabric of the national life'.

Image became all important to the snooker brand. And in 1981, they created a new superstar in Steve Davis. Like most rugby league players, Steve Davis was from a humble working-class background. Born in Plumstead, the son of a London Transport depot worker, he played snooker at his dad's local working men's club, where he soon found himself under the management of Barry Hearn. Hearn encouraged Davis to pursue a professional snooker career and instilled in Davis the idea that 'courtesy, politeness, smart presentation and always being on time for an appointment' would help him reach the top. Through Hearn's Matchroom programme, snooker embraced all the commercial opportunities that came before the sport, making its players millionaires in the process. To some, it was the selling-out of a sport to a branch of entertainment. Hearn disagreed. 'There's so many opportunities,' he told Gordon Burn. 'And if you can take ' em, why not take 'em?'

For people such as Harry Edgar, there were few people in rugby league who could be marketed in the way that snooker players were. The editor of the influential Australian *Rugby League Week* magazine advised Edgar to pick five players he could shape a season around and continually write articles and comment pieces to promote them to the public. In the early 1980s, he focused on people like Les Dyl, Steve Nash, George Fairbairn, Bruce Burton and Steve Norton. But although they were the big-name players, none of them presented the image that Edgar was searching for.

It was hard to promote them as stars when the supporters didn't see them in this light. International rugby league appeared to be at its lowest ebb when France defeated England 5-1 in a game where they failed to cross the whitewash. More worrying was the attendance. 'Only 3,229 spectators paid to see the game and they may have witnessed the final nail being driven into the coffin of international rugby league in this country,' wrote Harry Edgar in *Open Rugby*. Then, one afternoon at Leigh, Edgar found the exact sort of player he was looking for.

* * *

Des Drummond was not supposed to be a rugby league player. Born in the Jamaican coastal town of Savanna-la-Mar in the 1950s, his mother moved to Bolton to work as a sewing machinist. She encouraged Des and his brother Alva to engage in sports to help integrate them into the community. Alva played football and rugby league but Des was more interested in judo. In the middle of the 1970s, Leigh Centurions had taken a punt on Alva but he was in and out of the team and on the fringes of the club. One afternoon Des went along to watch Alva play a reserve game at Barrow. Short on players, the coach asked Des to make up the numbers to give them a hand. Out of nowhere he ended up being the star of the show by scoring three spectacular tries. A few weeks later he was playing for the first team.

The Leigh team that Des Drummond joined was in need of a spark. Leigh was a mining town that had often lived in the shadow of its neighbours Wigan, St Helens and Widnes. When the magazine *Picture Post* had wanted to capture a 'typical Lancashire town of the sort you find west of Manchester' in the 1940s, they chose Leigh because of its huge number of coal pits and mills. They found that it had endless straight rows of red-brick houses. 'There are few more unlovely towns,' the magazine declared. The rugby league club had been around since the 19th century but almost disappeared in 1945 after the war when fixture compilers forgot to include them in the new season.

The club needed to be rebuilt from the bottom up. Around 4,000 local people came together and their voluntary labour ensured that the club had a team and a ground. Supporters helped raised money for the revival of the club. When *Picture Post* journalists walked around the pubs and clubs of Leigh in 1949, they found that every way of raising money for the club had been explored: 'If your lighter blacks out in a Leigh pub, you can buy a refill for a penny – which goes into the supporters' club.'

The club had enjoyed a brief period of success in the 70s when Alex Murphy came to the club as a player and they lifted the

Challenge Cup for the first time. But by the late 1970s, the club were in the Second Division, and the town was starting to suffer the hardship of pit closures. Nobody knew who Des Drummond was when he found himself stood on the wing at Hilton Park one afternoon. But it wasn't long before he became a folk hero in the town. Drummond looked different from the wingers who had played the game previously. He was short and stocky in an age where wingers were often tall and glided around the pitch. In an early interview with *The Guardian,* he admitted, 'Yes, it is true that I am not that big. And I have had to work doubly hard to get over that problem.' But, he argued, 'Rugby league is like life, it is not height but heart that matters.'

In an age where many rugby league players were manual workers, their strength often came from working in heavy industry. But Drummond was unemployed and unable to find work. He was unusual in that he kept himself fit by going to the gym, by cycling and through judo. Few rugby league players had ever used judo to build up strength and that made him almost impossible to tackle. Drummond believed that players needed to focus more on fitness to succeed in the game. 'If you want something badly enough and are willing to work hard to get it, then you will get it,' he argued. 'I also like winning and you have to be good to win. You have to give 100 per cent effort to be good.'

When Alex Murphy returned to the club as a coach in 1980, he and Drummond brought the crowds back to Leigh. In one match against Warrington, the crowd was so tightly compacted that a barrier and three rows of seats collapsed at Hilton Park, leaving four fans injured. A spokesman for the club admitted that it could have been a lot worse. 'It was probably the sheer weight of numbers trying to get out after the match that caused the collapse,' said one official. 'Fortunately, most of the seats were not occupied, otherwise it could have been most unpleasant.'

Drummond was an integral part of the Leigh side that won their first title in 76 years, in 1982, scoring the try that helped them beat Whitehaven on the final day of the season. The *Leigh Journal* lauded him as the best signing the club had made in a generation. In the aftermath, Drummond was tasked with taking the Championship trophy round to the local clubs and pubs as well as the schools and community centres.

* * *

Des Drummond had helped revitalise Leigh Centurions and reconnected the rugby league team to the town with his attitude. A few miles west of Leigh, in Wigan, Maurice Lindsay and Jack Robinson were watching on with envy. Wigan had arrived back in the First Division in 1981 but soon found that they were not up to the top standard.

By 1981, the Wigan board had been cut from 12 to four with Maurice Lindsay, Jack Robinson, Jack Hilton and Tom Rathbone in charge of running the club. Dubbed the 'gang of four', they radically changed the way that decisions were made. But for all the changes that the new board had initiated in terms of streamlining the decision-making, they were unable to find the top players to come to the club. Likewise, Fulham struggled to score points in the top division. Wigan and Fulham were locked in a relegation battle that looked like it was going to the death. And when both clubs looked to find the spark that would keep them in the First Division, they ended up on the sidelines of Rochdale Hornets.

Rochdale were a club that had struggled for much of their existence in the game. Having won the Challenge Cup in the 1920s, their fortunes had been tied to the cotton industry, which suffered a serious contraction in the 1960s and 1970s. Yet they had always been on the lookout for exciting players, which often took them to far-flung corners of the globe. In the 60s the club took the rare step of putting an advert in the *Fijian Times* to try and recruit Fijian rugby union talent. A number of players answered the advert, and they became local celebrities.

But by the 1980s they had become one of the classic 'yo-yo' teams that continually fluctuated between the top divisions. The club had no resources to advertise or market players and instead turned its energy to keeping people out. One call was for the directors to keep an eye on the turnstiles to avoid 'freeloaders coming to watch matches' for free. 'That is working well and is a commendable practice,' agreed Stan Townsend in the *Rochdale Observer*. In 1981, it took two months for the club to secure their first sponsor for a match. It came from a director's building firm, who supplied just £25 for sponsorship of the match ball.

Where Rochdale seemed to operate well was in the transfer market. Fulham arrived at Rochdale with £30,000 in their kitty to pick up a talented youngster and found one in the exciting young forward called Sean Hoare. Hoare was 6ft 5in and 16 stone and a much-talked-about prospect in the Lancashire area. The Wigan coach Maurice Bamford was desperate for the club to sign someone like Hoare to boost their forward pack. But instead, Lindsay and Robinson came back with a young winger called Henderson Gill.

The Gill family had arrived in Huddersfield from Barbados in 1956 to work in the car industry. Henderson Gill was one of five children in the family who grew up in the Marsh area of the town. It was a tough area to live in with only a very small West Indian community. As he would later tell Ross Heppenstall, Gill went out to youth clubs and nightclubs; he had to go in a group because there was racism 'everywhere we went'. Unlike Drummond, he had won youth honours with Yorkshire and England as a stand-off and was talked about as one of the brightest prospects. But when he was picked up by Bradford, he was soon seen as a 'troublemaker'. When Gill missed training, coaches were fed rumours that he had been out partying. And when he missed games through injury, physios began to think that Gill's injury was 'all in the mind'.

Bradford lost patience with him and eventually sold him on for just £9,000 to Rochdale in 1980, where he looked destined for a lifetime playing in the lower echelons of the game. Initially, Gill failed to make an impact and the club were worried they'd signed a dud. Then, at the turn of 1981, things began to change. Striking up a combination with John Gilmore, the pair went on to score 14 tries in ten games. The *Rugby Leaguer* predicted that 'the Gill/Gilmore combination could soon become one of the most lethal scoring combinations in the game'.

What Maurice Lindsay noticed when scouting him was how the crowd responded every time the ball came towards him. Through his strength and power, and natural exuberance, the public expected him to make something out of nothing at any given moment. In one game against Batley, the *Rochdale Observer* remarked how he scored a try 'off the cuff' by accelerating past several players to touch down under the sticks. The problem was that only a few hundred people were there to see it. A week later, against Keighley, he scored another 'world class' try in front of less than a thousand people.

Wigan swooped in to sign Henderson Gill, who quickly became a crowd favourite through his effort and determination to carry the ball. And when he began to score important tries, the supporters responded to him as Wigan won their first game in eight. 'Gill is proving "electric" as far as the fans are concerned. As soon as he got one of few passes the crowd was on its feet,' reported the *Wigan Observer*.

Off the field, however, he was proving much more difficult to handle. He would often miss training to go clubbing in Yorkshire and London. The administrators at Rochdale, criticised for selling him too cheaply, warned that there was more to him than met the eye. The *Rochdale Observer* took great delight in announcing that Gill 'did not turn up for training with his new club this week'. After making a scoring debut at Barrow, 'It appears Gill had gone into hiding.' Rochdale were quick to brief the media that this was typical of Gill: 'This illustrates the kind of problem we had with him. It's something the fans don't always know about him.'

Yet as Wigan and Fulham battled it out for survival, the signing of Gill proved to be the decisive difference between the two clubs. When the pair met in London, Gill scored 'two more improbable tries' where 'as soon as he gets a pass, the crowd rises in expectation of some spectacular football'. Harry Edgar sensed that Gill was an exciting new talent that needed to be promoted on the pages of *Open Rugby.* He ran a special photograph of Gill scoring his tries against Fulham and began a campaign to have him and Des Drummond selected for the Great Britain side. Edgar identified Gill and Drummond as 'the people who have the kind of charisma guaranteed to draw the crowds'.

* * *

While rugby league had always been open to black players in the sport, the 1970s and early 80s were a much more hostile environment than the one that Billy Boston had faced in the 50s. The journalists cheered the day that Viv Anderson became the first black player to play football for England. In a sport where monkey chants and the throwing of bananas on the pitch was commonplace, there was hope that it would turn the image of the sport around. 'The coloured kids have arrived in a big way and have made a tremendous impression on the game,' argued the football writer Jack Steggles in the *Daily Mirror.* As Britain suffered an early cold freeze, the *Daily Express* commissioned a cartoonist to make light of the situation: the weather would be so cold that England 'would be playing with one black player and ten blue ones'.

Anderson's debut was immediately heralded as a significant moment for the country. A spokesperson for the Commission for Racial Equality said that, 'The more blacks can get involved in mainstream activities like football and other sports and be selected on merit, the more people will see them as part and parcel of the British game.' But when Anderson played each week, he was still subject to loud boos and monkey chants every time he touched the ball.

Rugby league's racism was perhaps more tribal than it was systemic. When a young Leigh supporter called Paul Mason watched Des Drummond play for the first time in 1976, he was shocked by the racist abuse he heard from opposition fans. Mason saw Drummond antagonise the crowd by scoring a try which resulted in pockets of fights between fans. 'To hear open racism was quite shocking,' observed Mason. Henderson Gill also found that the higher profile he received, the greater the abuse. Gill used the racist abuse as motivation, sensing that they had only targeted him because they 'were fearful of what I would do to their team'. But the chants were obvious. One was 'Zigger, Zigger, Zigger, Wigan's got a n****r!' Like Viv Anderson, Gill suffered racist abuse on the pitch but to block it out, he told Ross Heppenstall, he adhered to a simple policy: 'You can call me whatever names you want from distance, but you can't put your hand on me.'

Despite the racial tensions on the terraces, Harry Edgar had no hesitation in using Des Drummond and Henderson Gill as his cover stars at *Open Rugby*. At a time of heated debate about whether the children of the Windrush generation should be deported, Edgar acquired a picture of Drummond in his Great Britain jersey: 'The emergence of Drummond as a winger with true charisma and finishing power has been one of the few redeeming features of a disastrous international season.' And in October 1981, just as Conservative backbenchers were putting forward plans for voluntary repatriation, Drummond and Gill were picked to play on the same side together, becoming the first black wing pairing for the national side.

The question of whether they were 'actually' British was brought up in many media interviews. 'Their eyes glow with genuine emotion when they talk of acceptance by the country and sport of their adoption,' wrote Keith Macklin in *The Times*. Both players understood that by turning out for their national side they could change perceptions about what black people could achieve in sport. Gill admitted that 'at last I was a somebody, somebody with a big job to do for Great Britain'. Drummond likewise admitted to personal pride when cheered on by those who usually engaged in monkey chants and racist abuse. 'Usually, the Hull speccies give me stick,' he revealed. 'That day they got right behind me and cheered my tries. It was marvellous.'

* * *

Rugby league players were rarely profiled in the national media in the early 1980s. But in Drummond and Gill, the sport had two players that had captured the public imagination. Journalists were interested in their heritage and their culture. When one journalist from the *South China Morning Post* visited Drummond at his flat in Bolton, he was impressed at his 300-strong record collection and up-to-date modern hi-fi system. 'I like music and there is no point in playing a really good record on equipment that does not do it justice.' Journalists were fascinated by his interest in reggae music and the sort of food he ate. 'I like West Indian food, British food, European food. People should have the choice, but I do not think you should stick one way. You should adapt to get the best of all worlds.'

Meanwhile, Gill developed a reputation for creating his own mix tapes and handing them out in the changing rooms. Few people in the early 1980s walked around the dressing room with headphones and Walkmans, but Gill told the *Courier Mail* that music was a way of relaxing before a big game. 'People have different ways of relaxing and getting themselves psyched up. I like to listen to music. If there is anything important to be said I listen out of courtesy, but otherwise I like the music.'

At the end of 1981, Drummond and Gill would be joined by another young player who had ambitions of playing at the top level. Three years earlier, in the week that Viv Anderson made his debut for England at Wembley, the name Ellery Hanley appeared on a team sheet for the first time. Brought up in Potternewton, near Chapeltown in Leeds, Hanley's parents had arrived from St Kitts in the Caribbean in the 1950s. It was not an area famed for its rugby league, and Hanley had played football, basketball, cricket and tennis as a teenager. He could not, he told *The Guardian*, 'have cared less' about the league, until one afternoon his schoolteacher asked him to play to make up the numbers. Hanley refused. But the teacher threatened him with 'the slipper' if he didn't. Hanley played and soon realised that he could run through defenders and score tries at will. He kept picking up the ball, running and falling over the line again and again.

Hanley never argued about playing rugby league again. And when it came to turning professional he had seven clubs interested in his signature. He ended up at Bradford because they offered the best terms and aged 17 he was sat on a substitutes' bench watching as the Northern side struggled to break down the Rochdale team. With around a quarter of the game remaining, he came on and made an immediate impact. 'And then Northern made absolutely sure,' reported the *Telegraph and Argus*, when 'young Hanley marked his first league appearance by scoring after a fine Grayshon break.' But after a try-scoring debut he disappeared for three years.

Hanley was brought up in a village near Chapeltown which had been the subject of much media attention and scrutiny in the 1970s. Notorious as the area where the Yorkshire Ripper had murdered several women, its red light district was, to many in the media, a symbol of inequality and deprivation. Several reports by social researchers found that the Chapeltown area was impoverished and its population discriminated against. One study concluded that 58 per cent of the heads of households were born overseas, with many of them unemployed or working part-time. A quarter of their homes were overcrowded and deteriorating rapidly.

Community groups warned of rising racial tensions and civil unrest if conditions weren't addressed. But little was done. The police in the area talked about the growth of illegal drinking clubs – known locally as 'shebeens' – that had sprung up across the city. As the *Sunday Times'* Peter Paterson observed, 'The police are a kind of buffer state between the city and the noisome immigrant slum of Chapeltown.' Sympathetic observers admitted that the police had little power to turn the situation around. 'They can do nothing about immigrant complaints of poor under-equipped schools, sub-standard housing, upswept streets and racial discrimination,' argued one journalist. Others blamed the police for racial discrimination. People who ran an Immigrants Advice Service claimed to receive complaints about police harassment of young West Indian men who were stopped and questioned for no reason.

People who worked at Bradford said Hanley was 'mixing in ropy company' when they signed him. Hanley later told *Sportsweek* magazine that he kept the same company as he had when he was a teenager and that signing for Bradford had not changed him. 'I might have made more money than the others, but I soon wasted it.' He found himself 'getting into trouble' in the local area. *Sportsweek* magazine later reported that not long after his debut, 'the law caught up with him and his petty crime landed him in jail.' From a rugby league perspective, the Bradford chairman Jack Bates admitted being disappointed when he heard the news: 'We tried to keep him in the game, but he had to serve his time,' he told the *Sydney Morning Herald*. By the time Hanley returned to the fold in 1981, many commentators were expecting him to fall back into old ways.

Hanley admitted that the experience changed him profoundly. He revealed in the *Sportsweek* interview that he channelled the experience into his rugby league. When he went out on the field, whether it was against Hull or Doncaster, he remained utterly focused on the job in hand: 'My discipline comes from the lessons I learned in the hard times. They've stood me in good stead and there is great value to me in not forgetting what I've been through.'

The re-emergence of Hanley in the autumn of 1981 drew much attention to the Bradford side. The local paper found that Hanley's performance away at Leigh had 'really got the tongues wagging' and in his first outing in Lancashire, 'Leigh fans were full of grudging admiration for the youngster who made their hero John Woods take a back seat for such a long spell.' After just two games, Hanley was seen as a 'crowd pleaser' who had the ability to create opportunities from nowhere. Dubbed 'the black magic', Hanley was praised for his skill in the middle of the park, where he differed from the tradition of black players who had often been used on the wing to utilise their speed. 'Hanley has still a lot to learn, and his inexperience has shown on occasions,' but 'there has been no doubt at all about his flair for pulling tries out of the hat,' wrote one journalist in the *Rugby Leaguer*.

To the naked eye, it looked like Ellery Hanley was just another exciting young player with pace and the ability to find his way to the try line. But behind the scenes, he was developing a mindset that enabled him to deal with the racist environment in which he found himself. As a youngster, he found that he was 'going to be the focus for racial taunts from players and spectators', and quickly decided that he had to be as tough as he could be both mentally and physically to deal with the abuse. He later told the *Daily Mail* that he had to roll his sleeves up and 'get stuck in twice as hard' to avoid being the target that his skin colour made him.

He knew he was a marked man and would be the subject of dirty tactics off the ball and away from the referee. He would play on with injuries and never let on: 'Once you show weakness in this game you are finished. Everyone homes in on you. Every side in the league gets to know.' He soon realised that to survive in the game, he would have to have the edge over everyone else. He began training on his own and doing extra sessions. He even wore a weighted vest when running to replicate the heavy mud of the jersey when playing to give him extra fitness. It wasn't long before opponents realised that the racist comments would only spur him on to score more tries and win more matches for Bradford.

* * *

While Hanley, Drummond and Gill were redefining what it meant to be a rugby league star in the early 1980s, the undercurrent of racist attitudes still prevailed. An example came in a rare rugby league documentary that arrived in 1981 in a blaze of publicity. Doncaster Rovers had been the perennial rugby league strugglers since they were created in the 1950s. By 1981, their general manager, Tom Morton, had received a copy of the *Guinness Book of Records* for going the longest period without a victory. Yet the story of defeat interested filmmakers who wanted to understand what life was like behind the scenes of Britain's worst club.

Another Bloody Sunday followed the Dons as they tried to avoid finishing the season without winning a game and offered unprecedented access to the inner workings of a sports side. In the opening scene, the narrator introduces it as a study in 'resourcefulness, courage and sheer Yorkshire grit' as the team faces 'the inevitable prospect of yet another defeat and more derision'.

The television critics were enthralled by it. Richard Last put the story on a par with the best theatre Britain had to offer: 'The dressing room harangues could have been tapes transcribed and implanted bodily in anyone's script, down to the last despairing expletive, without changing a comma.' So too, the *Daily Mail*'s theatre critic who lauded it as a 'mesmerising documentary'.

What all the critics had overlooked, however, was the sub-storyline of *Another Bloody Sunday*. The filmmaker had decided to centre the documentary around the 'journey' of the Doncaster prop forward Tony Banham, who had 'overcome a troubled past' to make a new life for himself in Bradford. Banham admitted that racist abuse had been part and parcel of his everyday life, referring to it as a 'handicap'. He informed viewers how he had been born out of wedlock to an 'American negro – that's all I know'. His early life had seen many family members die, meaning he spent his teenage years living alone in a hostel: 'I ended up with nobody.' The tough start in life had, in his own mind, led him to become 'a bit of a swine' with people. But he was in no doubt that the racism he experienced had 'created a chip on my shoulder' that saw him go into dark places. He would often use his size to fight in pubs and intimidate the people who gave him abuse.

Banham was a bouncer at a nightclub as well as the prop forward for Doncaster. Drunk punters would call him a 'n****r' if he threw them out or barred them from the club. But he learned to deal with it. Banham was followed in the documentary as he did his work in the pubs and nightclubs of South Yorkshire. Having been dropped for a vital match against fellow minnows Huyton, he refused to train as a 'mini protest' against the club's actions. But in a moment of pure theatre for the documentary crew, Banham was brought off the bench to score a match-winning try. But when the camera cut to the club directors celebrating his try, the chairman Tom Morton turns to his fellow supporters and joyfully shouts, 'The Black Bastard!'

The casual nature of the insult, shouted in a scene of celebration, highlighted just what environment black players were up against when they entered a rugby league club. But as players like Des Drummond became integral members of the Great Britain side, they gradually changed some of those perceptions. Des Drummond soon attracted the attention of the producers of the BBC show *Superstars*, which moved him from the rugby league world into the wider public consciousness.

The BBC first brought the series of *Superstars* to screens in 1973 and it involved top sports personalities competing each week in various sporting contests. In the late 1970s, a Welsh rugby union convert called Keith Fielding was the first league player to appear on the show. Yet Fielding appeared uncomfortable with the limelight. Minor celebrity status didn't suit him because he was a teacher and wanted to focus on training. 'I was a little overawed at first,' he revealed. 'It was a little bit frightening lining up with so many world champions.' The *Daily Mirror* even nicknamed him the 'reluctant hero'.

Drummond, by contrast, appeared eager to use his opportunity to make a name for himself. His appearance was greeted by the rugby league community as an opportunity to make an impression on a global audience of up to 20 million people. Most importantly, Drummond was an athlete who challenged the conventional stereotypes about what rugby league players could do physically. He ran a time of 10.85 seconds in the 100 metres that would have seen him qualify for the Olympic heats a year later. He excelled at basketball and weightlifting. In a preview of the show, the *Leigh Journal* proudly wrote about how he was representing the town and the sport. 'For six gruelling days last week Drummond pitted his skills against some of the world's best all-round athletes in the stifling Hong Kong heat in order to become the undisputed champion sportsman.'

Chapter 4

Bleak Midwinter

AFTER MRS Thatcher's victory in 1979, the government had been determined to bring down inflation by cutting public spending and reducing employment levels. In 1980 alone, over one million jobs disappeared as the old industries struggled to compete with high interest rates and the value of the pound. The car industry was just one sector that reached critically low levels of production and exports. But in the first two years of the Thatcher government, rugby league had been able to ride out the storm. Redundancy money had kept many people going and the sport could still rely on significant attendance figures for cup games.

By 1981, there was no other Western economy where so many people were on the dole. Chancellor Geoffrey Howe introduced a budget which cut spending even further at a time when Tories were demanding increased borrowing and spending. Famously, 364 economists wrote to *The Times* to criticise the economic approach. Mrs Thatcher had promised not to 'U-turn' as her predecessors had. Not even in the much mythologised 1930s had so many people been unable to find work. 'Few sports have remained completely insulated against the ravages of the recession, and rugby league is no exception,' opened Paul Fitzpatrick in *The Guardian* at the beginning of the 1982/83 season. He wondered how 'the harsh financial climate that seems likely to get worse before it gets better' would impact everyone involved in the sport.

Employment and unemployment became a status symbol in the way that people had once been differentiated by the kind of work that they did. Traditional manufacturing declined sharply but even competitive private sector industries were causing concern for the government. When the Department of Trade and Industry established a unit to monitor the situation of individual companies, they were shocked to find the scale of the decline. A report on the huge employer in Widnes, Imperial Chemical Industries (ICI), one of Britain's most prominent industrial enterprises, spooked the government when it reported profits on export sales falling from 5.5% to –16%. The report said, 'The outlook is very bleak.'

The Thatcher government was surprised at how quickly unemployment had risen but there was little sympathy for industries not equipped for the new global marketplace. Thatcher had faced down those within her Cabinet that wanted to go in a different direction. By the autumn of 1981, when she addressed her party at Blackpool, she was adamant that unemployment was down to the 'enormous past wage increases unmatched by higher output' and 'the mistaken belief that, come what may, the government would always step in to bail out companies in difficulty'.

Rugby league towns were hit hard because of the dominance of single industries. In the 19th century, mill owners, textile bosses and factory owners had moved to the north to develop companies that exported across the globe. Firms such as British Steel, Vauxhall, Ford and British Leyland could employ over 20,000 people. It meant that there was a rock-solid community where workers had the same jobs, joined the same trade unions and enjoyed the same social life. Single industries came to dominate entire towns. And when they fell, a whole community went with it.

Unemployment fast became a national crisis. Night after night, news bulletins would announce the rising numbers and behind the headline figures was a tragedy. Every rugby league supporter had read in their local press about the human stories behind the statistics. In Leigh, one grieving widow recounted how her husband had become 'very depressed' after being one of 400 people made redundant at a textile mill. She told the *Leigh Journal* that for the last six weeks of his life, she had woken up to find her husband spending his days crying in his armchair until he couldn't face it any longer. She found him hanged, with a note that said he 'couldn't help it'.

Other tragedies made national headlines. In May 1981, the media reported on two unemployed teenagers from Widnes who stole a car and drove it to the banks of the river Mersey. The pair then ran a pipe from the exhaust into one of the windows and turned the engine on. They both died of carbon monoxide poisoning. When the bodies were found, there was a note in which they had said: 'What have we left to live for now there is no work for anyone?' At the inquest, the coroner concluded that there would probably be 'more cases like this' where the economic realities of unemployment would hit home.

In late 1981, a new sitcom called *Only Fools and Horses* situated the Trotter family in the ever-expanding black economy, as secure employment prospects vanished for millions of people. In the opening episode, 'Big Brother', Rodney Trotter is ridiculed for even thinking about getting a proper job. 'At the ripe old age of 23, you are a social leper,' Del tells him. 'Society has placed you in the darkest corner of its deepest cellar to grow moss and be forgotten about.' It was a pattern that was replicated when the US journalist Stephen Handelman took to the road to study the impact of Thatcher's Britain for his book *Uncommon Kingdom*. Visiting Bradford, he found young people who had simply given up hope of ever finding work again. 'They had developed a wartime fatalism. Joblessness was accepted as a cruel fact of life.'

* * *

Rugby league clubs could not ignore the scale of the deprivation that was now building up around them. At the beginning of the 1980s, Bradford Northern could still count on attendances of 6,000 and more. But as the recession took hold, they lost almost half of their support, despite the emergence of Ellery Hanley in the side. 'Northern cut prices for unemployed' ran one story in the *Telegraph and Argus*, which advertised a discount to any supporter who could produce their sign-on card at the Odsal ticket office. Discounted tickets for the unemployed was not universally popular nor without stigma. Coventry City tried to introduce a similar scheme in football but were heavily criticised when they designated a specific 'unemployed' gate. It was said to be a disaster because people did not 'want the stigma of going through a turnstile for the unemployed'.

The same economic problems were impacting Leigh, who needed help capitalising on their previous season's success. 'Cut price champions', announced the *Leigh Journal* in November 1982 as they slashed all admission 'for the rest of the season as the economic recession begins to bite deeper'. The chairman said it was done to 'assist people suffering from the recession in the town'. But the cut in prices had little impact on attendance. In 1982, when the Australian Kangaroos arrived in the country for their tour, few clubs could point to a boost in attendance. Only Hunslet, Leeds, Oldham and Wigan had increased their attendances, while 28 clubs were down. And while it was difficult for the traditional clubs, it was even harder for those areas that had set up new teams.

After the arrival of Fulham in 1980, the expansionists within the game had been excited about the prospect of a team in Carlisle.

For *The Times* rugby league writer Keith Macklin, Carlisle had a catchment area from Tyne Valley to Cockermouth and Keswick to tap into. Idealistically, he had suggested 'Workington, Whitehaven and Barrow enthusiasts might even divide their loyalties when fixtures do not clash'. There was even talk of fans combining holidays in the Lake District with away days to Carlisle. But the dreams of regularly drawing in around 5,000 spectators hit the reality of the recession. And soon they were facing a serious cash-flow crisis. Facing bankruptcy, the club agreed to reduce match fees to players to just £18 after tax. But still the attendances fell.

The club admitted that 'You can't force people to come and watch.' Their chairman even suggested a novel idea to level up the playing field. He proposed a new cup competition to stimulate interest that was based on a bookmaker's handicap system. Each team would be given an independent, bookmaker's-style handicap: for example, a poor side would be given a 20-point start against a good side'.

To make matters worse, the Fulham experiment appeared to be rapidly running out of steam. After the initial buzz of their debut season faded, the club returned to the Second Division where attendances fell and column inches dwindled. Colin Welland remained the prominent face of Fulham in the media and set out the dilemma they faced: 'It's £3.50 for a seat at Fulham, and that's a hell of a lot if you've a couple of kids to bring.' Welland also accused the club in *The Guardian* of not doing enough to publicise the game in London through advertising agencies and marketing campaigns. 'It's just not tradition – you don't see Arsenal or Spurs taking ads in the papers. We should open an account with an ad agency and get our name on TV, in the press, on the front of buses.'

If Welland was at a loss as to grasp why Fulham were struggling to draw in the crowds, the whole game struggled to understand why one of its former powerhouses was in deep decline. 'Of all the second division clubs battling to get out of the depressing rut of dwindling enthusiasm, crowds numbering in the mere hundreds and mountainous financial problems, none do so with a much heavier heart than Huddersfield,' argued Harry Edgar in *Open Rugby*. 'They may be only one of a dozen clubs in similar circumstances, but for the game's traditionalist, Huddersfield's pain cuts that little bit deeper.' People in rugby league circles often described the club as a 'sleeping giant' because of the size of its town and its illustrious past. Some still remembered the glory days of the 1940s when packed houses cheered on the great Lionel Cooper on the wing.

In the early 1980s, Huddersfield were in serious financial difficulty. They asked those running the game to help them out by moving a Challenge Cup semi-final to their ground to guarantee an immediate economic windfall. But their ground was in no fit state to accommodate such a big game. And the rejection was part of a much wider push from the RFL to take the big set-piece semi-finals to football grounds One of those changes was driven by the demand, as David Oxley acknowledged: 'There is a growing trend for people travelling to a major match wanting to sit down and watch the game. Seats, of course, mean more money, and people are happy to pay more to sit down.'

That philosophy didn't help Huddersfield. Their finances were so bad the *Rugby Leaguer* reported how they had 'taken the unprecedented step of offering to sell spare seats on the team coach to supporters to help offset the cost of the trip to Fulham'. A few weeks later, a player strike was threatened when training was abolished at the club – to save £20 fees – and cut the losing pay to just £5. Then, the new coach resigned after just one game of the season after being offered just £20 a week to coach the side. 'I am not in it for the money,' he argued. 'Any reasonable offer would have been accepted. But £20 works out at about 75p an hour.'

Life in the Second Division of rugby league was tough. But for all the problems facing teams like Huddersfield, there was a recognition that the sport had come out of the recession stronger than other industries that had gone to the wall in the early 1980s. One of the ways the game had sustained its financial model was by showing restraint when paying player wages. Economically, rugby league was no longer a route to financial security for anybody. In the 70s, player wages could not keep up with rising inflation and the cost of living. Players were not on annual fixed salaries but were allocated fees for winning or losing.

In 1976 the lack of money in the game had become a national story when the St Helens team decided that they would strike for extra pay. Capturing the industrial mood of the time, the *Sunday Times* led the way with an exposé of life at the heart of one of Britain's most successful clubs. The paper's industrial correspondent revealed that the players were on about £40 for an away win, £35 for a home win and £15 for a loss. The problem for the players was that they were not rewarded if they won more games and crowds and revenue increased.

In 1976, the Saints won the Challenge Cup at Wembley, the Premiership and the Floodlit Trophy. 'The only perk we got for winning the Challenge Cup was a sweater and a fucking bag,' said one player. Finances were so tight that the club refused to even increase the players' pay by £2 a man for fear of the economic consequences. Saints skipper Geoff Pimlett said that life at the top of rugby league was financially hard. 'For winning three trophies last season we got a big thank you of nothing from the club,' he revealed. 'No one could live off what we pick up. The money we get out of football hardly keeps the kids in toffees.'

Yet by the early 1980s people within the game argued that the restraint on wages had paid dividends. At the beginning of 1982, as the jobs crisis began to spiral further, Ray French claimed that the freeze had saved the game: 'The saving grace of our game in these harsh economic times has been the lack of high pay rises.' In his *Rugby Leaguer* columns he made a defence of the restraint. 'Long may our system continue to be the envy of other sports,' he argued. There was, however, one major consequence of that approach. It made playing rugby league in Britain a totally unattractive prospect for Australians.

* * *

The biggest financial protection the game placed upon itself in the 1970s was the self-imposed ban on foreign players entering the British competition. At the beginning of the decade, there had been open trade between the Australian clubs and their counterparts, resulting in one-way traffic to Sydney. Ambitious players tapped up by Australian clubs were told that if they moved down under for more money, they would be banned from turning out for Great Britain. But money and the Sydney lifestyle was more appealing than an international jersey. In the 1970s, much talk had been about the 'brain drain' of talent across industries as people left the country to work overseas. For some rock stars, such as David Bowie, the prospect of living in Germany appealed; others, such as the Rolling Stones, exiled themselves in France. Australia became, in the mid-1970s, a popular spot for Brits who wanted to start a new life. In 1974, applications to move down under were so high that they had to begin restricting the number of people coming in.

Rugby league officials in Britain were desperate to stem the flow and reverse the tide back in their direction. Their lowest point came at the 1977 World Cup when Great Britain was forced to put out a second-string side because of the number of players involved in the Sydney competition. Yet rather than come up with an economic plan to entice people to return, the game decided to simply pull up the drawbridge. They asked for a watertight international ban that stemmed the flow of all players. They got their wish. Even if clubs agreed on transfer fees, English players could not sign for overseas clubs. And no Australians could ply their trade in the English game either.

The international transfer ban was supposed to level up the British game. 'With all our top players available, Australia won't beat us for six years,' argued the Great Britain coach David Watkins. Bill Fallowfield agreed it would be the silver bullet to wrestle control away from Australia and back to the British game: 'This ban will benefit rugby league the world over – for far too long, England has been bled of its best players.' But when that theory was tested out for the first time in 1979, the British game was shocked by the advances made by the Kangaroos. The Australians beat the British convincingly and won the Ashes 3-0 without a competitive fixture. The Australian public voted with their feet when a record low attendance turned out for the final dead rubber.

* * *

By 1982, David Oxley and David Howes were convinced that they had made serious progress. Ashes tours had declined in revenue over the course of the 70s and people were beginning to ask whether they were financially viable. But despite the economic problems at club level, Oxley had secured a major new sponsor for the series thanks to the development of the game in London. Dominion Insurance Company offered a record £40,000 to sponsor the tour. The fact that it was an insurance company was a significant win for Oxley. In the previous series held in Britain in 1978, it had been sponsored by Forward Chemicals, a Widnes-based firm that manufactured liquid, powder and aerosol chemicals. Their managing director had wanted to align with the Great Britain side because it was a 'man's game'. Dominion had been attracted to the game because they felt it had evolved under Oxley's stewardship.

The investors had been sold on the idea that rugby league was 'extending its field of attraction to other areas of the country'.

The £40,000 sponsorship was funnelled back into the game and spent on Britain's 'most intensive preparation' ever, involving coaching conferences and a special summer-long training programme centred on endurance, strength and speed for the players. The Great Britain coach Johnny Whiteley claimed that the squad were 'discovering a new pride in their fitness'. Whereas before, 'A top player in his position would not have to worry about his level of fitness,' he told the press, 'that's all changed now.' Training at a camp in Grimsby, Whiteley talked about how the gym and swimming pool facilities at a local school would give them a great chance of winning: 'We've got everything we need here.'

And when the Australian journalists arrived to cover the tour, they were impressed by the level of detail that had gone into their plans. 'Great Britain geared to beat Kangaroos after 12 years,' reported one Australian journalist in the *Canberra Times*. Veteran British writer Roger Halstead of the *Oldham Evening Chronicle* could see visible signs of change. He applauded the idea of each member being provided 'with an individually designed training schedule'. 'Ready steady go-go Britain' opened Jeff Goodwin in the *Rugby Leaguer*. 'Great Britain is finally on the verge of producing a team good enough to match Australia.' By the time of the first test, there was a groundswell of support for the British side. The *Rugby Leaguer* went with a patriotic front page entitled: 'Britain Needs You'.

The confidence that emanated from the British camp reflected a general change of mood in the country in the autumn of 1982. The royal wedding of Diana and Charles in 1981 had turned the eyes of the world on to Britain again. In the wider sporting context, the England cricket side had captured the hearts and minds of the nation. In what became known as 'Botham's Ashes', the England side had at one stage been 500/1 to win the Test at Headingley before taking out the series. Then, closer to home, the Fulham director Colin Welland gave the British film industry a revival when *Chariots of Fire* won the Oscar for best screenplay in the US. *Chariots of Fire* told the true story of two runners who ran to glory at the 1924 Olympics in Paris, and quickly became seen as a British success story at a time of national decline. His words to the Oscars audience were reported around the world: 'The British are coming!'

A few weeks after Welland's Oscar success, in April 1982, Argentina launched a surprise invasion of the Falkland Islands. Only a few people in Britain had heard of the Falklands or cared about how they were governed. But once British territory had been invaded, there was a political consensus that it would need to be recaptured. In 1982, Britain was a country that still remembered what it was like to live through the Second World War. The occupation of British territory by a military dictatorship revived talk about the way in which the country had responded to the rise of Hitler in May 1940. The Labour leader Michael Foot, who had been one of the authors of the anti-appeasement pamphlet *Guilty Men*, drew a comparison to the fascism of that era.

As the conflict progressed, the public largely supported British actions in the Falklands. And as approval of Mrs Thatcher grew, the islands were swiftly recaptured. For the newspapers who had spent the decade talking about decline, the idea of Britain back as a major player on the world stage held much appeal. Mrs Thatcher tapped into the patriotic sentiment in the country by using it to define her ambitions for Britain. 'We have ceased to be a nation in retreat.' She urged the people to 'rejoice that Britain has rekindled that spirit which has fired her for generations past and which today has begun to burn as brightly as before'. Her approval ratings increased from 34% to 52% in the aftermath. Support for the Conservatives, which was slowly rising, dramatically increased from 31% in March to 46% by July 1982.

The Australian Kangaroos who arrived to tour Britain in late 1982 fully understood what they were walking into. The Australian coach Frank Stanton asked the players to make notes and keep newspaper cuttings whenever a patriotic British 'expert' questioned their ability. 'These and many other comments made by the English,' revealed the *Rugby Leaguer*, 'ended up in Stanton's hotel room and were subsequently used as motivation material.' Stanton decided to combat British patriotism with some motivational techniques of his own. He used a novel approach of cutting videos of his players to the themes of *Rocky* and *Chariots of Fire* to keep them motivated. Another method was to use the footage of the cricket star Ian Botham winning the Ashes to remind his players of how painful it was for the country.

By the time of the first Test at Hull, there was huge expectation about what the British team could do. Oxley and Howes anticipated a big crowd and warnings were put out in the *Hull Daily Mail* for fans to arrive early. League fans were promised an extensive preview on *Grandstand* but no live coverage. Instead, a highlights package would be put together in between an afternoon of racing from Ascot, tennis from Brighton, snooker from Reading and updates from football across the country. For some, this signalled that the BBC still did not treat the game respectfully. 'I know this is a rugby league touring team and not a rugby union one but surely Test matches of either code should be given the same coverage,' complained one supporter.

Australian viewers, by contrast, would be able to stay up late and watch the game beamed into their homes by satellite. But the lack of live coverage meant that the only way to witness the action was in person. Boothferry Park, the home of Hull City Football

Club, locked the gates early with a capacity crowd. Organisers had been caught off-guard by the demand for entry and there had almost been altercations between supporters outside as kick-off approached.

* * *

For four minutes of the game, Britain led the Australians. And the first 40 minutes proved to be a classic 'backs against the wall' effort. 'There had been a certain dogged quality to Britain's play in the first half,' concluded *The Guardian* writer Paul Fitzpatrick. 'But the second half exposed mercilessly the barrenness of British rugby compared with the fluent, exciting play of the Australians.'

Any delusions of British superiority were shattered by full time when eight different players had found their way over the try line as the Australians won the game 40-4. In the *Sunday Times* write-up the morning after, Peter James encapsulated the speed at which the players had gripped hold of the contest: 'To get the feeling of the game you only had to see one extraordinary spell in the second half when the tireless Australians scored three tries, boom, boom, boom, in a few minutes and ran the British to a standstill in doing so.' One supporter in the crowd joked that the fans had had their money's worth, having watched two games: 'One when Britain had the ball and another when Australia had it.'

Paul Rylance in the *Daily Telegraph* delivered a more stinging verdict: 'There was no British fire, passion, or hero. Tackling was dreadful, passing amateurish and tactics seemingly confined to one-man charges at a mean defence modelled on the American gridiron style.' Oxley and Howes had thought that the British game had been moving in the right direction and were proud to be hosting the Australians. But they had been utterly humiliated. When Oxley returned to the hotel after the game, he was shell-shocked and unable to speak to anyone. But as he checked in on the players afterwards, he found that many of them had just taken it in their stride. 'The players just seemed normal,' he later told the journalist Adrian McGregor. It was a wake-up call for David Howes. 'We'd been selling the domestic game on its general image, and suddenly that drubbing showed it was not worth its salt internationally.' For all the pre-match talk of preparation in Grimsby, the training camps were shown up for what they were. 'Like swotting on the eve of an examination,' said one Australian journalist.

Never had one 40-minute period of play had such an impact on everyone who had witnessed it. Comparisons were quickly made to the way in which Hungary had come over to England in 1953 and shocked a nation who believed they had a right to ownership of the game. The *Rugby Leaguer* newspaper received letter after letter from supporters who were dazed and confused at what they witnessed. The editor of the newspaper dedicated a special double-page spread to letters to deal with the demand: 'We have got to get back to the game of the forties and fifties.' Others wrote about the stages of grief they went through: 'Shock, disbelief, embarrassment, dejection and, finally, resignation. After everyone has blamed everyone else we will have to accept that, as a rugby league nation, we are second best.'

Organisers began to worry about what impact this would have on the rest of the tour. The Kangaroos were scheduled to play to supporters across the country in places as diverse as London, Carlisle and Bradford. A few days after the first Test, over 7,000 people turned out to see whether Leigh, the British champions, could match the Australians. 'If this had been a boxing match,' argued Mike Hulme in the *Leigh Journal*, 'the referee would have stepped in long before the final bell to save "punch drunk" Leigh from further punishment.' The second-string Australia side ran in 12 tries. Had Mal Meninga kicked the goals they would have been over 60 points, which was almost unheard of in an era when it was three points for a try.

But as the British champions took a hammering, organisers realised that supporters were still leaving the ground satisfied. 'Superlatives are inadequate to describe these Aussies,' concluded Hulme. 'Suffice to say it was a privilege to witness this exhibition, and judging from the standing ovation at the end, I wasn't alone in that view.' As the tour wore on, people began to turn up to matches hoping and expecting they would witness a Kangaroos 'box office' performance. One journalist quoted a member of the Kangaroos squad who said that he'd 'never seen so many people ecstatic after their team was thumped'. 'The crowning achievement,' reported the *Canberra Times*, was the announcement that reserved seating had sold out for the next two Tests 'even though the home team has just been dealt the second-heaviest defeat of all time.'

In the second Test at Wigan, where Great Britain were again unable to score a single try, spectators sat back and admired the show. At one point, when the Australian team worked the ball through various players' hands, the supporters spontaneously applauded the way the Aussies kept the ball alive. The *Rugby Leaguer* noted how 'the Central Park crowd duly applauded a sight which has gradually passed away from the domestic scene'.

With the advent of home video, word of mouth soon spread throughout the sporting world that the Kangaroos were doing something radical across the rugby pitches of northern England. When Ray French was travelling through the country as a schoolteacher, he found in places as diverse as Colwyn Bay, Shrewsbury and Fleetwood that all people wanted to do was speak about the Aussies. When Brian Batty at the *Daily Mail* secured a copy of the highlights on VHS, he urged British supporters to pick up a copy: 'This should be compulsory viewing for everyone interested in the game in this country.'

In rugby union circles, tapes began to circulate amongst players and coaches. The war between league and union meant that people could be ostracised publicly for admitting to learning anything from the league code. Brian Batty used one of his columns in the matchday programme to emphasise how popular it was amongst union coaches. England Under-23s coach Dick Greenwood managed to obtain videos of each of the Tests and told everyone who would listen that it was 'compulsive viewing for every rugby union player'. Steve Smith, the England and Sale player, admitted that he had studied the videos and identified how the Australians tackled: 'The Aussies go forward to meet the player and they stop him dead in his tracks. They hit him with the shoulder and drive through.' Lancashire's Des Seabrook was taken aback by what had been achieved with 'simple moves with straight lines of running done with great skill and pace'.

Devoid of any big-name rugby league writers to talk about the game, the London newspapers asked legendary rugby union players to offer their verdicts. *The Observer* sent former Wales player Clem Thomas up to Wigan to report on the second Test and he found that they lived up to the hype: 'There can be little doubt that these great Australians are one of the greatest rugby teams ever to visit our shores.' Thomas ranked them alongside 'the 1951 Springboks, the 1967 All Blacks and the 1971 Lions in New Zealand'. So too, Carwyn James, who had coached the 1971 British Lions in New Zealand – he believed they had revived a spirit of attacking play missing from union: 'They have clearly restored the art of collusion rugby allied to support play which leads to thrilling sustained movements.'

* * *

About halfway through the tour, the *Rugby Leaguer* started to write about the 'invincible' performances that occurred every time the team stepped on to the pitch. Over time, the term 'Invincible' would be attached to the group as they became the first touring side to go through an entire tour unbeaten. They had started out in Papua New Guinea, won 15 games in Britain and then followed it up with nine wins in France. For the people who understood the game's history, there was an immediate recognition that something significant had happened that might never be seen again. Harry Edgar at *Open Rugby* commissioned a special souvenir brochure called *Kangaroos 82* in a bid to write the first draft of that history. 'Their exploits in going through Europe undefeated deserve to be recorded,' he wrote. 'Maybe, many years in the future, old men will dig out fading copies of this magazine and remember Max Krilich and his men.'

But for one journalist, the tour proved to be a defining moment in his life. Paul Fitzpatrick had been a late arrival to the rugby league scene after spending many years covering cricket for *The Guardian*. He had never been on a tour to Australia and had never covered the Kangaroo tours in Britain. In 1978, Fitzpatrick had been a cricket correspondent for *The Guardian*, and the league side had little impact on his thinking. 'I must admit that their play came as a shock to me ... as well as a revelation and a delight.' The way they played the game was so different from everything he had seen in Britain that it made him wonder what sport he had been watching these past five years. Even those that had been covering the game for years were left spellbound. It was enough for Ray French to conclude, in his weekly *Rugby Leaguer* column, that the tour was already the biggest post-war embarrassment to the sport.

For Fitzpatrick, the tour was a reality check against those, including him, who thought the game had done enough in the 1970s just by surviving: 'As 1982 draws to a close, however, illusions are being peeled away like tangerine skins.' The Kangaroos' time in the UK radically changed people's thoughts about the game.

As they left France and departed for Sydney, Fitzpatrick summed up the feeling amongst supporters: 'Rugby league is not the same sport it was seven weeks ago.'

* * *

The Australians, too, did a lot of thinking about what had happened. Their general manager, Frank Farrington, observed how the British game was behind the times: 'Britain played football which went out of fashion years ago,' he told the *Daily Mail.* The journalists were even more scathing. The most potent criticism came from Bill Mandle in the *Canberra Times*, who believed it wasn't just about a difference in class. For him, the tour symbolised British decline and a lack of competitiveness that expanded well beyond the pitch. 'It is not solely a matter of money,' he argued, 'it is pride in performance and a recognition that there is intrinsic value in doing anything, even playing rugby league, as well as it can be done.' The Australians had a determination to win and were willing to do whatever it took to do it. 'They are built on taking the game seriously and seeing what the wit of men can devise when brought to bear on a problem.' It left Mandle wondering 'how two once reasonably closely matched heartlands of league could drift so far apart'.

The British game had been spooked by what had happened. Phil Larder had been appointed as the new director of coaching for the British game a few months before the Australians arrived. As early as 1979, Larder questioned whether the game had the right structures in place to develop top players. Reflecting on British coaching in his testimonial programme, he believed that 'Many professional coaches have usually qualified on the basis of having been a great player. But is that a suitable qualification to coach?' Back then, he argued for a radical overhauling of the system to introduce novel ideas such as coaching badges. 'I would also recommend coaching weekends where top coaches trade ideas.' But ahead of the 1982 Kangaroo tour, Larder had been just as unaware of how far advanced the Australians had become. 'I expected the tourists perhaps to be fitter than British players,' he wrote in 1982. 'But I still expected British players to be more skilful.'

Aussie coach Frank Stanton implemented ideas like team meetings behind closed doors where players could criticise and evaluate the players and how the coach operated. Performances were discussed openly, with solutions offered to reflect the individual person. He gave senior players free rein to take training sessions and guide the young players. It was about creating a culture and getting buy-in from the players. Only after he had seen it up close did Larder understand how much planning had gone into the lead-up to a match. Larder noticed that Stanton carried a book around all day: *The Psychology of Coaching*. He looked at how each player was psychoanalysed before they left Sydney, and the findings were used in different ways. Everything was carefully considered, even down to the allocation of rooms in the Leeds Hotel.

British coaches in the 1970s and early 80s often transitioned straight from playing to coaching via the player/manager route. Players such as George Fairbairn had been appointed Wigan coach aged 29, as had Reg Bowden at Fulham and Geoff Fletcher at Huyton. An insight into Fletcher's coaching standards was found in the documentary *Another Bloody Sunday* where Fletcher was filmed giving his pre-match speech to the team, ranting and raving about the importance of tackling. 'Get stuck in amongst them' and 'tackle and go in like a lunatic and knock 'em down!' Players who weren't deemed tough enough were nicknamed 'posers' and told to run hard and straight. To his wingers who couldn't score tries, he asked them to 'score a couple because we haven't had any for a bit, have we?'

The Australians not only better developed their coaching standards, they spoke in a completely different language to their

British counterparts. In the language of the changing room, there were discussions about the game plan, the tackle count, the possession count, yardage metres and ball control. The adoption of a new language was happening across other industries in the early 1980s as well. Across industries, people such as Ian MacGregor were being hired from America to initiate a very different type of working culture. MacGregor was brought in to reorganise and decentralise British Steel, cutting over 100,000 jobs in the industry by 1982. Thatcher saw people like MacGregor as essential to the development of her industrial strategy and subsequently recommended him for the role of chairman of the National Coal Board to oversee a dramatic change in the way that it operated.

In the wake of the Invincible tour, people began to wonder if British rugby league needed the same treatment. After the tour, Phil Larder made a trip to Sydney to pick the brains of Frank Stanton. Over schooners in a Manly pub, Stanton warned him that the British game was in deep trouble: 'Your professional game is weak, hamstrung by the selection of outstanding ex-players as coaches at your top clubs, positions which they don't deserve by virtue of coaching experience or depth of knowledge about the game,' Larder would recall in *The Iron Curtain.* Larder put together a plan to redevelop the way that coaches were trained and bring it up to modern standards. The concept of the 'professional' coach was indeed a new one. British managers, in many sports, still ruled by discipline and fear. Paul Fitzpatrick noted that it was unusual to find an English coach with 'obsessive attention to detail and [who] is a remorseless searcher after perfection' in the way the Australian coaches were. Larder, too, admitted that there couldn't be anyone working in Britain who could say, after the 1982 tour, 'that he knew it all'.

PART TWO: AFTERSHOCKS

Chapter 5

The Miners

THE AFTERSHOCKS of the Kangaroo tour reverberated around the sport for the next few years. Nobody, any longer, talked about the British being 'exceptional' or 'unique' in the way that they played the game. To people such as Ray French, who longed for a return to the golden age of the 1950s, there was a fear of what might now happen to the sport if it did 'not grasp the realities of life in the eighties'. One Christmas he wrote a lengthy piece in the *Rugby Leaguer* arguing that the game was on the verge of extinction. His favourite phrase was warning that the game would become 'a pleasant backwater in the sporting life of this country!'

Harry Edgar at *Open Rugby* had immediately identified 1982 as the year that 'time caught up with rugby league', when 'the old myths were shattered and all the years of allowing rugby league to slip down the road to mediocrity came home to roost'. Everyone had their own thoughts on what had gone wrong but David Oxley welcomed the debate: 'The time to worry will come when people no longer think deeply about RL or bother to argue its issues, for then no one will care.'

The immediate problem facing the game was a financial one. The day-to-day running of the sport was increasing at a time when the areas that league was being played in suffered. The aftershocks of the recession were now creating systemic long-term unemployment in many rugby league towns. And it was clear that there was a growing north/south divide. In 1981 the TUC organised the People's March for Jobs – a march of the unemployed from Liverpool to London to highlight the issue just as the Jarrow March had done in the 1930s. It had run through towns like Warrington and generated much publicity. In one rally, the Labour leader Michael Foot said he had 'seen the feeling of growing anger about unemployment and I have seen a rising determination to translate that feeling into political action'.

But when the general election came in 1983, Mrs Thatcher was re-elected on a landslide. In the aftermath of victory, it was clear that the Labour Party had struggled in the south. 'In the 186 seats outside London in the area from the Wash to the Severn, Labour held only three,' concluded the authors of the 1983 British election guide. Richard Rose was an academic who had long argued that the Labour Party needed to change the way it appealed to people in Britain. In 1983 he observed how you could no longer divide the British electorate by class as the parties had done for much of the post-war years. The 'traditional bowler hat v cloth cap' model was dead. 'Most voters are literally and metaphorically hatless.' The Conservative Party had won in 1983 because they forged an alliance between the new working-class voters and the middle class in the south. 'Labour is lagging behind because it is appealing to an ageing and shrinking minority of the old working class.'

One look at the map of rugby league landscape showed that over 80% of the areas that had a professional club had elected Labour MPs. And there were many people within rugby league that still wanted the game to appeal solely to the 'cloth cap' workers. But David Oxley was adamant that the game needed to continue with the idea of expansion. A phrase started to emerge which divided the game between the 'glamour' clubs, such as

Hull and a revived Wigan, and the 'shoestring operators' such as Featherstone and Castleford, who relied on traditional methods of fundraising to survive. Oxley believed the game needed more entrepreneurs and in 1983 he was excited by a proposal for a new club in the south.

Maidstone was deep in the heart of Conservative Britain but, following the arrival of Fulham, people running their football club set their sights on developing a rugby league team. Kent Invicta began lobbying the rugby league in 1983 by sending glossy promotional brochures to the northern clubs. Maidstone was seen as the ideal rugby league town for the 1980s with 'bars, restaurants, training facilities, a greyhound track and a pitch for dual use'. Most importantly for Oxley, the club sold itself on its ability to tap into a new, affluent market in the South East. 'Maidstone is at the heart of the so-called golden triangle and has an unemployment rate of less than 8%' ran a promotional feature in the *Rugby Leaguer*. This, it was argued, would be 'tremendous' for the game from a 'commercial development aspect'.

Fronting the application was a new and ambitious chairman who promised to do things differently to the clubs in the north. Aged 29, Paul Faires was a successful businessman through a record-importing company and immediately impressed those running the game with his enthusiasm and ambition to shake things up. Central to the idea of Kent Invicta was 'razzmatazz', a word which popped up everywhere in rugby league circles in the 80s. Due to increased coverage of the NFL on Channel 4, supporters had increasingly looked at the way that the Americans packaged their entertainment. When *Open Rugby* investigated the rise in support amongst fans, they studied the NFL and concluded that it worked because it is 'safe to attend and comfortable to watch. You can take your girlfriend, your wife and your grandmother in complete confidence.'

Others suggested more radical ideas. In one letter to the *Rugby Leaguer*, a fan proposed a US idea 'to help rid us of the old fashioned cloth cap and hooped jersey image'. He argued that clubs should adopt nicknames: 'Leeds Jets, Widnes Bears, Bradford Cardinals, Keighley Falcons, Castleford Cougars, Wakefield Eagles and Hull Kingston Dodgers.' Rugby league still lagged behind in terms of any pre-match entertainment or 'razzmatazz' but Faires told the *Rugby Leaguer* that he saw himself as someone who could change that. 'There will be razzmatazz, but nothing is wrong with that. We are looking at all sorts of ideas for matchdays to surprise spectators because we are there first of all to entertain, and that means mum as well as dad and the kids.'

Faires promised to create local celebrities, 'personalities proud to play for and proud to promote the club' in return for being well paid. Another idea was that the team would not travel across the country by coach. Instead, the squad would travel by British Rail from Euston. 'A deliberate decision to keep the team always in the public eye.' It wasn't long before the media wanted to know about Faires and his ideas. In *The Observer,* Simon Kelner wrote of how important 'image making' was for the project – 'He is marketing the game as family entertainment' – and revealed that pre-match gimmicks included the match ball being dropped by parachute. In addition, the team would walk out to the sounds of 'Jerusalem' while Queen's 'We Are the Champions' would ring around the stadium when the team scored a try. This sort of pre-match entertainment had never been seen before, and some journalists warned that 'It may be hard to take the accompaniment seriously.'

Mrs Thatcher had placed image at the centre of her election campaigning in 1983 and using Saatchi and Saatchi had contrasted a professional operation with a Labour Party that appeared to be stuck in a bygone age. Those excited about Kent Invicta sensed that this was league's opportunity to fashion a similar image of change and modernisation. David Oxley was blown away by the brilliance of the Kent application to join the league. On the eve of the vote to let them enter, he warned the clubs that if they rejected it, they would be 'condemning themselves to a parochial, tin-pot sporting organisation rather than a wide-ranging and expanding national sport'. For Harry Edgar at *Open Rugby*, Faires was exactly 'the type of young go-ahead official Rugby League is crying out for', who understood business and public relations.

There was little doubt that they would be accepted. And when they were, in the summer of 1983, they enjoyed a similar boom in media coverage to the one Fulham received in 1980. When *The Times* sports writer Simon Barnes was dispatched to Kent to meet the 'hip' chairman who would 'shake up the sport', he was shocked and impressed to find him dressed in a New York Mets T-shirt and faded blue jeans.

* * *

It wasn't long before the Kent Invicta bubble had burst. There had been much talk of crowds of 10,000 flocking to Maidstone to see the new venture but when they opened the gates for their first game, they were shocked to see just 1,815 people turn up. 'Kent Invicta's bold attempt to bring professional rugby to all and Sunbury floundered on all fronts,' opened *The Guardian*. Spectators instead visited 'the counter-attractions of vintage cars at Brands, aerobatics at Rochester, cricket at Folkestone or an afternoon on the coast'. Things quickly went from bad to worse and they were soon playing in front of crowds of just 700 people. 'One extra car load turned up,' reported *The Guardian*, 'under the misapprehension that the entertainment involved the racing of Afghan hounds.' One solution, to pump free tickets into the community, backfired when over 1,000 tickets were issued for the game against Workington and fewer than 100 were used.

The problem for Invicta was that they had committed to over £150,000 of players in the transfer market and now needed to pay the clubs. Hard-up Workington, Swinton, Oldham and Whitehaven all revealed that they had yet to be paid for the players that had been purchased. Other struggling clubs began to complain that they didn't want to travel down to Kent if they weren't guaranteed a return fixture at the end of the season as speculation mounted that they were going to fold. 'Invicta's plight,' argued Paul Fitzpatrick in *The Guardian*, 'is sad not only for the game's expansionist ambitions but also for its image.' The Kent experiment was another symbolic blow to the people who wanted the game to expand into new areas.

At the same time, one of the game's 'shoestring operators' was trying to work out new ways that it too could sustain itself in Thatcher's Britain. Featherstone was a town that had always prided itself in being one of the smallest catchment areas in the entire sport.

Often described as 'a set of traffic lights on the road from Wakefield to Pontefract', the area was known around the globe as a hotbed of young rugby league talent. Its amateur scene was responsible for creating some of the best British players such as Jimmy Thompson, Steve Nash, Mal Dixon and Gary Jordan, who had played for Great Britain.

In the 1950s a group of sociologists studied the town in a bid to understand what working-class life was like. In *Coal is Our Life*, the group calculated that almost half the population could be found at a rugby league match at the weekend. They found that the local supporters' clubs were integral to the community as they organised ballroom dances, local beauty pageants and outings for fellow supporters. 'No other sport can be compared with rugby league in its importance for the general life of the community.' Rugby league was adjudged, alongside the working men's club, the pub and the cinema, to be 'the only institution bringing large numbers of people together'.

For much of the post-war period, the club was run by the community and the committee. In the 1960s, the *Daily Mirror* ran a profile on the club and its attempts to challenge the financial might of the big clubs. They found the vice chairman of the club, Clive Asquith, working in his butchers selling weekly draw tickets, to raise funds for the club, alongside the sausages and steaks. 'We've got to keep raising funds this way to keep going,' he revealed. 'All our lads are local born and bred.' Most significantly, the club's fortunes were tied to the coal industry.

Coal and rugby league was central to life in Featherstone, with the railway track in the middle of the town symbolically separating the ground and the colliery. The Featherstone team remained rooted in the coal industry. It was often remarked how players would head straight to the training ground covered in coal dust after just finishing a shift. On the field, the miners of Featherstone were renowned for their physicality. When they won the Challenge Cup in 1967, the Queen and Prince Philip watched the action from the Royal Box and were enthralled by what they saw. When someone joked to Prince Philip that he should play a game, he replied, 'Not likely. Life's dangerous enough without going out there.'

The fortunes of the team were intrinsically linked to the fortunes of the coal industry. The 1930s was often described as the club's 'darkest hours' as the troubles in the industry hit them hard. During the 1926 General Strike, the club responded to hardship by allowing striking miners into the ground for free once enough money had been collected from those that could afford to pay to go in. By the 1970s, as the miners enjoyed the best pay and working conditions for a generation, it was little surprise that Featherstone Rovers enjoyed a period of success. They won the Challenge Cup in 1973 and the Championship in 1976.

The early 1980s had seen them again struggling to make ends meet as the coal industry geared up for an inevitable battle with Mrs Thatcher. To break even, Featherstone Rovers needed to attract another 1,500 supporters each week. They also needed the people in the community to buy lottery tickets, sponsor players and organise the day-to-day running of the club. In one appeal, the club secretary Terry Jones urged supporters to stop drinking in the local pubs and use the clubhouse instead: 'Have a drink at the Social Club, buy a lottery ticket, for unless we get more support for Rovers, I cannot see a future for them.'

As attendance began to slide in the early 1980s, the coach Vince Farrar used his programme notes to criticise a fan who came to the social club for a drink and moaned about the poor quality of the radio coverage he had just listened to. 'I was flabbergasted,' he wrote. 'People staying at home and listening to games on the radio will seriously harm our progress.'

The club invited supporters to suggest ways they could raise extra money to support them. One fan committed to running the London Marathon to raise funds which would be 'used to carry out much-needed improvements to the ground and buildings'. One strategy was to send season tickets out to schools in the local area, which could be shared with pupils in the class. Another was to tap into the booming video market by opening a rental store at the ground to loan movies to fans. But attempts to generate extra revenue were often thwarted by the restrictive rules around business practices. When the club tried to hold a Sunday car boot sale on the ground, the local authority closed it down because of an ancient Royal Charter that prevented Sunday trade. The same charter prevented them from staging a weekly market under the stand.

But whenever Featherstone were in trouble financially, they could often rely on the players on the pitch to pull them through. Featherstone was always seen as one of the toughest places to win. And in 1983, the team went on a cup run that took them all the way to Wembley again. For the people who believed that the game needed to expand, the prospect of Featherstone at Wembley caused deep concern. For Keith Macklin in *The Times,* there was a fear about what would happen to the attendance. 'Even if every able-bodied man, woman and child in Featherstone were to go to Wembley, along with the population of Sharlston and other surrounding villages, the exodus would have difficulty in mustering 10,000 souls.'

The 1983 Challenge Cup Final was seen as the ultimate 'David and Goliath' clash. Featherstone had, at the beginning of the year, been quoted as 100/1 to lift the Challenge Cup. Hull, their opponents, were seen as the model template for a modern league club. Not only were they the best-supported club in the game, but they had been heralded for investing in New Zealand players at a time when few clubs looked overseas. Their director, Dick Gemmell, captured Fred Ah Kuoi, James Leuluai and Dane O'Hara when there were few foreign players in the English game. He said it was a reward for the booming success of the Hull club: 'Without them, we would not have the money to buy such players. This is their reward.'

When the BBC arrived in Featherstone to film a pre-match feature on the town ahead of the final, they were inevitably drawn to the romanticism of coal life. The found that every shop was decked out in blue and white, as was the winding gear of the colliery. 'Featherstone is an isolated mining community with two fixations: rugby league and coal,' said the presenter Richard Duckenfield. The press reported that the only person who probably wouldn't make it down to Wembley was the signalman at the main-line level crossing in the middle of the town. On the morning of the game, special prayers were said by the town's clergy members and parishioners who wished for success.

It was fitting that the guest of honour that afternoon was Lord Gormley. Born in Ashton-in-Makerfield, between Wigan and St Helens, Gormley had been as famous as most of the country's politicians, as president of the National Union of Mineworkers (NUM) throughout the 1970s. He was central to negotiations with Labour and Conservative prime ministers in the decade as the miners became the most militant workforce in the country. In his autobiography *Battered Cherub* he put his negotiating skill down to the fact that he was born in between two rival rugby league towns. As he walked on to the pitch to meet the players before the match, some joked whether he could help sort out a day off from the pits on Monday.

In front of Lord Gormley, Featherstone Rovers pulled off one of the biggest shocks in Challenge Cup Final history. 'The little mining town from the West Riding of Yorkshire have beaten the might of Humberside,' was how Ray French called the result. When David Hobbs was interviewed by journalists in the wake of his Lance Todd Trophy win, he talked about how everyone had written them off: 'I think we gave a good advertisement for rugby league but more important is the fact this has put us back on the map.'

And the victory was seen as a win for the 'shoestring operators' in the game in the face of those who wanted the game to expand. The *Rugby Leaguer* concluded that it might be the best thing to happen to the game for years. 'The name of the game at the moment is professionalism: image-building on a large scale with the glamour clubs encouraged to set the standards.' But then along came Featherstone 'to pump life back into ailing hearts; show the shoestring operators what to do and how to do it'. Politically, there was a belief that the town would benefit from the boom. After the club's success was celebrated in a motion in the House of Commons, the local mayor suggested that it might just rekindle the town's economic success.

* * *

The Monday morning after the Challenge Cup Final, the Featherstone Rovers players were back at work. The players took the trophy to the colliery and posed for a photograph in full mining gear. When the club had returned home on an open-top bus, players saw that almost everyone had turned out on the streets to cheer them home.

Over the summer, the Featherstone Rovers loose-forward Keith Bell began preparations for what was to be his testimonial year. In the 1970s and 80s, a testimonial for a player was seen as the ultimate accolade of loyalty and commitment. In an age where players worked around playing and only received £50 to £100 winning and losing bonuses, the prospect of a fundraiser was seen as something that could set a player up for retirement and security afterwards. The club would run events and fundraisers throughout the year to celebrate the player's success.

Having signed for the club in April 1971, Bell had been due one in 1982, but he had delayed it because there were other players who were also celebrating their ten-year anniversaries. Bell was unusual amongst the Rovers side in that he didn't work in the mines but as a maintenance fitter at the local glassworks. He received no special treatment despite playing and captaining Featherstone in the 70s. When bosses used to post leave requests on the work notice board, Bell still had to scramble to ensure he had Boxing Day and New Year's Day off to play. He would have to ask the bosses for time off to play and compensate for lost time in the winter by working more shifts in the summer.

Bell had helped other players with their testimonials each season and had been around the team long enough to have picked up lots of ideas for his. More than any other club in the game, Featherstone were well adept at fundraising. In 1982, players heard that Mick Gibbins had earned a five-figure sum for his efforts, including a match against France. His testimonial brochure was packed full of advertisements for local businesses such as Celia's record and tape shop, G & K Motors and John Barrie menswear store, which helped boost his fund.

But just as Bell was putting together his plans, the miners in the town started an overtime ban. Just weeks after the 1983 Challenge Cup Final, Mrs Thatcher had won her landslide victory in the polls. Throughout the campaign, there had been little discussion about what would happen to the coal industry. In 1981, Thatcher had attempted to instigate a round of pit closures but had been forced to retreat in fear that it would sink her premiership before it had even begun. Instead, there was just one sentence included in the manifesto: 'In the next Parliament, the interests of the whole country require Britain's massive coal industry, on which we depend for the overwhelming bulk of our electricity generation, to return to economic viability.'

The miners, by 1984, had developed a unique position within the Labour movement. Buoyed by successful strikes in the 1970s, which brought down the Heath government, they had developed an increasingly political outlook to their work. Their trade union, the NUM, saw themselves as opponents of the government, acting on behalf of other, weaker unions. The NUM outlined their position in *Miners and the Battle for Britain,* placing themselves at the forefront of resistance to Conservative economic policies. They argued that 'the country's miners are in the frontline trenches' in 'a unique position to observe the effects of good Government and bad Government'. The miners could resist the Coal Industry Act because 'history – and especially recent history – is on our side on this'.

A note prepared for Mrs Thatcher by her press secretary Bernard Ingham in February 1981 warned her that any plans to take them on would be a tough battle. He argued that she had taken a 'relaxed approach' towards pit closures. Ingham was a rugby league supporter who had been on a journey from left to right during the 1970s. As a journalist in the 50s he had covered the sport in Halifax and was often seen by Mrs Thatcher as someone who understood the motivations of the working man. Ingham's note concluded that the miners were unique compared to other public sector workers, who would accept redundancy. The miners 'are more resistant' due to them being 'the most cohesive industrial force in Britain who are prepared to defend the basis of their livelihood – i.e. pits'. Ingham wrote that miners were not 'as corruptible as the next man'.

After winning the election in 1983, the government began to prepare for a strike by stockpiling coal across the country. At the same time, the miners had elected a new leader, the Yorkshireman Arthur Scargill, who made no secret of his eagerness to confront the Thatcher government head-on. Scargill was adamant that the NCB would begin closing down the coal industry pit by pit over the course of the 1980s. And while the NCB focussed in on the ones that were said to be 'uneconomic', he urged the miners to fight to keep each one open. Scargill's problem was that the miners did not support him. Scargill had tried to ballot his members to vote for a national strike, but they voted 'no' three times. Then, in March 1984, the NCB announced plans for a new wave of pit closures and the confrontation that Thatcher and Scargill had been waiting for was a reality. But instead of calling a national ballot, each region was encouraged to strike individually. The Featherstone miners, alongside those in Castleford and Wakefield, immediately came out in support while others, in Nottinghamshire, did not.

Keith Bell hosted one of his testimonial events at the club just before the strike began. He had put on a darts night that involved the player John Lowe who had become world champion in 1979. The club was packed, and Bell's event did well. But he immediately sensed that it was a last hurrah before money would run out and the strike would take hold. For the Featherstone Rovers players, the off-season of 1984 was spent picketing and mobilising support for the dispute. Over the summer, Keith Bell started work on one of the power stations nearby. One afternoon he stood on the hill outside the workplace and looked across the area – all he could see were mountains of coal. He thought to himself that this strike would be a lot different than before.

* * *

Featherstone Rovers had prided themselves on being able to construct a team around local players who worked in the local industries. When the game introduced a ban on Australian players, it suited clubs like Featherstone, who had a strong and thriving amateur scene. Their model of success was based on a simple economic premise that they developed players and sold them on to major clubs like Hull FC for a substantial profit. That money was then filtered back into the club to start the cycle again. But the shock of the 1982 Kangaroo tour prompted a move to overturn the ban on Australian players and open the market back up to competition. The newly formed Professional Players Association had promised legal threats if they were prevented from moving clubs. In the workplace, the Thatcher government had loosened up the labour market to encourage businesses to recruit from overseas and make hiring and firing people easier. Players began to write to employment minister Norman Tebbit to explain the restrictive practices within rugby league that prevented players from moving between countries. And in 1983, the ban was finally lifted.

David Oxley was convinced that few clubs would be able to sign Australian players when the gates opened. He revealed to *Open Rugby* that it would be a costly business for clubs: 'Return airfares, accommodation, the use of cars, match fees and some kind of living allowance still need to be found.' Consequently, Oxley didn't personally 'anticipate a high degree of movement either way'. Others believed that they would be unpopular with fans. The first Australian had yet to arrive when the *Rugby Leaguer* reported on its front page that 'imports worry club chiefs. There is a danger of home-grown talent being overlooked as continual steps are taken to brighten up the British game.'

But those experimenting with signings soon saw that it paid off in increased attendances. In late 1983, the Australian superstar Wally Lewis had made a surprise decision to spend an autumn at Wakefield. Trinity, who were bottom of the First Division and threatened with relegation, signed Lewis on a record pay deal of £1,000 a game. The club didn't see the best of him. But they were astonished to see that the wages were covered when there was a dramatic increase in revenue. The club had sought local businesses to help fund the transfer and were widely praised in *Open Rugby* for the 'great courage and enterprise in bringing such a big-name footballer to the game in this country'.

As clubs began to hunt for the next 'big-name' signing to turn their fortunes around, Featherstone resisted the changes. Rovers didn't have the money, nor did they believe that their supporters would respond to a change in policy. When some fans did ask why the club had yet to invest in Australian talent, they admitted in the programme notes that 'the progress of youngsters may be halted by players who may well be no better than our own'. The club also needed clarification about the money involved. 'The big names from abroad are demanding ridiculously high fees and unbelievably are getting them.' Instead, they remained loyal to the English players.

* * *

St Helens, like Featherstone, was a town built physically and metaphorically on coal: the original motto on their coat of arms was 'Ex Terra Lucem', which translated to 'Out of the Earth Came Light'. But unlike Featherstone, the town had also benefited from its close links to Liverpool as the city became a port for goods from across the world. Other industries that were reliant on coal to burn furnaces soon popped up in the town. Thomas Beecham moved to St Helens to build Beecham's pill factory while William Pilkington invested in a new project that would make St Helens the home of glass-making. The Pilkington Brothers would quickly become a major St Helens employer with an international reputation in the manufacture of flat glass.

People used to joke about St Helens just as they did about Wigan. But industrialists and economists often pointed to St Helens' 'long tradition of innovation' in the business world. 'At its worst, it is authentic L.S. Lowry country,' wrote one economist in the *Financial Times*. 'At its best, it excels in the activity it knows best – manufacturing.' The work population growth made it a prime location for a rugby league side at the beginning of the 20th century. And by the 1960s they matched Wigan as the dominant club in the Lancashire region.

But by the 1970s, coal was in decline. In the 1950s there had been around 15,000 working in the mines. That was quickly halved. St Helens was hammered by the recession in the 1980s as British companies looked to cut costs and streamline their businesses to survive. Part of the change was technological. There were protests in the workforce when Pilkington announced that the new 'flow line' would cut in half the number of people it needed to man machinery. Between 1978 and 1982, there were 15,000 job losses across the town in various other industries. The government system for calculating unemployment put the figure between 18.5% and 20% of the working population. One journalist in the *Financial Times* who visited the town admitted that, 'Many of those will never get their jobs back even if the boom were to come tomorrow.'

If anyone doubted how difficult the recovery would be, they only had to look at Liverpool. Where once the success of Liverpool had spilled over into St Helens, the city was now seen as beyond saving. With unemployment rising, and a housing crisis spiralling out of control, it became the symbol of Britain's 'managed decline'. Since the 1950s, the population had been dropping faster than any other city in Britain. It fell from 900,000 to less than 500,000. In 1981 riots broke out following long-standing tensions between the police and the black community. As the clean-up began, rival factions within Mrs Thatcher's Cabinet talked about evacuating the city and leaving it to market forces. Chancellor Geoffrey Howe set out the Treasury's approach in bold terms: 'Should our aim be to stabilise the inner cities ... or is this to pump water uphill? Should we rather go for "managed decline"?'

St Helens rugby league side appeared to be in no position for a revival. While Featherstone had built a solid team around its youth system, St Helens were in crisis.

St Helens didn't face the cold, hard shock of relegation like Wigan had but they too had faded into mediocrity. Paul Loughlin had signed for St Helens in 1983 when the club was at its lowest ebb. 'Just as the coal and glass industries had sustained the town in better times, the star-studded power of the Saints side had flickered then died,' he later observed in his autobiography *From Glass to Grass*. As Loughlin pointed out, they were 'hard times for both club and town alike'.

Attendances stuck around the 5,000 mark but were decreasing each year. 'Fans cannot continue to live in the past,' declared the *St Helens Reporter* in September 1984, after fewer than 7,000 spectators turned up to the first two matches of the season. Sympathetic observers blamed the miners' strike which was beginning to impact workers at Sutton Colliery. But others refused to hide behind a strike for a trend that stretched back to the 1970s. 'The miners' strike may be affecting attendances slightly,' wrote one journalist, but, 'the main reason is born of stubbornness – a stubbornness of fans living in the past.'

When the market opened to Australia, St Helens could have joined Featherstone and decided not to bother signing anyone. But the club sensed they were rapidly losing ground to neighbours Wigan and Widnes. They needed to signal to the town that they wanted to be a major force again. And the name of the person at the top of their list was Mal Meninga. Of all the players who had come to Britain on the Invincible tour in 1982, Meninga was the one who captured the hearts and minds of the British public. Sporting profiles of rugby league players were rare in the early 1980s but, during the Kangaroo tour, journalists had obsessed over the skills of the goal-kicking centre. The *Telegraph* believed that Meninga was a special talent. 'Despite results being a foregone conclusion, large crowds have flocked to see Meninga and his colleagues.'

For the journalist Dave Hadfield, the fascination with Meninga was down to the fact that you didn't need to understand the game too deeply to relish him in full flight: 'A huge, powerful man, he nevertheless moved with the grace of a dancer,' he observed in his book *Playing Away*. Meninga was less brash than other Australian players and appeared to think deeply about the game. Even as his Kangaroo side tore apart every English side in 1982, he understood that it was not good for the game. 'Progress is crucial in every aspect of life and it would be disastrous for rugby league if the game stagnated in Britain,' he revealed. Part of this came from the affinity he had with the British way of life. He enjoyed some of the anonymity and the ability to go to a country pub and 'settle in' for the afternoon.

The price on Meninga's head for a winter stint in the UK was going to be high. Rumours spread throughout the game that it would cost £30,000 to get Meninga over to Britain. That was the sort of money you spent on a player who would play with you for his whole career. Leeds and Wigan were seen as the only viable club with sufficient funds to bring him over. But the St Helens board believed that he would be the silver bullet to revitalise the club in the town.

The St Helens directors made a late-night journey down to Heathrow Airport to collect Meninga, his wife and another player, called Phil Veivers. The board called on the town to now match the ambitions of the club. 'We have provided what the fans wanted – a world-class star. Now it is down to them to attend the matches.' The director, John Clegg, told the media that 'all we want is for the town to get behind the team'. The buzz within the town was immediate. Two days later, the three of them were snapped on the front page of the *St Helens Reporter*, 'Aussie aces astounded by their welcome'. Meninga was humbled by the support. 'Everyone has been extremely helpful, and we have been impressed with the St Helens club, the people and the town.'

As soon as Meninga landed, local businesses were maximising his marketing potential. Helena Housing, a housing association, had secured Meninga to come and open their centenary exhibition where supporters were told they could meet the new superstar. And business interest was matched by media support. The *St Helens Reporter* called on the people in the town to bring back supporters, 'It is time the stay-away fans rallied', to improve attendance figures. And the effect was immediate. The prospect of Meninga's name on the team sheet added almost 3,000 people to the attendance for a game against Castleford. Even the journalists sent from West Yorkshire to cover the game were impressed. 'All sports need heroes, and for too long now rugby league has had too few of them, but St Helens have found a real star in Australian centre Mal Meninga who, like a true showman, gave the expectant crowd just what they wanted.' As the hooter sounded, hundreds of youngsters flooded on to the pitch to get close to him and pat him on the back. 'Castleford must have wished they had impeded his progress as well as those children did.'

After just two games, journalists such as Paul Fitzpatrick in *The Guardian* concluded that Meninga was already paying for himself: 'The town has come to life and more displays of this quality are sure to sustain interest.' St Helens were soon finding innovative new ways to cash in on their Australian superstar. In the run-up to Christmas, the club announced that they had produced exclusive 'Mighty Mal' T-shirts, available for £5. Anyone hoping to purchase one for Christmas was told they would need to make an order by the end of November, such was the demand for merchandise. 'The glass town is buzzing with the feeling that Saints are making it back into the big time of Rugby League,' declared one feature in *Open Rugby*.

The arrival of Meninga had an immediate impact on the Lancashire Cup which had been in decline for most of the 1970s. Wigan and St Helens had not contested a final since the 60s but in 1984 they managed to do so. The final was usually held at a neutral venue such as Warrington or Swinton. But both Wigan and St Helens sensed they could make more money for each other if they hosted it at one of their grounds. The clubs flipped a coin, and Wigan won. St Helens sold 8,000 tickets immediately. Journalists noted that there had been a shift in the atmosphere within the supporters. Fans were decked out in scarves, hats and rosettes, fervently waving banners – signalling the roaring trade for the street souvenir merchants. Meninga 'earned every penny' of his fee by scoring two tries and setting up another two. It was the first time the Saints had lifted the Lancashire Cup since 1968 and their first trophy for seven years.

The size of the crowd that afternoon was the first shot that the Lancashire clubs had fired across at Yorkshire in almost a decade. And it wasn't just the St Helens supporters who were happy with the result. Burtonwood's Brewery had sponsored the cup for nearly a decade but had never seen interest quite like it: 'Ten years ago, the Lancashire Cup was struggling financially, and yet, this year, I would say the competition generated more interest than for 20 years.' Over on Humberside, the two Hull clubs had also produced a Yorkshire Cup Final to boost the coffers as their big-name Australian signing Peter Sterling for Hull drew in the crowds. The two attendances brought in over 50,000 spectators to what was usually considered a pre-season tournament.

* * *

The financial boom enjoyed in Lancashire completely contrasted with the events in the pit towns of Featherstone and Castleford. Before the season had even begun, as the miners' strike edged into the autumn, Featherstone had been angered by the way that the RFL had compiled its fixture lists. The Featherstone chairman, Bob Ashby, was shocked that they were set to play eight matches in the first 28 days of the season with the strike still ongoing. 'There can be little doubt that the town will still be suffering the effects of the stoppage, and many fans won't be able to afford so many early season games,' argued one club official. 'Last week's attendance of under 1,800 was evidence enough to show that, at this moment in time, the people of this mining community do not have the money for rugby.' Ashby admitted that the structure of the season was hurting them. But when they approached other clubs about swapping games, they found little support: 'We've had no luck because the list suits other clubs.'

Keith Bell had quickly realised that he was not going to enjoy a testimonial like some of his team-mates. As the strike had begun to hit the local economy, he felt ashamed about asking people for money when he was at work and others were in dispute. His brothers and his team-mates were doing everything they could to survive. Unemployment in the Pontefract and Castleford area soon hit its highest levels. The local MP Geoff Lofthouse warned that there would be a rise in public disorder if it carried on rising. 'Human nature will stand so much,' he argued. People needed to feel they were part of the broader national story. 'This is not the case in the North and South nations that Thatcher has created.'

Bigger firms soon began to follow suit by leaving the area. John Collier, the Leeds-based tailoring firm, closed its Pontefract and Castleford shops before Christmas because takings had dropped. Local traders were 'forced out of business' because of a massive slump in takings. The Castleford Chamber of Trade president said, 'The effect of the miners' strike on takings is forcing businesses to cut staff or even sell up.' Other traders found that without the miners, they had no customers. When Currys, the electrical store, opened, they found that they needed help with passing trade: 'Another problem is that the street is half empty and there doesn't seem to be any movement to fill the vacant units.' With many of the men in the town out on strike, it started to affect other small businesses. One of the first things the striking miners started doing was stopping getting haircuts, which hit local salons in the area.

The Featherstone Rovers committee soon realised it needed to do something to bring supporters back in and mobilise support for the team. In the past, the coal mines had linked up with clubs to ensure that ticket membership was removed from monthly wages. But without the pay packets, the club found that people no longer had the tickets or the means to attend. To tempt back the striking miners, the club launched a 'watch-now-pay-later' plan in case the dispute continued through the winter. Throughout the season, the club thought of different ways to financially support the club. They developed a bottle-bank scheme where fans could return glass bottles, with funds coming back into the club. To raise 'much-needed cash', the club appealed for supporters to bring in old newspapers, catalogues and telephone directories for a waste-paper collection.

And what was a problem at Featherstone was also a problem at Castleford. When the shareholders announced that the club was losing money, it was put down to several factors. One was that sponsorship and ground advertising was much lower than they had been 20 years earlier. The strike's impact hit the lottery scheme, which, due to administration costs, had actually turned into a loss for the club.

* * *

Shaun Edwards understood the day-to-day hardship of the mining industry. Over the summer of 1983, as millions of young people left school with the prospect of no jobs and little work on the horizon, Edwards had been the most-talked-about teenage rugby player in the country. In his home town of Wigan, people had been talking about him since he was a toddler. One of his first appearances in the media came as a child when he was photographed by the *Wigan Observer* with his father Jackie ahead of their trip to watch a Challenge Cup Final together. Over the summer of 1983, clubs across the league promised to battle hard with Wigan for his signature. Hull KR, St Helens, Widnes and Warrington had scouts watching him, as did rugby union clubs.

The hype around the teenager had people in Wigan sending Maurice Lindsay letters begging them not to miss out on signing him. But it wasn't long before the national newspapers were focusing on him. While he was still an unsigned 16-year-old, the *Daily Mirror* ran a profile on Edwards as a future sports star. The writer observed how Edwards had the chance to make the big time. 'Mirror Sport's search for the stars of the future has unveiled a whizz-kid with the rugby world at his feet ... So gifted is Shaun at both rugby codes – union and league – that he can choose to play for love or money at the highest level.'

Edwards admitted in the interview that he had yet to make up his mind. 'I love both codes ... I've had tremendous help from people in both games, but I'm going to keep my options open for the future,' he revealed. If profiles and in-depth interviews with rugby league players in the southern editions of newspapers were a rarity, lengthy interviews with 'schoolboys' who had not even signed professionally were beyond the realms of possibility.

One of the ways that Jackie Edwards had kept his son motivated to make it as a rugby player was to warn him about what might happen if he didn't put in the extra effort: 'If you don't go out training, you'll end up down the pits like the rest of your family.' Edwards came from a long line of miners. His grandfather Tommy had been involved in several pit accidents, which impinged on his mind and the family. In one incident, Tommy had been trapped underground for over a day waiting to be rescued. Shaun Edwards would think about what his grandfather went through every time his own father took him out training as a teenager in the depths of winter.

There was, too, an added motivation for Shaun Edwards to make it as a rugby league player. His father Jackie had not only been a miner but one of the most talented half-backs of the 1950s. Growing up in Wigan, many people within the town were shocked when Jackie signed for Warrington. But a neck injury had ended his career at the age of just 23. The injury meant he not only had to retire – destroying his dream of playing at Wembley – but he could no longer work down the mines.

Shaun watched as his father spiralled into a depression at the thought of what he had lost. And as a youngster, he channelled his father's energy into his own game instead. To call Shaun Edwards a 'schoolboy' was to grossly underestimate just how much work he had put into his game by age 16. His dad would push him across Blackpool Beach for stamina training and started him doing weights at 13. Edwards immersed himself in the culture of the game. In the 1970s, very few British players took much notice of what was happening in Australia. But Shaun Edwards was different. As a child he would knock on Maurice Lindsay's door, hoping to borrow rugby magazines. Jackie had a video recorder with tapes of Australian RL long before most people had them and he studied the game extensively.

In 1983 ambitious young players signed for Widnes rather than Wigan and the prospect of playing at Wembley with Widnes could fast become a reality for Edwards. Since his birth in 1966, Widnes had reached the Challenge Cup Final six times compared to Wigan's one. But just as he was approaching his decision, Jackie wrote him a note that summed up the situation in front of him. He asked Shaun to think about what he would want to achieve, 'Playing in a Challenge Cup Final in front of 15,000 Widnesians or 35,000 Wiganers.' It was enough to tip Edwards towards Wigan. 'If I ever become a great player, which I hope to … I want it to be before the Wigan spectators,' he told the *Wigan Observer*.

When Wigan finally got his signature over the line, on his 17th birthday in 1983, there was a blaze of publicity when they used breakfast television to announce it to the world. News that Edwards had received £35,000, even though it was staggered over several years and milestones, made him a target on the pitch. After ten games playing at stand-off, he'd dislocated his shoulder, had three teeth knocked out, broken his nose and had about 25 stitches in various head wounds. Playing against the hardest of men, he began to wonder if he'd made the right career choice. At the same time, life as a rugby league player was financially tough. Edwards was one of many people in the town struggling to find work. He admitted that life on the dole was a struggle. 'I can really sympathise with anyone who is, or has been, on the dole,' Edwards said. 'It's something which saps your confidence and leaves you feeling helpless and an outcast.'

Like the striking miners, Edwards could channel his energy into his rugby, and winning bonuses became ever more important. Everyone knew that when they went to play against Featherstone that season they were playing against men who were fighting to feed their families. Featherstone had always been a tough place for Wigan to play at, even in their glory days of Billy Boston and Eric Ashton. Between the years 1944 and 1984, Wigan only came away from Post Office Road with a victory on one occasion. But Featherstone had only won one of the opening four games of the season. Without wages and collecting only losing pay, they faced up to Wigan desperately.

Wigan took a good crowd over to Featherstone and were experiencing a revival on the back of the Edwards signing and the arrival of John Ferguson from Australia. It was a combination of those two who set up the game's first try for Edwards. Edwards was quickly learning that to survive he had to defend well. That night he formed a partnership with the centres and wingers to try and nullify the Featherstone attack by encouraging players to race up in the line, cut down space and put pressure on the attackers.

With Keith Bell in the pack for Featherstone, it was always going to be a tough battle for Wigan. Bell scored a try and led the Rovers team to a famous victory. As Brian Heseltine reported in the *Pontefract and Castleford Express* the next day, it was a game in which the Rovers players played with 'relish and enjoyment' at the physicality. Edwards walked off the field again battered and bruised and wondering what career he had let himself in for. Edwards later said it was 'probably' the 'hardest match of my life'. But he learned a lot about the importance of defending that would stay with him.

* * *

Featherstone Rovers continued to play on through the 1984/85 season, picketing and protesting by day and training in the evenings. The wives of the players who helped organise the matchday functions were now helping organise food banks for striking miners. The rugby league pitch remained an escape and beating the Australian imports became an obsession. One victory over Leeds at Headingley went down 'as one of the best league displays in the club's history'. 'Perhaps the most pleasing aspect was the way in which our local lads overwhelmed the antipodean stars in the team to prove that they are not superhuman after all,' concluded one note in the Featherstone matchday programme.

But while the players battled to feed their families on the pitch, the strike was turning increasingly more violent off it. The picket lines had become a site of battle between the miners and the police. In the 1970s, the miners had won popular support for their pay campaigns by launching a massive promotional campaign around their low pay and poor working conditions. Mrs Thatcher had watched from the Cabinet table as the Heath government had 'surrendered' to the miners' demands and been ousted from office.

Advisors had presented her with information about the cost of coal to the economy but, at the same time, they outlined why the public often supported the miners. The coal issue was presented to the Prime Minister as a 'psychological one'. A wide-ranging report on the 'NCB/NUM problem', given to her in 1981, argued that 'the fact remains that miners are seen to be (and most people with any direct contact would say they are) the "salt of the earth"'. Mrs Thatcher was advised that any attempt to reduce the coal industry's power must first 'counter a public tendency to sympathise with miners, based on the history of the mining industry and the bad conditions under which underground miners still work'.

The attempt to demythologise the striking miners, to turn them into the 'enemy within' as Mrs Thatcher would call them, was central to the reporting of the strike in the newspapers each day. On picket lines, miners would burn copies of Rupert Murdoch's *The Sun* to keep warm as the coverage of the strike grew ever more hostile. Their reporters descended on rugby league towns from London to generate news stories each day. In January 1985, a journalist for *The Sun* managed to go undercover in St Helens as a flying picket after befriending an elderly widow, and revealed the 'secrets' behind the life of the striking miners. The report, it was argued in the *St Helens Reporter*, was a complete fabrication: 'He saw one picket at Sutton Manor on Monday morning and one in the afternoon at Bold – that's his countless hours.'

And the suspicion of 'flying pickets' – groups of striking workers that move from one workplace to another to persuade them to not work – was high. When the Featherstone Miners' Welfare amateur rugby team were on their annual training session in Bridlington, locals believed that they were flying pickets. When they had been confronted, the police reported that a crowd of 49 people had been engaged in a half-hour street battle. 'The rugby coach was given a police escort while some players spent a night in the cells,' according to the *Pontefract and Castleford Express*.

In order to police the strike, southern police officers had moved into mining towns, and their presence caused much friction. Keith Bell continued to work in the power stations throughout the year and would have his car stopped and searched every day to ensure that he was not a flying picket. He had been issued with a document to show that he had the right to travel and the right to work, which he had to show the officers each day. To some people it felt like Featherstone had been turned into a 'police state'. Bell and his colleagues would try and get their own back in the only way they could. If it rained, they would make the police officers stand and wait outside their car while they tried to find the relevant documents that allowed them to go and do their job.

Stories were shared about police officers waving pound notes in front of the miners to show them how much overtime money they were making from the dispute. Over Christmas the tensions spilled over from the picket lines and into the crowds. Both Featherstone and Hull enjoyed a reputation for being the toughest fans in the rugby league community. There was no organised hooliganism as there was in football but if tempers flared in pubs before a game, each club had fans who could take and land a punch.

Despite the impact of the miners' strike, the whole town turned out for the biggest game of the season against Hull. The club had asked for an early kick-off to prevent trouble with fans on the drink all day. But pockets of fights between the sets of supporters sprung up. The *Rugby Leaguer* concluded that 'the main cause of the trouble was alcohol'. However, the paper reported that 'another theory is that the police presence of mounted police in crash helmets an hour before the kick-off could have been seen by some as a red rag to a bull in view of the industrial situation in the town'.

Events at Hull prompted Bob Ashby to launch an appeal to his supporters to report disorder in their own ranks: 'Six coachloads of Hull supporters were attacked with stones and half bricks by a bunch of drunken thugs as well as elderly men being knocked unconscious and suffering broken limbs.' The letters pages of the *Rugby Leaguer* showed little sympathy for the town's plight as the miners' strike entered the New Year. 'The sight of a gang of youths' stoning a bus was 'my worst moment in more than 30 years supporting the game,' one supporter wrote. Another recalled how they had seen a friend knocked unconscious and beaten up for wearing a black and white scarf. 'It hardly gives me reason for optimism that the fortunes of the Featherstone club are going to improve.'

With tensions running high, it was inevitable that the abuse would filter down to the terraces. The dark humour between rival rugby league supporters became political. The young Featherstone supporter Mark Kirby remembers travelling across the north to watch Rovers play in 1984/85 and found Hull supporters unsympathetic to their situation. 'Here they come, the flying pickets!' one supporter shouted. 'Get back to your soup kitchens!' said others. Words like 'scroungers' were thrown around. To Kirby, this was 'hard-edged' working-class humour from old dockers and fishermen to the miners. But it was clear that the image of the miner was changing and that the longer the strike went on the less public support they would receive.

* * *

Memories of the 1983 Challenge Cup Final were quickly becoming distant for Featherstone as problems mounted. At the beginning of the strike the club had been rocked by a fire at the social club which severely impacted their ability to raise funds. And then, as the season and the strike drew to a close, the club was hit by another hammer blow when a fire engulfed the main stand of the ground at Post Office Road. Thought to be caused by a faulty floodlight, the stand was burned to the ground in the spring of 1985. The club admitted that it was devastated by the news and launched another appeal to raise money for the club. One family arranged a sponsored walk around the training ground, while another supporter raised £255 after losing a stone in a sponsored diet. The former Featherstone player Mick Morgan organised a special fundraiser while local businesses offered up furniture and carpets to raffle off to supporters. Even a referee for one match donated his fee to support the club. LINPAC offered up their £10,000 sponsorship of the club in advance.

After a year of organising to support the miners, the club continued in its battle to keep rugby league played in the town. But when he reflected on the whole period at the end of the year, chairman Bob Ashby admitted that the 1984/85 season was 'one of the most disastrous periods in the history of the club' with attendances well down on previous seasons. Just like the wider country, a divide was emerging between clubs tapping into the new commercial opportunities that the 1980s provided and those that were living day to day. As the strike drew towards the one-year mark, attendance at Featherstone, Castleford and Wakefield inevitably fell. The teams that had invested in Australians – St Helens, Wigan and Halifax – all added over 2,000 spectators.

The contrasting fortunes of Featherstone and St Helens on the pitch were evident when the two sides met at Post Office Road in March 1985. St Helens still dreamed of winning the Championship and the Premiership to add to their Lancashire Cup, to send Mal Meninga back home in style. Due to the fire, which damaged the main stand and facilities underneath, the players of both sides used the junior dressing rooms to get changed. There was a flare-up between groups of young supporters before the game. Steve Nicholson of the *St Helens Reporter* wrote of a running battle between the two sets of fans from kick-off. A no-go area was created between the two groups, creating a 'tense atmosphere' throughout.

As usual, the Featherstone players fought a tough, intense battle and almost gained a victory over the stars of St Helens. At the same time as the match was being played, hundreds of miles away in London, the NUM was facing up to the realities of their situation. After 12 months on strike, people had begun the drift back to work as the miners realised they were not going to win this battle. While Featherstone and St Helens had been going toe to toe, the NUM executive had been coming to a decision. Outside the TUC building in London, Arthur Scargill announced that the miners were going back to work. Much of the nation had been watching a repeat of *Dad's Army* as the news was announced. A BBC news alert appeared on the screen to say that the miners had lost, and the strike was over. The main pit in Featherstone, Ackton Colliery, never opened its doors again.

Chapter 6

Family Game

THE MINERS returned to work in the spring of 1985, and as media attention turned away from them, it shifted its focus to another working-class male: the football hooligan. If the early 1980s had been a disaster for the image of the national game, the six weeks between March and May 1985 turned it into a serious political crisis that threatened its very existence.

In early March the sport had been rocked by violent scenes at Chelsea's League Cup semi-final with Sunderland when hundreds of fans had been arrested. Then, ten days later, an overcrowded Luton Town v Millwall match descended into a large-scale riot between fans on the pitch. Ten thousand supporters crammed into a 7,000-seater stand after organisers had underestimated Millwall support, which had been joined by Chelsea and West Ham supporters. And when the police attempted to control the overflow, fans charged at them, triggering a night of fighting, looting and rioting in and outside of the ground. Hooligans destroyed the ground, ripped out plastic seats and smashed shop and pub windows outside.

Until the Millwall–Luton riot, the Prime Minister had shown little interest in sport legislation. There was the occasional intervention against England hooligans fighting abroad and she had attempted to stop Britain from competing in the Moscow Olympics for political reasons. But as media interest in the miners' strike dissipated, interest turned to the football pitch. The Millwall 'riot' was said to have shocked many within government because it 'bore all the hallmarks of a riot in which police officers, not rival fans, became the main target'. Police officers had been knocked unconscious and of the 47 people reported injured, 33 of them were police. The officer who had been in operational command at the game told the *Sunday Times* that it was the worst violence he had seen and that 'it was directed at police as opposed to anyone else'.

Mrs Thatcher took attacks on the police seriously. She immediately put herself at the head of a special 'war-cabinet' task force which included the Home Secretary Leon Brittan and the Minister for Sport, who were to 'fix the problems with football hooliganism'. In the eyes of the government there was no difference between the violence on the terraces, the violence on the picket lines and the violence on the streets of Northern Ireland. Central to the new Thatcher vision of 'restoring football to its proper place in society' was bringing families into the game and neutralising hooliganism's threat.

The government floated the idea of toughening up the Safety of Sports Grounds Act 1975 by giving police more powers to control supporters. The outdated stadiums were also thought to be part of the problem. In early 1985, the *Sunday Times* outlined how the government envisioned a different future for football based on the modernisation of the stadiums: 'The new generation of soccer stadium would be set on a purpose-built site outside towns and cities as the centrepiece of a sports and recreation complex.' Technological additions included fixed closed-circuit television cameras, family enclosures, identity swipe cards and spectator areas divided by fencing. The newspaper proposed that alcohol would be banned 'outside executive boxes'.

And just a few weeks after the *Sunday Times* splashed on the futuristic proposals to revolutionise the 'fan experience', the game was confronted with one of the worst disasters in football history. Thousands of supporters in Bradford had crammed into an old wooden stand at the side of Valley Parade to witness the club celebrate its promotion to the Second Division. The stand had been deemed 'unfit' for purpose by inspectors and was set alight when a cigarette was dropped into the debris underneath. Fifty-six supporters lost their lives and around 265 more were injured in scenes which were broadcast live on television.

The next day, newspapers printed front-page photographs that graphically depicted supporters with their clothing alight clambering over hoardings on to the pitch. The *Sunday Times,* under the stewardship of Andrew Neil, had, throughout the 1980s, been a strong advocate of Thatcher's attempts to revive British industry. The morning after the fire, an editorial urged her to do the same to football, which was 'wallowing in the lowest reputation it has ever held'. Comparing the sport to the decaying nationalised industries, it argued that 'the game needs cleaning up and revitalising every bit as much as the rest of Victorian industrial Britain'. It was a sport in crisis. 'A slum sport played in slum stadiums and increasingly watched by slum people who deter decent folk from turning up.'

While football hooligans inevitably drew the media attention and prompted concern in government, it was clear that football grounds were becoming unsafe for everybody. Sports fans knew that the Bradford fire could have been so much worse. Had the ground had high metal fences – as many did in the 80s – the death toll could have reached an unimaginable level. As one card sent to the disaster appeal put, it 'could so easily have been my family'.

The sport had little time to recover from the Bradford fire before another tragedy struck. Following an evening of simmering tension between Liverpool and Juventus fans at the European Cup

Final at Heysel, fights broke out in one of the stands. The stadium was old and crumbling and supporters found that they could easily put holes in the walls. The stand collapsed under pressure and crushed the Italians. The weight of fleeing supporters caused a fall, and Italian fans became buried in the rubble, with many trampled and crushed to death. Liverpool fans were blamed by the football authorities and the morning after the Prime Minister called for hooligans 'to be isolated from society', linking the Liverpool fans to violence in Northern Ireland and the picket lines of the miners' strike.

Encouraged by the success of the tough policing of the miners, Thatcher pushed for legislation that would give the police greater control over all football fans. English teams were banned from playing in Europe for the rest of the decade. The events of spring 1985 finally had people questioning whether football could survive into the next century. The *Daily Mail* produced a rosette for its coverage, saying, 'Association Football: Born in 1862, Died 29th May 1985 RIP'. An editorial in the *Financial Times* urged the government to do something radical and threaten to ban professional football altogether. 'One even wonders if a ban would be particularly unpopular anymore with the general public. It would not stop people playing the game. It might help them to do it in a more civilised way.' It had, the paper argued, 'become corrupt to the point of murder'.

* * *

Rugby league had always prided itself on having a more family feel on the terraces. And in the middle of the football crisis, people within the game believed that it should make it their main selling point to the wider public. David Oxley and David Howes increasingly spoke of modernising the fan-day experience to encourage families to attend. Over at Wigan, Maurice Lindsay spoke of 'the family game' that had no problems with hooligans. 'Rugby is increasingly becoming a family game and we believe it will take over from soccer as the main sport in the next ten years,' he declared – part of which was down to Wigan's new offer to fans. For the first time, the club offered a crèche service 'so that parents with very young families can have their children looked after while the grown-ups watch the match', he told the *Wigan Observer*. As part of the new scheme, trained staff were recruited, and the social services department at Wigan Council agreed to support the venture. A new family season ticket was priced at £85 and proved to be a top seller. 'It is always safe to bring the family to a rugby match and you won't find any hooligans at Central Park,' Lindsay said.

Paramount to Lindsay's drive to change the standards off the pitch was attacking and coming down hard on any 'football-style behaviour' from the crowd. Throughout the 1980s, pitch invasions had increasingly become part of the rugby league culture. The *Wigan Observer* reported that there was 'some worry about the growing habit of youngsters in the crowd to mob the Wigan try scorers'. And while it may have seemed like harmless fun, Lindsay worried that it might lead to other type of disorder. The club announced that it would severely punish pitch invaders. 'We will not tolerate people running on to the pitch at Central Park, no matter how well intentioned they are. Such disrupters of the game will be ejected by the police and barred from the ground.'

Maurice Lindsay demanded that supporters shoulder some responsibility for policing behaviour in the ground. Lindsay called on supporters to keep an eye on the behaviour and report any hooliganism: 'We want our fans to be as disciplined as the players,' he wrote in one *Wigan Observer* article. To hammer the point home further, the club printed one letter in the match programme that criticised the 'obscene football-type chanting' that now accompanied the big matches. 'These foul-mouth yobs are apparently missing when the crowd is below 10,000 but any needle match brings them out.'

Rugby league crowds were beginning to rise as football attendances appeared to be in irreversible retreat. In the immediate post-war period, football had attracted a peak of 41 million people through the turnstiles in just one season. That had declined, as it had in many spectator sports. But by the 1985/86 football season, after Heysel and Bradford, there was an immediate 9% drop in support across the board. People questioned whether this was part of a wider change in working-class life. The 'serious' political writers took the debate beyond arguments about hooliganism into a wider 'state of the nation' analysis. Peter Jenkins, the influential political commentator in *The Guardian*, believed football symbolised a violent society rooted in inequality: 'Its perpetrators grow out of cities in which youth employment is epidemic, where ignorance triumphs over education, where housing conditions are often sub-human and where poverty is rife.'

Others, such as Ian Jack, wrote about the emerging underclass now engulfing Thatcher's Britain. That the question of inequality was still up for debate 'says a lot about the nature of the country, so much of which – video Britain, tinned-beans Britain, heroin Britain, council-estate Britain, Britain on the dole – remains under-reported and little understood'. Anthony Burgess, the author of *A Clockwork Orange*, used his column in the *Daily Mail* to present football fans as the worst of English values. Burgess said he was sick of belonging to a nation that 'in the name of sport, exhibits on foreign soil a pretty wide spectrum of human degradation'.

But it was clear that the football hooligan was not representative of the working class as a whole. And when people looked at rugby league they understood that it was appealing to a different group. The *Sunday Times* praised it as a sport which appeared to have none of the problems that football now had. 'Rugby league does not need segregation or an army of police,' an editorial argued. 'And there is no more working class sport.' And if the game needed an advertisement for the game it wanted to sell to the world, the stars aligned in May 1985 when Wigan and Hull met at Wembley.

* * *

As the Australians had arrived in the UK as part of the 'gold rush', there was some scepticism that the people who traded a summer on Bondi for a winter in Blackpool really wanted to be in England. The money was inevitably a factor. But there was one other dream that every player who landed at Heathrow had: the prospect of walking out at Wembley for a Challenge Cup Final. Over in Australia, the cup final had often been the only opportunity for people to check in on the 'mother country' in the 1960s and 70s when coverage of the British game was rare.

A mythology grew around the fixture and Wembley as a Challenge Cup winners' medal became the most coveted prize to take back to Australia. The bookmakers had made Wigan and Hull the joint favourites, but rarely in the Challenge Cup have the two favourites managed to avoid each other to reach the final. Brett Kenny and Peter Sterling had been the big-name signings for Wigan and Hull in 1985, and when they carefully navigated their two teams to Wembley, there was a sense that something spectacular could happen. 'Once in a while, a final comes along that seems to contain every possible appetising ingredient and Wigan and Hull is that final,' concluded Paul Fitzpatrick in his *Open Rugby* match preview. 'Two of the best-supported and most attractive teams meeting in the sport's showpiece occasion.'

As Harry Edgar arrived on the ground to cover the game for the magazine, he soon realised that the crowd was much bigger than anything he had experienced in the past. For all the hype around the mythology of the Challenge Cup, attendances had been in decline. Between 1978 and 1982, the final had at least 92,000 people at each one. Yet in 1983 and 1984 the attendances were around the 80,000 mark. But in April 1985, over 98,000 people packed into the stadium. Shaun Edwards looked out and thought that there was a lot more than that. The terraces were so packed that supporters had spilt over on to the running tracks at the side of the pitch.

For Maurice Lindsay, there was an added incentive to the game. At the beginning of the decade he had demanded that Wigan modernise to become as popular as Hull were on Humberside. Wigan had copied much of what Hull had done in the early part of the decade. They even had the same shirts, made by Umbro, and the same tracksuited jackets. It meant that when the two teams entered the Wembley pitch, the jerseys were the mirror image of each other. For the casual television viewer, such as the teenage Martin Offiah, you could easily pick a side between the black and whites and the cherry and whites. Offiah tuned in to *Grandstand* and watched his first rugby league match. He was immediately drawn into the colour and scale of it all.

Wembley was supposed to be the place where players froze. In the build-up to the game, there had been much talk about how Australians like Brett Kenny and Peter Sterling would handle the big occasion. Alex Murphy believed that the game was often won and lost inside a player's head as they walked out on to the pitch: 'It is very hard to describe your feelings as you kick your heels in the players' entrance and then move out on to the pitch. As you emerge into the daylight it's a strange sensation,' he wrote in a book called *Wembley Magic*. Murphy argued that people became 'terrified' at the scale of the event. 'Even though you may be waving to spectators or flexing your muscles, nothing can break that isolation from the world.'

Much of the mythology around Wembley was built on how long you had to be on the pitch before kick-off. There was the walk out of the tunnel, then the meeting of the special guests before each player was introduced one by one to the crowd. Brett Kenny refused to buy into the mythology. As the players walked out on to the pitch, he kept his hands firmly in his pockets. Even when he was introduced to the Earl of Derby, Kenny casually took one hand out of his pocket and shook his hand. On the television, commentators Ray French and Alex Murphy wondered why he looked too casual, 'slouching' and 'sulking' on the biggest day of the year. But Kenny didn't understand nor care for the Wembley traditions and mythologies. And over 80 minutes, he proved that the size of the event didn't impact him at all.

Just a few weeks earlier, another sporting battle between two individual greats had gripped the nation. Snooker was fast becoming the most popular television sport in the country. The World Snooker Championship 'black-ball final' between Dennis Taylor and Steve Davis had kept over 18 million people glued to their television sets. Central to the appeal was the personal battle between the two men. Davis was the consummate professional while Taylor was a maverick who wore his glasses upside down. In an epic battle, Taylor had dramatically fought back from 8-0 behind to take the match. For 80 minutes at Wembley, Brett Kenny and Peter Sterling fought their own individual battle to see who would take home a Challenge Cup medal to Sydney. And it resulted in a remarkable attacking game that was immediately seen as the greatest in the history of the sport. Kenny won the Lance Todd Trophy as Wigan edged over the line after Hull staged a Dennis Taylor-style comeback of their own.

The play was so fast that nobody could remember ever seeing a game of such high skill. Within a few hours, Paul Wilson in the *Wigan Evening Post* argued that it was one for the ages: 'If there was any such thing as a neutral spectator at Wembley, he probably knew straight away he was witnessing the greatest Challenge Cup Final of all time.' Richard Tingle filed his copy for the Saturday night *Sports Mail* for the Hull fans returning from Wembley. He noted that people had already started calling it 'the greatest final in 50 years at Wembley'. For Henderson Gill it marked a moment of personal triumph. He scored an incredible 50-metre try which wowed the millions of television viewers watching across the country. In the aftermath he told the press that it was a historic moment. 'You are looking,' he told the press, 'at the only West Indian to hold an unbeaten goal-kicking record at Wembley!'

The Challenge Cup Final delivered the game of a lifetime in a country increasingly looking at sports other than football. As Harry Edgar would write in *Open Rugby*: 'The script came to life to produce a marvellous match and send rugby league soaring into the nation's consciousness like never before.' The viewing figures were high, and the Australian media had paid extra money to ensure that they could beam it live across the world. What impressed the Australian press was the atmosphere in the ground. 'While soccer violence hogs the headlines, league is billed as the family game, and indeed it is. Mums, dads, kids and grannies all make the trek from Northern England.' Ambitious administrators began to wonder whether the 'family game' could take over from football as a national sport. And as BBC *Grandstand* ended its coverage for the day, the host Des Lynam summed up what he had just witnessed: 'If you weren't a rugby league fan before that, then I'd be very surprised if you weren't one now. A tremendous occasion here at Wembley.'

* * *

For all the talk of rugby league becoming a family game by appealing to a broad audience, there were lots of areas where women were still excluded from participating in the game. On a cold, wet afternoon at Craven Park, one supporter was increasingly unhappy with the way the referee was performing. Unhappy, they shouted that they could do a better job than the referee on the pitch. 'I bet you £5 that you couldn't do a better job,' said another fan. Fuelled by a few pints, the supporter took up the challenge and immediately followed up the bet by answering an advert that was asking for referees to join the sport. After signing the request J. Lee, the respondent received a welcoming letter thanking them for their interest in participating. 'Dear Sir …' It hadn't even occurred to the people running the referees' association that J. Lee might actually be a woman.

Julia Lee had been hooked on rugby league since the late 1970s when she watched her uncle follow Hull Kingston Rovers each week. Julia had wanted to go to games at an early age but had been stopped by her mother, who didn't think it was suitable. And while rugby league had always prided itself on the number of women that watched the game on the terraces there was little doubt that it was a masculine environment. In the 1970s, when the Caine Report had been produced, it had expressed concern about the inability of the game to attract women. In his 'Ask Eddie' sports column, Eddie Waring said that he would welcome women attending more sports matches 'if it will improve manners and bad language'.

The image that the game created was one that centred around hyper-masculinity and aggression on the pitch. The game was proud to call itself 'a man's game'. In films and television shows such as *This Sporting Life* and *Fallen Hero*, the central characters were depicted as aggressive, angry men with short tempers who abused the women around them. The female characters are anti-rugby league and believe that it brings out the worst in the men who play it who translate their anger into the domestic setting. And while the reality was somewhat different to the way it was portrayed in drama, league was comfortable presenting itself as a 'man's game'.

Newspapers such as the *Daily Mirror* had often referred to rugby league players as 'he-men' due to their superhuman strength and toughness. And anything which undermined the idea that they were tough was criticised. In the 1960s, there had been a moral panic within the game at the rise of players kissing each other after they scored tries. 'We like to think rugby league football is a man's game. To give a player a kiss after he has scored cannot be considered in the manly category,' one administrator told the *Daily Mirror*.

In the early 1970s, as the game struggled with declining attendances, an idea was floated that women should be allowed to play touch rugby before the game to bring in new spectators. The *Daily Mirror* reported that Bill Fallowfield's plan was to get more women into the game – 'Once girlfriends became interested in the sport, their boyfriends would have no difficulty in taking them to matches.' But when the plan was floated, people within the game immediately criticised it. The Wakefield skipper Neil Fox said he thought rugby league should be 'for men only'. Others, such as Alex Murphy, warned that it would be 'treated as a joke'. The *Daily Mirror* interviewed the wives of Fox and Murphy, who both agreed that women didn't actually want to play the game.

The Sex Discrimination Act, designed to outlaw inequality on the basis of gender and marital status, was passed in 1975. However, it had exempted any sport 'where the physical strength, stamina or physique of the average woman puts her at a disadvantage to the average man'. This meant that women had no right to play rugby league with boys and schools rarely created girls' teams. There were rare examples of individual schools who had decided to allow it. But when it did, it was such a surprise that it often made national headlines.

In 1972, the *Daily Mirror* again ran a story on two eight-year-olds who wanted to play rugby at Clapgate Junior School in Leeds. Yvonne Davis and Carole Whitaker regularly played for the boys' team and were encouraged to do so by the deputy headmaster Harry Jepson. 'These two relish getting knocked about and show a fair bit of skill,' he argued. Carole admitted it was a tough game, saying she had knocked a tooth out and busted a lip playing against the boys' team. 'It doesn't put me off,' she said. 'It's better than netball.' Meanwhile, the paper reported that Yvonne had been underestimated as a player: 'Boys used to treat me gently. Now the ones who know me treat me as a boy.'

By the early 1980s, the role of women within the game was still restricted to supporting players and coaches in their job. In the pre-match Wembley programme for the 1983 Challenge Cup Final the publishers ran a feature on the 'Big Match wife'. Margaret Bunting, wife to Hull's Arthur Bunting, was profiled as a 'rugby widow': 'I suppose that is what I am really ... we women like to make Wembley special too. As wives, we sit and discuss what best to wear and how we can play our little part.'

The 1970s had been a period of transformation for women's rights within British society. In the late 1960s, a famous equal pay strike at the Ford car plant in Dagenham highlighted the discrepancies between male and female pay in the workplace. It led to the long, and at times slow, road towards the Equal Pay Act and Sex Discrimination Act in 1975. Women were also benefiting from changes in the nature of the welfare state in the post-war period. A generation of women born after the Second World War could now benefit from the NHS, the 1944 Education Act – which had allowed women access to schooling – and the expansion of university education.

Much of this has led to changes in the workplace and by the 1970s, there had been a rise in what was called 'working mothers'.

Yet many people argued that the legislation had still not done enough to change attitudes and open up opportunities in the workplace. Some employers simply re-graded women, so they still earned less money than men. The Sex Discrimination Act was meant to bring about equality within the workplace, but you still needed individuals to test cases. And rugby league was a sport that had rarely been challenged.

Julia Lee had challenged the way things were done from a very early age. At school she had asked why she wasn't allowed to play rugby league and demanded that she be given the same treatment as her classmates. Lee was told that she and a friend could stand at the edge of a pitch and pass a ball to each other instead of playing against the boys. As a young person, Lee had felt that women didn't really 'have a voice' over the way things were done. Feminism in Hull in the late 1970s was not 'a cool' thing to be a part of. She found people were hostile to the idea of feminism and women pushing boundaries. 'Are you one of them feminists?' would be a regular insult. 'It was like a form of abuse and a dirty club to be in.'

Julia Lee didn't think about refereeing as a feminist issue but couldn't understand why she didn't have the same opportunities as male friends had. When she pushed back on her application, the local referees' committee realised that there was nothing in the laws that could stop her from becoming a referee. They could, however, try and make it seem as difficult as possible to do. After the committee agreed to listen to her application, they arranged for an interview in a working men's club. Women were not usually allowed inside but they had to make an exception. When she arrived she was hit by the clouds of cigarette smoke that emanated from the hall.

The committee challenged her on how she would operate as a woman in a 'man's game'. The first question was about how she would deal with a mass brawl between the two sets of players. Mass fights on a rugby league pitch were a central part of the spectacle in the 1970s and 80s and the role of referees, such as John Holdsworth, was to get stuck in the middle and sort it all out. Lee admitted that she would not be able to do that. Instead, she stuck to the rule book: 'I would stand away from the fight so I could identify who the perpetrators were.' They scoffed at her answers and warned her that she would find the role difficult. But, ultimately, nothing in the rules said women could not referee and eventually they gave her a position; refereeing the under-11s in the area.

* * *

There was, however, one area in which women were placed front and centre of rugby league culture. In the 1980s rugby league believed that 'personality girls' were essential to the promotion and marketing of the sport to supporters and journalists in the media. Beauty pageants had long been associated with rugby league clubs in Britain. The sociological study of Featherstone in *Coal is Our Life* emphasised how selecting a beauty queen was a highly glamorous and sought-after role in the community. In the post-war years, beauty contests had been a central part of life at seaside resorts and holiday camps such as Butlin's. Local newspapers would often select a 'beauty queen' and ask readers to send in pictures of themselves to represent the newspaper each year. Beauty pageants especially held popular appeal in the north of England. Morecambe held the Miss Great Britain competition in the 1950s and when rugby league clubs began to elect their own, they became a feature of events such as testimonials and end-of-season awards dinners.

The 1970s, however, had ushered in a different type of glamour modelling. Under the stewardship of Larry Lamb, *The Sun* became the first tabloid newspaper to use photographs of topless women when they introduced the 'Page Three' girl to readers. It sparked an immediate backlash amongst protest groups. But it helped turn *The Sun* into *'The Soar away Sun'* as it replaced the *Daily Mirror* as the favoured paper of the industrial working-class male. The *Daily Mirror* soon followed with its own version of Page Three followed by the *Daily Star* and the *News of the World.*

Rugby league fans were the people who read *The Sun* and the *Daily Mirror* each morning. As Oxley and Howes sought to increase their coverage in the biggest-selling tabloids, they ensured that 'personality girls' were front and centre to the promoting and marketing of the major rugby league events. In the 1980s the promotional photoshoots with the 'Miss Rugby League' each year would see players lift up the women in various different poses. At the press call before the 1982 Kangaroo tour, the Australian Rod Reddy joked with journalists that he was holding her up with 'no hands', to the delight of the press pack.

What began to change over the decade was the way in which the women themselves were photographed. At the start of the decade, the Miss Rugby League Geraldine Fuller was used by various clubs to help promote shirt sales and new sponsorship deals. Fuller was pictured wearing promotional sweatshirts for JPS and Slalom Lager, who pumped money into the game. In 1983, Wigan recruited her to a promotional campaign to sell the new Wigan jersey in posters and in the programme each week as shirt sales became ever more lucrative revenue for clubs. But as the decade wore on, the models were increasingly 'sexualised' in the imagery and were asked to take more and more clothes off to sell the sport to the public.

Girls were asked to start wearing bikinis and were placed in positions where sexual innuendo could be inferred between the players. For one shoot, the Great Britain captain Brian Noble was pictured being chased around the pitch by Val Moss in a 'Benny Hill style' skit. The photo, which made the pages of the

Bradford *Telegraph and Argus*, were shot so that it looked as if she was stood naked, with her long hair covering the bikini. In another promotional campaign, Des Drummond was pictured in a changing room as one glamour model lifted her jersey over her head. Readers were asked to caption the image to win a prize.

Desperate to attract more media attention, clubs saw personality girls as a route into the tabloids and drawing supporters into the game. Tracey Elvik was one of *The Sun*'s iconic Page Three girls during the 1980s and, as someone who was born in Warrington, she was recruited by the club's main sponsor Vladivar Vodka. Elvik was tasked with handing over the £60,000 cheque and was invited to attend future Warrington games. Peter Higham, the Warrington chairman, admitted that she would be a welcome motivation for players: 'What an inspiration she'll be.'

At the same time, politicians were increasingly critical of the way that women were being objectified in the media. *The Sun* was criticised by the Labour MP Clare Short when she introduced a Bill to ban 'the display of pictures of naked or partially naked women in sexually provocative poses in newspapers'. The Bill didn't get too far, and it put Short on the radar of the right-wing media who dubbed her 'Killjoy Clare'. But even Larry Lamb appeared to suggest that the sexualisation of women in the papers had gone too far. In his autobiography he commented that after he had left, and been replaced by Kelvin MacKenzie, the women got 'younger and younger and more and more top-heavy'.

The *Rugby Leaguer* newspaper believed that it too needed more glamorous personality girls to help sell their product across the country. Each year the newspaper asked readers to send in pictures to crown the Miss Rugby Leaguer who would help promote sales at events throughout the year. At the beginning of the 80s, the photographs sent in were often of women at home wearing casual clothing or business attire. The competition in the early 1980s asked readers to judge faces to identify the most 'beautiful' candidates. But it rapidly turned into a much more competitive battle. Images of the applicants were increasingly sent in via professional photographers and agencies. Readers were encouraged to look at the body as applicants were asked to send pictures of themselves in a 'swimsuit'. By the end of the decade the age range was switched to between 18 and 25.

Ahead of the 1986 season, the *Rugby Leaguer* announced that Elaine Burr would have a 'busy year' and 'it looks like she will measure up nicely'. Elaine was introduced to readers as the person who would add 'a dash of glamour to the game' at promotional events across the country. The image they chose was of her stood in a bikini and high heels standing over the Great Britain and Hull winger Gary Clark.

By the time Wigan's Amanda McGugan won the competition later in the decade, she was introduced to the rugby league community via a centre-fold poster, wearing bright-blue swimwear.

Some spectators believed that the personality girls were being objectified and exploited purely to sell the game to men. But at the same time, many of the women who applied for the roles and won the competitions didn't see it that way. There was a pride in being selected as the face of the game and, as the magazine industry boomed in the 80s, modelling as a profession was becoming more attractive and more lucrative. Page Three girls such as Samantha Fox had become major celebrities, developing television and pop careers off the back of it. For Tracey Elvik at *The Sun* it had been a complex industry: 'I had to fight not to be classed as thick or a bimbo,' she told *The Guardian*. 'I struggled with bulimia for five years; going into that industry makes you more paranoid. But if it wasn't for Page Three, I'd still be an insecure doormat in Warrington.'

By the late 1980s the competition to become the Miss Rugby Leaguer was part of the business to create glamour models across the industry. One year the *Rugby Leaguer* offered the winner a ten-week modelling assignment courtesy of a special agency in Huddersfield. The winner would be invited to take part in a modelling, charm and etiquette course with the hope of breaking into the industry. One of those was 21-year-old Amanda Dyson, who, after being the face of rugby league, went from working as an apprentice boiler fitter to becoming Miss Great Britain.

* * *

Julia Lee wasn't the only person challenging the traditional hierarchies in the game. In 1985, a writer called Margaret Ratcliffe wrote to Harry Edgar to ask why there were no features written by women in the magazine. She suggested that it would benefit from a different style of interview, and she pitched herself to him as 'a fan with a notebook'. In September 1985, *Open Rugby* decided to dedicate a column each month to appeal to the growing number of female spectators. 'A Female Angle', penned by Ratcliffe, was launched as a 'feature written by a woman for women'. Ratcliffe wanted to move beyond the traditional articles about tactics and statistics and address the cultural impact of the game on wives and families: 'How are players' families affected by publicity? What sort of jobs do they have outside of the game? What do antipodeans do all day when they play for English clubs?'

Those interviews yielded different answers than the ones a man might have given to another man. Halifax centre Brian Juliff talked about some difficulties in being a father and a rugby league player. 'I feel guilty that the children are growing up and without me seeing them,' he admitted. 'I just don't have time to play or go shopping.' Edgar noticed that she had added something new to the magazine. Ratcliffe asked questions that male journalists wouldn't have asked. Edgar realised that she had a different type of confidence to approach players and ask them difficult questions in a way that he did not'.

More broadly than the media, there had been few women around the game in positions of power in the early 80s.

Gary Hetherington's passion was to coach and manage, and after being turned down for the coaching job at York, he and his wife, Kath, decided to form their own club in Sheffield. Using money from Kath's earnings in selling double-glazing, the Sheffield Eagles arrived in the sport in 1984 as a new expansion club with ambitions of turning the steel city into a rugby league heartland.

Kath Hetherington had deep roots within rugby league. Brought up in Featherstone, three of her brothers had played the game, including Gary Cooper, who toured Australia in 1962 with Great Britain. When the Eagles needed someone to be their representative on the RL Council, Gary's application was refused because he was still playing the game. Instead, Kath put her name forward to try and become the first woman to sit on the council. When she arrived at the meeting, they first had to decide whether she could stay in the room while they decided on her membership. There was, as Cynthia Bateman reported in *The Guardian*, 'one or two misgivings among the all-male establishment confronted with voting to allow a pregnant woman in their ranks'. Some clubs still operated a 'men-only' boardroom where no women, even club secretaries, were allowed to sit inside. But after inquiries, the staff found no law against a woman becoming an RL Council member and she won the vote to stay in the room.

Across the game there were individual women challenging the natural order of things. But as Julia Lee admitted, it often felt as though it were a solitary pursuit. There was little opportunity for women to meet and share experiences of their time in the game. And more broadly, each was often finding that there was little in the way of 'female solidarity' on the touchlines. Lee found that when she drank in the social clubs after games, there would be questions from players and referees' wives about what her 'motivation' was. Margaret Ratcliffe found that at *Open Rugby* there was initially some scepticism from players, many of whom had never been interviewed by a woman about rugby league – 'Most players like the wife to be in attendance when I'm grilling,' to prevent any potential accusations.

In the male-dominated world of rugby league, it became about finding ways to become accepted and respected against the conventional norms. Julia Lee quickly found that people made assumptions about who she was and how she would act. In the 1970s, Mrs Thatcher had been advised to change the way she dressed to look more powerful, and she had been trained to change her voice to be more assertive. Lee found herself doing the same to fit in. She found herself adopting a more masculine and assertive tone on the pitch than she used in her day-to-day life. Lee very consciously wore smart women's suits and clothes that emphasised she was a professional woman who took the job seriously. 'I realised quite quickly what I looked like was key to how they would respect me,' she said.

Kath Hetherington too was inspired by the way that Mrs Thatcher had adapted to the demands of leadership and argued that there should be more women in decision-making roles. Ahead of a Challenge Cup Final she was asked to comment on the role of women in the sport. 'Women are more used to making logical decisions with their children and running a home,' she said. Hetherington pointed to the way that Margaret Thatcher had run the country. 'You don't have to agree with her politics to recognise that she has done very well in her chosen career and nobody can accuse her of not being able to make a decision under pressure.'

The changes were enough to prompt the BBC into running a special television segment on the rise of women in the game and what it meant for the players. On *Grandstand*, the BBC documented how Vivienne Gleave, a physio at Widnes, was altering perceptions about what women could achieve in the sport. When she met Reg Bowden for the first time he joked that, 'You're not too good, looking but you'll do.' She worked while expecting twins and wore 'big smocks' to cover it up in order to fulfil her duties. She admitted that she faced challenges to succeed: 'I know this sounds sexist. But being a woman in rugby league, I think there is a lot more pressure on you. You've got to be that little more brisk.' Gleave had found that players were 'dubious' about taking her advice when she first arrived at Widnes. But over time, as she had proven herself medically, the players had started to listen to her. When asked how she dealt with the abuse, she said that she stood her ground: 'If you get the wisecracks going in the other direction, it soon shuts up.'

Viv Gleave had to keep up with all the latest technological and medical developments. 'Because I am female I have to be better than any man at my job,' she said. 'You can't just be average because people would always be comparing you with a male counterpart.' This, however, meant that she had an advantage over other physios in the game. She began to challenge the way that players had trained in the past. When there was a growth of groin and pelvic strains in the game, she made the case in *Rugby Leaguer Review* that the training was wrong. 'It's down to over-training. The problem is coming because clubs are using people from other sports disciplines to increase their fitness levels.'

In a male-dominated environment there were still those who believed that women should not enter the changing rooms. The most revealing aspect of the *Grandstand* feature came from the panel of men who were asked for their thoughts. The BBC asked the comedian Les Dawson, who was attending a function at St

Helens, what he thought about women in the game. 'They should be used as the forwards!' he joked. Meanwhile, Alex Murphy, who was still the game's biggest name and co-commentator on the BBC, argued that employing women would be a 'problem' for him. He believed that you couldn't possibly have a woman working in a male changing room, 'You would have a lot of people saying my groin is struggling and some of these lads don't need excuses!'

Chapter 7
Box Office

THE ARRIVAL of Australian players into the British game had led clubs to open chequebooks to varying degrees of success. For every Mal Meninga, Brett Kenny and Peter Sterling, there was Kerry Boustead and Mario French who were accused of coming to Britain purely for a holiday. Clubs were paying Australian players one-off fees to release them from work and compensate them for flying over to the other side of the world. But there were also several young British players who were beginning to match them. When Peter Sterling came to Hull, he was amazed at how good young players such as Garry Schofield were in their application in training. 'He's a world class player,' Sterling revealed to *Open Rugby*. 'I'm impressed with the way that they think … these lads have taken success very professionally.'

In early 1983 the British players needed to come together in a training camp to begin the long fight back to match the Australian standards. New Great Britain coach Frank Myler decided that it was an opportune moment to regenerate the squad. 'I was disgusted with the players' attitude in the 1979 and 1982 series against Australia,' he revealed. He set about creating a squad that would 'set the ball rolling' on a new era. The important point was that Myler did not expect to take a team down under in 1984 to win the series. He wanted to select a squad that could gain experience, players who 'if beaten, will come back as the nucleus to create our future attitudes'. Letters were sent out to the most talented players in the game such as Lee Crooks, Andy Goodway, Joe Lydon and Andy Gregory.

Fitness was the key. Each player would need to engage in a run of five miles, three times a week, plus sign up to their own individual weights routine. An academic called Rod McKenzie was brought in to lecture the players on the importance of training and developing muscle strength. It's important that 'they see the relationship between their exercise and the game of league itself, thereby giving them a greater incentive to train', said McKenzie. At first there was scepticism as they were asked to compete with each other through press-ups, sit-ups and dips. But young players such as Widnes star Joe Lydon took it seriously. And some of the older lads didn't want to be embarrassed. David Topliss, the veteran Hull half-back, recognised that there had already been a shift in mindset: 'Here are younger, keener players who want to take part and are very eager to get fit. Last year many didn't want to know anything about fitness schedules. They merely lazed around and sought the easy way out.'

Fitness became the focus of everything that the British game did in the years following the Invincible tour. Before a match between Great Britain and France in 1985, McKenzie outlined his thoughts for the future in the pre-match programme. 'I would like to see every British player relate at all levels to new world standards.' He talked about creating a quicker game and removing the image of the players with the 'big stomachs'. 'My main ambition is to turn the rugby league player into a rugby athlete.'

One player who had impressed McKenzie from the beginning was Bradford's Ellery Hanley. While Brett Kenny and Peter Sterling had captured the headlines after the 1985 Challenge Cup

Final, it had been Ellery Hanley's year. As one journalist summed up his season, 'Trying to write a report of a Bradford Northern match without mentioning Ellery Hanley is almost as difficult as trying to tackle him.' For much of the 1970s the shadow of Billy Boston, Brian Bevan and Tom van Vollenhoven hung over the modern player every time the try-scoring charts were pored over. By the mid-1980s, scoring 30 tries would be considered a good year while 40 seemed almost impossible.

But Hanley kept finding ways to score. And when he broke the mythical 50 tries in a season record, there was a sense that something special was happening. In the review of the season for the *Shopacheck Rugby League Yearbook,* he was judged to be the year's personality: 'Hanley was a throwback to the days when people went to matches to watch particular players.' Unfortunately for Hanley's club Bradford Northern, they had not seen the people flock into the ground to watch him. Bradford had opened their season with 5,567 people watching Northern against Hull KR, and the number steadily dropped throughout the winter. By the end of the season, attendances were down over a thousand on the previous year. And they were almost 3,000 down at the beginning of the decade.

Nobody had any solutions to the problems of Bradford's attendances. After a few months of the season, the club chairman Jack Bates appealed to the city to come out and support the club: 'I am most distressed at the apathy of rugby league supporters in Bradford. Don't they realise what they are missing?' he appealed to the *Telegraph and Argus*. Bates believed that the club's reputation was so low that they couldn't even get them in to watch Hanley. 'The public has been told so often that we at Odsal have limited playing resources that they are prepared to believe it.' Other supporters believed the club was still as badly run as it had been in the 1960s and refused to watch a game with those administrators in charge.

The 1980s were a tough time for the city of Bradford. After the Bradford City fire came the continuation of the economic decline that had begun in the 1970s. Difficulties in the wool and textile industry amounted to job losses as imported suits and the rise of denim battered the local firms. It had given rise to 'black spots' and pockets of deprivation across the city. The decline even drew national attention when a BBC *Newsnight* programme controversially identified Bradford as one of the country's most deprived areas.

The *Telegraph and Argus* mounted a defence of the city in the weeks after the documentary was broadcast. But producers had only chosen Bradford because their council had produced a report that said you were more likely to die younger in the city than in any another area in Britain. The local MP Max Madden urged the government to treat Bradford as a 'special case' just as they had with Liverpool a few years earlier: 'I think Mrs Thatcher owes it to the Bradford people to come and see what the problems are in terms of increasing unemployment and hardship.'

Bradford Northern had a major cash-flow crisis and struggled to maintain debt payments and transfer fees. But as clubs across the country increasingly spent money on Australian imports to draw in the crowds, players such as Hanley began to wonder why they weren't also being paid their market value. Hanley engaged in a renegotiation of his pay deal with Bradford to match some of the other players in the league. A stand-off quickly ensued. The Bradford club sought to embarrass Hanley publicly by revealing the extent of his 'unreasonable demands' to the club. 'What he is asking for,' declared Bates, 'amounts to one-third of our total income at the gate.'

The Bradford sponsors, SGS, were brought in to see whether they could negotiate a settlement. But they soon tried to bounce Hanley into a decision. They briefed the press that Hanley had demanded almost £100,000 a season to stay. Hanley was offended by the way they had treated him and put confidential information into the public domain. 'The contract I have asked for will not make me the top-paid player in the game by a long way,' he argued. Instead, he felt that there should be recognition for his efforts. 'I give 100 per cent on the field and in training. I am a professional. Rugby is my bread and butter. To say I am making unreasonable demands is unfair.'

The negotiation quickly became the dominant news story within the game and opened Hanley up to criticism that he was a difficult player to deal with. Keith Macklin of *The Times* was one person who believed that Hanley had gone too far this time. Drawing on his past, Macklin wrote that Hanley was 'a likeable lad who looks as if butter wouldn't melt in his mouth' and could 'be good fun off the field depending on one's point of view'. But he dismissed his demands for a new contract: 'Hanley is indeed crying for the moon at a time when clubs are struggling to make ends meet.'

Others believed that Hanley's demands would destroy the relationship between supporter and club. In *Open Rugby*, Harry Edgar commissioned a controversial piece from the writer Mick Fielding who believed that Hanley's wage demands would signal the beginning of the end for the sport in Britain: 'Does the game go professional and pay its top stars more for a season's football than the average fan on the terraces earns in a decade?' Fielding warned that player demands for high wages were selfish and contradictory to the spirit of the game: 'They threaten to seize control of the game, purely for their own egotistical gratification.' He pondered whether demands would turn players from 'heroes to contemptible mercenaries, alienated from their working class roots and supporters by their perfidious paymasters'. Alex Murphy warned in his *Daily Mirror* column that Hanley may 'finish' rugby league for good if wages spiralled.

The accumulation of wealth and the idea that people should be paid their 'market value' was becoming a mantra of the new Thatcher government as changes were made to the tax rates. In 1979, the top rate of income tax was 83%. By 1988, this had been reduced to 40%. The basic rate of income tax was reduced from 33% to 25%. Growing ever more confident after the end of the miners' strike, the government encouraged businesses to recruit top people from across the globe to run industries. But while the discussion in the media centred around Hanley's attempts to gain what he thought his market value was, there was something much bigger at stake for Hanley.

He had seen how Wigan and Hull had packed out Wembley and wondered whether he would ever make it there with Bradford. Playing at Wembley was Hanley's dream, but he remained trophyless for almost seven years. 'I've got to get to some finals,' he told *The Guardian* in 1985. 'I look in my cabinet upstairs, and I don't have any winners' medals.'

* * *

Over at Wigan, Maurice Lindsay had overseen a revolution in professional standards off the field. Since 1982, Lindsay had been constantly flying back and forth to Australia to understand how the Sydney clubs operated and marketed their teams. Central to the new regime at Wigan was to invest in youth and overseas stars and install a professional mindset in all aspects of the organisation.

Part of this was driven by his close work with local businessmen such as Dave Whelan who urged the club to operate as a business in a competitive marketplace. When Whelan had stumped up the cash to put his JJB Sports on the Wigan jersey, he demanded that players act professionally when representing the town and his business. 'I want standards applied by all players. I want to see them smartly dressed with a collar and tie at all times when on club duty off the field, not walking about in shirt-sleeves in any old fashion. I want to see them conduct themselves as one would expect from players of the Wigan club.' Whelan believed that the sponsor and the players should be aligned with business values, 'I want them to back JJB Sports by showing everyone that they don't belong to a tuppence ha'penny club.' Lindsay agreed and believed that the club had to offer the best in class to supporters to get them through the gates. 'We are competing with *Dallas* and *Dynasty* for attention,' he said.

The revival of Wigan through the new 'gang of four' directors had prompted businesses to buy into their project. Heinz stepped forward to fund a new scoreboard to align the factory in the town with a winning side. A spokesman for Heinz said that the move was significant for the future of the business: 'With our close community involvement for nearly 40 years we are pleased to be associated with the many sporting activities in Wigan and we particularly welcome the opportunity of supporting one of the country's most famous rugby league clubs.'

Over the summer of 1985, *The Times* was invited to run a special feature on the professionalisation of the club. Keith Macklin observed how Wigan's 'impressive Central Park organisation begins backstage' with offices and dressing rooms renovated and 'warm, sophisticated hospitality for visiting players, directors and VIPs'. The club had employed a new team of caterers which kept 'the large Wigan boardroom supplied with a sumptuous variety of food after each game'.

The drive in standards off the pitch was matched by an ambition to bring the most talented players to the club. When Hanley came on to the market, Wigan broke a world-record transfer fee to bring him to the club. While every other club in the league baulked at Hanley's demands for a salary, Lindsay calculated that he would pay for himself over time if he could increase the attendances. When the deal was done, Hanley admitted that he was ready for the bigger stage. 'It's fantastic playing in front of so many people,' Hanley told the *Wigan Observer*. 'The atmosphere at Central Park is tremendous, it's like playing in a cup final every week.'

Hanley immediately responded to the bigger stage. Hanley saw himself as an entertainer who thrived on the energy of the crowd. He would rally the public with try celebrations and quickly struck up a dynamic combination with Henderson Gill. The pair quickly developed their own try celebrations. Sometimes he would dive through the air, and other times, he would give a hand signal in the air to drum up support. One afternoon on *Grandstand*, the BBC's Harry Gration asked Hanley and Gill to replicate their celebration for the viewers. 'I think the crowd appreciate it,' said Hanley. 'I always feel that you should give something back to the crowd because they come along and they are enthralled by the game and they like to see individuals doing things.'

Hanley's move to Wigan came at a time when the media was beginning to expand and wanted more and more access to players. In January 1986, a year-long industrial dispute began at Wapping, when Rupert Murdoch moved production from Fleet Street to a secretly equipped new printing plant. It was the latest in a long line of disputes between the newspaper industry and its workers that had seen various newspapers off the shelves in the decade. In Warrington, Eddie Shah had, in 1983, announced that he was introducing new technology ending the 'closed shop' policy which he believed was preventing changes. When he launched a new newspaper, *Today*, in 1986, it marked the beginning of a new era that used computer photosetting and allowed for more coverage and photographs.

After Murdoch moved to Wapping, his papers too changed in production quality, increasing their number of supplements and colour photographs. Hanley was increasingly appealing to the newspaper and magazine industry that wanted more images and more features. Papers such as the *Manchester Evening News* began to run in-depth profiles on him, which tried to understand who he was and what motivated him. Hanley was sold to the public as a sports fanatic whose hobbies encompassed chess as well as running and basketball. One profile found him to be a complex, 'slightly schizophrenic character, mixing a flamboyant dress sense with an endearing, if not totally credible, shyness'.

In the 1960s and 1970s, you rarely saw rugby league players without wearing their official club blazer or training kit. But Hanley had earned a reputation for being interested in fashion. Newspapers would report that he thought nothing of 'flying to Italy to buy designer clothes'. And when *Grandstand* ran a feature on Hanley, Henderson Gill and Des Drummond in 1986, it was fashion that they were interested in. 'I am going to outdo them on the pitch, and I'm going to outdo them in dress as well,' joked Drummond. 'Star quality from the boys,' declared Des Lynam.

Rugby league had never really embraced the idea of celebrity but Harry Edgar was determined to help make Hanley a star. Edgar had been watching Hanley since he was a teenager and championed him as one of the brightest prospects in the game. As the magazine grew increasingly popular, he realised that Hanley was going to be the superstar of the 1980s. After 83 issues of the magazine, Edgar had only ever put people on the front of the magazine in their playing jerseys. Rugby league players, unlike footballers, rarely posed for 'serious' photographs. But after Hanley signed for Wigan, Edgar commissioned a special cover shoot to emphasise that rugby league players could be stylish, cool and aspirational. Hanley was captured walking round the streets of Leeds wearing a long, black trench coat.

The role of image and 'image-making' had been central to the way the Conservatives had campaigned in the 1979 and 1983 elections. At the end of the 70s, Mrs Thatcher understood the importance of appearance to the modern political campaign. Saatchi and Saatchi – along with Thatcher adviser Gordon Reece – performed a makeover the like of which had not previously been seen in British politics, with her hair, clothes, voice and personality all undergoing dramatic change. And image was going to be central to the marketing of sport in the 80s.

Andrew Varley was a photographer who recognised that rugby league players were becoming more fashionable and image-conscious too. The son of the *Daily Mirror* photographer John Varley, who took a picture of Pelé and Bobby Moore as they embraced each other at the end of the 1970 World Cup match, Andrew had always been interested in rugby league. But he felt that the way it had been photographed had often portrayed the wrong kind of image. Varley struck up a relationship with the northern editions of the *Daily Mirror* which had ramped up its rugby league coverage. Arthur Brookes, the rugby league writer, wanted to start running a feature on a different player each week.

Varley understood what kind of images the tabloid newspapers wanted. The arrival of the *Daily Star* newspaper had added to the circulation war between the *Daily Mirror* and *The Sun*. Varley studied rugby league closely in the early 1980s. He looked in the press each week for diverse stories that might make an interesting narrative. He looked at the statistics to see whether any record would be broken. He spoke with clubs to see if there were any PR opportunities. He also thought about what was newsworthy. Before the 1983 Challenge Cup Final, he heard that the Hull coach Arthur Bunting was from Featherstone and his whole family would be cheering against him at Wembley. Varley snapped them together, posed against each other, grimacing, ready for battle.

Varley sensed that the game was 'going places' under the leadership of David Oxley and David Howes and offered to do more photographs for the game. Varley was constantly thinking about how images could help sell a story about the game and its players. And it was only a short time before a meeting was set up between Varley and Harry Edgar at *Open Rugby*. Edgar believed that there was a failure to capture the vibrancy and colour of the game, and as the magazine grew, the pair thought of different ways to shoot the players. Varley invested in the best equipment he could find, meaning he had the advantage over many other people working around the game. Most importantly, he could shoot in colour, radically changing how the players could be photographed.

Ahead of the 1986 Kangaroo tour, it was clear that Hanley was rapidly becoming the star of the British game. The magazine *Sportsweek* tasked Varley with photographing Hanley for a special feature on the man that was changing perceptions of the sport. In a wide-ranging interview that focused on his past, present and his future, the journalist Alan Lee believed that Hanley was the person who could carry the sport into a new professional era: 'The men who run rugby league are very image conscious; they promote their product more vigorously and more effectively than the administrators of most traditional sports, and Hanley is a priceless gift to their marketing efforts.'

The immediate success of Hanley at Wigan drew in the attention of people well beyond the traditional sports pages and pushed him into other parts of the media that had usually ignored it. When Andy Spinoza had arrived in Manchester from London to attend university in the autumn of 1979, it was a city that was seemingly in managed decline. Just a few hundred people lived in the city centre and a combination of factory closures and slum clearances had reduced it to a ghost town in the evening. Rubble piled up everywhere and the impact of the war was still present everywhere you looked.

Slowly, however, young people within the city were refashioning its image around its new music scene. Spinoza set up a news, arts and listings magazine in 1983 called *City Life* which was a cross between *Time Out*, the *NME* and *Private Eye*. Run as a workers' cooperative, the magazine aimed to project the city in a different light to the way newspapers such as the *Manchester Evening News* reported it. Spinoza wanted cover stars that encouraged the arts and presented its culture as modern and dynamic.

One day, a young writer called Mike Barnett approached Ellery Hanley about doing a profile just weeks after he moved to Wigan. Spending an afternoon with Hanley, Barnett drove through the town as he listened to him outline his rugby league philosophy. 'It is up to each individual player to do their best and play well at all times,' he said. 'The spectators who pay the money to come through the turnstiles, they obviously deserve something back.' After watching Hanley train and seeing a group of teenage girls hovering around for an autograph, Barnett concluded that Hanley was fast becoming 'the Pelé of rugby league'.

Part of the *City Life* feature involved a photoshoot with the *NME* photographer Kevin Cummins who was also working for the magazine. Cummins was building a reputation as the best photographer in Manchester after documenting the early punk scene. Cummins photographed Joy Division in the late 1970s, and his atmospheric black and white pictures came to define the image of the band and the post-punk music scene in industrial Manchester. When Cummins came to shoot Hanley, he borrowed a rugby ball and had him pose in similar positions at various locations across the town. Barnett had expected it to be a small feature in the magazine. The picture, the copy and the subject appealed to the editors of *City Life*. When he went to collect a copy the next week, he was shocked to find Hanley staring back at him from the front page under the caption: 'In a rugby league of his own'.

* * *

The fact that the editors of *City Life* believed Ellery Hanley represented the new Manchester emphasised how far the game was developing in the 1980s. When the Kangaroos arrived in 1982, it would have been unimaginable to think that a Great Britain player would have appealed to such a magazine. David Oxley and David Howes understood that the game was appealing to more people. And with the Kangaroos set to return in late 1986, organisers wanted to do something seismic to honour their arrival.

One afternoon in the spring of 1986, rugby league journalists were summoned to Old Trafford in Manchester to hear the announcement of the new tour schedule. Throughout the early 1980s, Oxley and Howes had advocated using football stadiums such as Elland Road to sell more seated tickets for the big matches. But the decision to take the first Test of the Ashes series to Old Trafford was a gamble.

Manchester, unlike Leeds and Hull, was not a rugby league city. Letters immediately flooded into the *Rugby Leaguer* to express concern at why grounds such as Oldham and Swinton had been overlooked. In *The Guardian,* Paul Fitzpatrick argued that 'many traditionalists could be upset that the sport finds it necessary to hold one of its showpiece occasions at a soccer ground'. But Oxley was adamant that the game was worthy of the biggest stage. 'You've got to put on the best in the best,' he said. 'Great Britain versus Australia is the best rugby football in the world. And Old Trafford undoubtedly is the best stadium.'

The decision to take the match to Old Trafford was Oxley's attempt to respond to changing supporter demands in the 1980s.

He had noticed how more and more people had been asking for seated tickets at semi-finals and finals of the cup competitions: 'The genuine rugby league fan increasingly demands a seat. It has been proved time and again that supporters will watch quality football in comfortable surroundings. They will not go to watch rubbish standing in squalor.'

In the 80s, many rugby league fans complained that the sport should only use rugby league grounds to keep revenue in the game and boost the clubs' finances. But Oxley didn't believe the sport had the facilities to do it. Under fire, he called on rugby league fans to buy a ticket for Old Trafford to put on a show for the world. He said, 'We are often claiming that we have the best and most exciting product in the world. It is up to the fans to get off their backsides and prove it with their support.'

Oxley was banking on the rising interest in Australian rugby league to fulfil his target of getting 30,000 people to Old Trafford. As the writer Brian Murphy acknowledged, in 1982 you wouldn't have been able to find more than a dozen people who knew who Parramatta, Canterbury and Manly were. But in the space of four years, everything had changed. Channel 4 had started to show highlights from the Winfield Cup while clubs such as Wigan were ordering copies of *Rugby League Week*, which was available to read just 72 hours after they had hit newsstands in Sydney. 'Aussie-mania seems to be sweeping the country,' Murphy concluded.

The first video cassette recorders (VCR) had gone on sale in the 1970s. But priced at £799 (around ten times the average weekly wage), they were far too expensive for most people. As the historian Alwyn Turner has noted in *Rejoice Rejoice*, the rise of the VCR had boomed after the wedding of Charles and Diana in 1981. Adverts had tempted people in with the offer of being able to record the event for posterity, just as the Queen's Coronation had led to an increase in television sales in the 1950s. By the following year, one in five households owned a VCR, which continued to grow into the middle of the decade. By 1986, there were more homes with a VCR than with a car. Cinema attendances continued their post-war decline and video rental stores opened across the country. Rugby league supporters were soon recording matches and sharing them amongst each other. But there was still very little rugby league on television to satisfy supporters demands.

Video companies such as Micron began recording and selling matches to supporters. Most importantly, they imported the Australian tapes each week to offer a glimpse into the way the Sydney competition was run. The Welcome Feature Pub in St Helens began showing repeats of the game at regular intervals for supporters who wanted to rewatch the game during the week. And soon video companies began sponsoring players as well. Pricefighter video store, which opened in St Helens, invested in lots of rugby league videos from across the world. As part of their promotional campaign, they agreed to sponsor Paul Loughlin and give him a free video hire for every try scored or goal kicked. 'The more this costs us in video hires the better,' argued the store manager.

For £2 a night, people could hire the highlights of the week's action with coverage using 'multi-camera coverage, complex camera angles, stylish commentaries, rousing music and visual statistics'. Video nights were held by clubs and in the run-up to the Kangaroos tour, clubs held parties to show supporters exactly what they were in for. Shops selling Australian jerseys opened across the north and supporters began adopting their own teams.

The first club to properly tap into the British love affair with Australia was Halifax. Halifax had enjoyed success as a club in the 1950s but by the time the 1980s arrived they were a classic yo-yo side who bounced from First to Second Division each year. In one season, they even managed to finish below the perennial joke teams of rugby league in Doncaster and Huyton. After five seasons of fluctuation, the club president David Brook travelled to Sydney to see if he could pick up a few Australian players. Brook's plan was to take advantage of the loosening of the market and bid for the Australian players that wouldn't catch the headlines and, most importantly, not cost too much money.

Unknown figures such as Kevin Moore, Martin Bella and Bob Hudson were signed from Australia, and they were soon joined by more. By October 1985, Halifax had a full team of Australian players – 13 in total – to try and stay in the First Division. Crucially, Brook decided to do what no other club had thought of. He decided to appoint one of the players as a coach as well. Chris Anderson was a winger with the Canterbury Bulldogs who had been one of the last Australian players to come to England before the ban was imposed.

When he returned Anderson radically transformed the fortunes of the Halifax side in the 1985/86 season by bringing in an 'Australian mindset' to the coaching set-up. He quickly observed that the British game may have improved standards on the pitch, but the coaches still needed to catch up: 'You've got the same coaches running around for the last 20 years, introducing no new ideas.' Anderson quickly realised that he was miles ahead of them, by introducing some structure to the defence and set plays. 'It's the same guys doing the same old things,' he revealed in *Open Rugby*. 'All you get is inward thinking that stifles progress.'

Having begun the season as 100/1 outsiders for the title, events seemed to turn in their direction as they entered the winter period at the top of the table. But being top in December meant very little. The crucial test for any rugby league team was how they managed the inevitable backlog that came in the last month of the season. Rugby league games over winter would often get cancelled due to frozen pitches. These games were then added on to the end of the season. In 1981, for example, Warrington had started the season by winning the first two trophies on offer. They looked in a prime position to complete a league and cup double. But they came unstuck when tasked with playing ten games in 23 days. They crashed and burned on both fronts.

Chris Anderson had studied this system and worked out that if you could keep matches being played then you could avoid the crash at the end. He began to think of ways around the fixture system. In 1986, when the weather again disrupted the schedule, Halifax boldly decided to play fixtures at neutral grounds with undersoil heating. Others were played when they probably shouldn't have been. In a home game against Bradford, 'Fans of both sides stood to applaud the teams from the field' as 'the pitch disappeared from view beneath a torrent of rain that poured from the heavens like somebody forgot to turn off the tap.' In the aftermath, the *Halifax Courier* made the Halifax kit lady a front-page star by photographing her entering a bath of mud to collect the dirty jerseys: 'It was a labour of love for Margaret as she waded into the black water of the players' bath to fish out the shirts and shorts of the local heroes.'

Halifax's title bid developed momentum when rivals Hull KR faced the mammoth task of playing nine games in 17 days. Everything fell into place for Anderson as over 7,000 people witnessed Halifax's final match of the season when they secured a 13-13 draw to deliver the title. 'Tension crackled round the ground,' reported one journalist at Thrum Hall, 'taking a stranglehold on everyone before finally relaxing its grip and unleashing a tidal wave of unbridled emotion.' Nobody was in any doubt that it was the Australian culture that had swung it for them. Chris Anderson admitted that market forces had worked in their favour: 'Wigan can pay £100,000 for a top British player – we were getting players of the same quality for nought.'

* * *

The 1986 Kangaroos landed at Manchester Airport to much fanfare and expectation in the British media. There were only five survivors from the 1982 tour but there was excitement that the country was about to witness something special. *Sportsweek* magazine acquired Andrew Varley's photograph of the touring side standing with each other in a V shape and placed it on the front cover with a simple question: 'Best team in the world. Or is it Liverpool, West Indies or the Bears?' Inside they asked the rugby union coach Chalkie White to explain why they held mythical powers over both codes: 'They are as near the ultimate best you can get. They are offering the best team performance anywhere in the world in any sport at present.'

The Australians were keen to point out that they were professionals who wanted to entertain the English crowds. 'We are coming to play rugby league in a professional way – our players are not professional for monetary influence, but professional with their skills, their attitude, and their presentation of the great game of league,' said a publicity statement. 'A professional is not necessarily a paid player. He is a player who is dedicated to portraying his skills for the entertainment of the patrons. What follows is rewarded for excellence,' it read. 'Don't miss out on the opportunity to see them.'

The decision to take the game to Old Trafford had given the first Test a gravitas and a profile that took it beyond the traditional rugby league newspapers. Manchester United legend Bobby Charlton was brought on board to help promote the game and publicise it to the city. Meanwhile, the BBC brought the Great Britain coach Maurice Bamford to the stadium to shoot a pre-match walk around the stadium with Charlton. The RFL had spent £20,000 on posters in the Manchester area and put adverts and prize competitions out on Piccadilly Radio to generate publicity.

Most importantly, Oxley and Howes had worked on bringing the top sports writers to Old Trafford to showcase the game to them. On the morning of the match, *The Independent* chief sports writer Ken Jones penned a lengthy article which argued that rugby league was moving into the big event world: 'Soccer can no longer command the nation's complete attention, and the impetus is towards other pursuits.' Jones sensed that the country was exploring new sports that could tap into a 'moment'. 'This week it is rugby league and what real men will bring to Old Trafford.'

At the *Daily Mail*, the veteran rugby league writer Brian Batty was joined by their rugby union correspondent Terry O'Connor for a special feature on the game. O'Connor told readers that he was a 40-year devotee of the other code but 'depressed at the present state of the game'. O'Connor announced he was joining a group of London Welsh supporters to sample 'what should be the best game under either code of rugby'. Even the *Financial Times* found an angle on the match by running a feature on the contrasting fortunes of each economy and whether this would give the Australian team the edge.

Perhaps the most symbolic shift, however, was the way in which the BBC had responded. To capture the event's scale, the BBC broke with convention to send Steve Ryder and the *Grandstand* production team up to Manchester to cover the event pitch-side. Previously, such an honour was reserved only for the Challenge Cup Final. Believing that rugby union fans would be watching the game, the BBC controversially selected the Welsh rugby union full-back JPR Williams to guest-summarise the match. Williams admitted that it was only the second time he had ever watched a game live but hoped the two codes would work together in the future.

As fans queued to enter the ground, organisers knew that they had made the right decision to take the game to Old Trafford. With

20 minutes to go until kick-off, Steve Ryder announced that a new Test record had been broken as 43,000 people entered through the turnstiles. And by the time Great Britain walked on to the pitch, there was a crowd of over 50,000 in the ground.

The bookmaker William Hill gave Great Britain a ten-point start on the handicap, and Australia easily covered it. Despite the defeat, Britain's full-back Joe Lydon gave the crowd something to cheer when he scored a full-length-of-the-field try. 'The bedlam of noise set up by the crowd when Joe Lydon went 70 yards to score must have been heard for miles,' observed Keith Macklin. 'Even in the press box, where journalists are taught to remain objective and detached, veterans of many campaigns with notebook and pen stood up and thumped the desk in glee.'

The result was irrelevant. 'Rugby league took a giant step forward in its determined bid to be truly recognised as a national sport at Old Trafford on Saturday,' argued an editorial in the *Rugby Leaguer* a few days later. For supporters who had been used to watching games on grounds such as Bradford, Oldham and Rochdale, the scale of the event was life-changing. A young supporter, John Drake, admitted that it was unlike anything he had seen before: 'This is what rugby league could be like,' he thought.

Manchester United officials were equally as impressed by the partnership. In the early 1980s the club had often struggled to fill Old Trafford as they drifted further and further away from the top of English football. There were 10,000 more people in to watch the rugby league than there was on average watching United. In the aftermath, United chief executive Martin Edwards speculated that rugby league may now become a permanent fixture at the ground. 'It proves there is sufficient spectator interest in the game,' he told the *Courier Mail*. 'Practically every town and city in the north of England has its name involved in rugby league, so why should Manchester remain the odd one out?'

What surprised the organisers most was where the applications for pre-match tickets had come from. The accountant in charge of the game's finances admitted that the match had 'really taken off' in the public imagination. Not just from the north or from London but from 'Scotland and Wales, Norfolk and Devon and places you wouldn't normally associate with the game'. Having loaded the big-name fixtures at the beginning of the tour, organisers could point to a huge success after over 120,000 people came through the gates in just five games. 'Financially, it looks like being the best Test series for 30 years,' David Howes said.

The influential Australian administrators such as Don Furner and Ken Arthurson began to look differently at the British administrators. 'We based our whole marketing strategy on the appeal of the Australians,' admitted David Oxley. In just four years, the British organisers had repackaged the game and placed it back in the 'box office' sporting-event list. 'I don't think you could find a more fantastic atmosphere for the players, spectators and those involved with the game who were there,' said Australian tour manager Don Furner. 'Even Saatchi and Saatchi could not have presented a better and more impressive package had they been asked to sell the game,' declared John Yates in the *Rugby Leaguer.*

Chapter 8
Yuppie League

NOBODY HAD expected the 1980s to be Mrs Thatcher's decade but after the defeat of the miners it was clear that Britain was developing into a very different country via its economy. The decline of manufacturing in the industrial towns had given way to the rise of a new service industry in London and the South East. The tax system had been reformed so that workers were now able to accumulate more wealth. No longer occupied with trade union battles, her government became focused on rolling out what she called 'popular capitalism'. In a confident speech to the party conference in 1986, she defined it as her goal for the next phase of her leadership: 'Popular capitalism is nothing less than a crusade to enfranchise the many in the economic life of the nation.'

Things were moving fast and the gap between the rich and the poor was expanding. In October 1986, the London Stock Exchange was deregulated, leading to the 'big bang' which firmly established London as one of the world capitals for finance. Around the same time, British Gas was privatised following a long advertising campaign which used the slogan 'If you see Sid … Tell him'. Sid – meant to represent the man on the street – was seen as Thatcher's attempt to bring in a shareholder society. The poster campaign depicted a new image of the working class. 'Soon anyone can buy a share', with pictures of miners stood next to bodybuilders to attract people of all classes to become shareholders.

A sign that Britain was increasingly divided by wealth came during the reporting of the 1987 general election on the BBC. As seat after seat in the north remained solidly Labour, the BBC spoke to groups of people in the city who represented the new affluence. David Dimbleby cut across to the city of London 'where the Yuppies live, the people who drive down there between 4:30 and 7:30 in the morning in their Porsches'. The Yuppie was a term used to describe the 'young, urban professional' and increasingly seen as the embodiment of the Thatcher Years. The BBC decamped some of their election coverage to a new 'trendy wine bar' to judge the mood. In the middle of the street, people could be seen posing with bottles of champagne and giant mobile phones. 'The city's young brokers and commodity dealers raise many a glass to the prospect of making lots more money!' reported the BBC's Joan Bakewell.

In the late 1980s, it wasn't just the Yuppies working in the city of London who benefited from the economic changes. One afternoon the comedian Harry Enfield noticed how a group of Tottenham fans were walking past his flat and were waving £10 notes at northern supporters. What was noticeable about the people was that they weren't the Yuppies of the square mile, but working-class tradesmen, plasterers and bricklayers who were earning money from the boom in housing refurbishments. Enfield turned the incident into a sketch for *Friday Night Live* and coined the catchphrase 'Loadsamoney!', which quickly became seen as a symbol of a confident working-class affluence.

For Philip Gould, who was working for the Labour Party as a strategist, there was now a disconnect between the 'aspirational' upper-working-class voter and the way in which Labour seemed wedded to the politics of the industrial world. As early as 1985, John Smith had argued, privately, that the party needed to organise campaigns to neutralise the image of the 'cloth cap' and move appeal to the new 'aspirational' middle-class voter. Neil Kinnock, who had been elected in 1983, talked about the need for the party to adjust to rising affluence, to win over the docker who now 'owns his house, a new car, a microwave and video, as well as a small place in Marbella'.

The people who wanted rugby league to develop and expand understood that it needed to appeal to the Yuppie if it wanted to grow economically. At *Open Rugby*, Harry Edgar was keen to explore whether rugby league could appeal to the new working class. For one special investigation for the magazine, he tasked a series of writers to examine the future of the game. Neil Hanson argued that image remained a problem and people didn't want to talk about it: 'Talk about image and you're immediately suspected of being a poser with a Porsche and a portable telephone.' But there was a growing sense that the sport needed to adapt to the demands of the new working class. David Oxley angered some within the game when he tried to talk about its problems. 'We're still lumbered with the cloth cap image,' he argued. The Sheffield Eagles coach Gary Hetherington concluded that the game 'always had a cloth cap image' because 'we've tended to foster that image'.

One club that was looking to change its image was Wakefield. In the late 1980s, the club tasked Brian Whorrall and his company Sportsmaster Marketing Limited with selling their club to the community. Whorrall believed the game needed to use market research to understand why it wasn't attracting new people. He found that there was still a view within society that rugby league was a game 'played by people in grey towns in the North of England where it is always raining' or it was the sport that people occasionally caught on *Grandstand* when they had nothing better to do.

Ellery Hanley remained the embodiment of the changes that people hoped the game could make as the 80s progressed. As Wigan became increasingly more successful, he was attracting the attention of more media outlets. In addition to his try-scoring ability on the pitch, journalists were increasingly interested in how he made his money and how he spent it. For a long time, rugby league players were listed in programmes and magazines by their profession. Ellery Hanley was unique in that while he had still been making his way in the game, he listed his job as a 'property developer' on the pages of the *Rugby Leaguer*.

The decade marked a major shift in social housing policy as Margaret Thatcher's 1980 Housing Act had allowed tenants to buy their council homes at a significant discount through Right to Buy. Suddenly, people who had never had the option before could realistically think about owning their own home. And it quickly became the status symbol of the age. Thatcher continually talked about the idea of a 'property-owning democracy'. 'The great political reform of the last century was to enable more and more people to have a vote. Now the great Tory reform of this century is to enable more and more people to own property.'

At the same time, the power and resources that local authorities previously had to build and manage council housing faced new restrictions. By 1983, the level of building had halved and a divide emerged between those who could afford mortgages to buy and those who could not. Often it was the low-paid, single parents who remained on estates which became the focus of much media attention. Likewise, those with the least amount of money in 'undesirable' estates had little incentive to buy.

For Mrs Thatcher the house sales debate was centred around freedom. In one speech she talked about what it would mean for people. 'We want more choice because choice is the essence of freedom. We want more personal ownership of property because that brings independence and responsibility.'

Ellery Hanley was a player that saw property as a way of creating the 'freedom' to develop a professional rugby career. In the late 1980s, most rugby league players were still part-time. They had midweek job commitments that meant training full-time was difficult. Winter tours could cause problems for players that needed time off work, with employers that were reluctant to let players go. He had recognised that, to be a professional, he would need an income that allowed him to train when he wanted. He decided to invest in property at the beginning of his career. And the media were always interested in how he had decided to invest his money. One profile in *Sportsweek* outlined how he was 'an old-fashioned landlord and he makes the monthly rent and facilities calls himself'. Part of it was financial. But it was also about committing himself to the sport. 'I didn't want a nine-to-five job anyway. It wouldn't have suited me.'

Hanley's wealth was a continuous talking point for tabloid journalists in a sport that was still viewed through the prism of the 'cloth cap'. 'Ellery Hanley drives fast cars, buys his clothes from the country's leading fashion houses and is heavily into soul music,' wrote one journalist in *The Sun*. The press talked about him 'living life in the fast lane', of driving his Audi Coupe to London for concerts and shopping sprees. 'He has snapped up property, investing money in offices and shops.' But the more Hanley tried to assert control over the way the press reported on him, the more they kept digging into his private life and his past.

Hanley organised himself like few other rugby league players in the 80s. He was serious about being a professional and employed an agent, before others, to help with contract negotiations. He angered tabloid journalists, making himself a target when he started to control which media appearances he did and asked them what the benefit to him was. Rugby league journalists believed the sport should remain accessible to them. In one incident, the *Daily Express* sports writer Andrew Elliott was not impressed when he tried to do a feature on him: 'You used to be able to go to the miners' welfare or the dog track and talk easily with the latest local hero. Now you must get past an answering machine, an agent, even a solicitor.' He was increasingly angered at the way journalists would twist his words. And when he reportedly found a *News of the World* reporter hiding in the bushes of his house, he decided that he would disengage from the tabloids altogether.

* * *

Wigan were a club that had embraced the professional age of the 1980s on the pitch as well as off it. The appointment of the New Zealander Graham Lowe in 1986, following Halifax's model, amounted to a radical change in the way that the players thought about the game. Lowe had been a highly sought-after coach who Wigan believed could bring an extra 'professional' mindset to match their ambitions off the field. Young players such as Shaun Edwards noted how he radically changed the training regime to focus on fitness and defence. Lowe introduced professional standards across the club, from insisting that the club invest in training gear to forcing players to train in muddy conditions to match the intensity of the winter pitches each week.

The effect was immediate. In his first season, Wigan won the League Championship for the first time since the 1960s. And soon they were moving faster than the game and ever more desperate to find ways of making money to accelerate revenue. To figures such as Maurice Lindsay the game remained hamstrung by the clubs at the bottom of the pyramid who needed extra funding to survive. In 1986, the big clubs, including Wigan, Leeds, Hull,

St Helens and Warrington, had come together to work out how they could earn a bigger slice of the revenue. Lindsay became the face of the campaign to change the power structure, and in doing so, he introduced a new word from the world of business: 'Streamlining'.

Streamlining had become a buzzword in British industry in the 1980s as companies cut costs of staff to bring them into the modern age. In St Helens, companies such as Pilkington had engaged in a streamlining programme to reduce numbers and introduce new technologies to equip themselves for the demands of the global marketplace. The theory was that the companies who were aggressive in their approach had survived. Those who tried to work on the models of the post-war years would die. Lindsay talked about how he and the board had 'streamlined' the Wigan club at the beginning of the decade by replacing the traditional way of running things.

Now he had ambitions to do it for the rest of rugby league.

A statement was issued from ten clubs outlining how they hoped to 'streamline and improve the playing structure of professional rugby league'. The stated aims were 'to gain a more direct influence and control over the game'. They sent out a warning that they hoped to do it within the current structure of the constitution – but would nevertheless 'carefully consider the implications of setting up a separate organisation'. Leeds chairman Harry Jepson coordinated the Yorkshire clubs while Lindsay mobilised the Lancashire teams: 'This is not a bunch of radicals, selfishly trying to break away and abandon the remainder.' Instead, Lindsay claimed that it was clubs who had become 'frustrated by what we consider to be the slow rate of development in the game'.

Lindsay and Jepson believed that the game needed to adopt some of the new business practices and employ high-quality administrators from outside of the game to run things differently.

'The game is only as good as its administrators,' he claimed. He called for managers, sales teams, and office and transport managers who understood the demands of running a modern business. 'Some of our clubs just haven't got those sort of administrators. They've got some very nice people – smashing people to go on holiday with, who probably love rugby league more than some of the administrators at the bigger clubs – but a love of the game is not what it needs.' What was needed, argued Lindsay, was 'the ability, time and determination to get some growth'.

Rugby league still prided itself on the way in which money was shared between clubs. The way the money was collected was that the First Division clubs paid 15% of their gate receipts into the central fund, while the Second Division reaped some of the benefit. At the end of the season, the levy money was shared out between the clubs when the costs of running the game had been considered. The big clubs were also annoyed that a further 15% was taken in VAT, meaning that 30% of the gate revenue never reached the club. For some, it was the scheme that made rugby league equal and allowed many of its traditional clubs to survive.

For Lindsay and the rebels, this needed to change. 'It is our contention that the bigger clubs are underwriting the smaller and less successful clubs,' said Lindsay, who demanded that the rules be changed or that the bigger clubs get extra powers in voting rights at council meetings. 'We are simply asking for recognition of the fact that we should be free to control the game and our own clubs – rather than Doncaster and Batley in a position to control the Wigans of this world.'

Lindsay was fast developing a reputation for himself as someone who wanted to break the game up between the rich and the poor. Warrington chairman Peter Higham was one man who was 'desperately disillusioned' with the way the game was being run. Higham supported the moves to give greater powers to the bigger clubs and used *Open Rugby* to outline his vision: 'They all have a vote on major issues facing the game and they are in the majority.' He found that other club chairmen laughed in his face when they proposed breaking up the power structure. 'We need another body to look after national affairs and development – a small group of very capable people whom we can trust.'

In an interview with *Open Rugby*, the other influential, but much less public-facing, Wigan director Jack Robinson floated the idea that the game should create a 'Super League' of the elite clubs. 'The time has come to create an elite competition, which rugby league can use as a showpiece for the game.' Robinson talked about how the country was changing and that rugby league would have to play a crucial role in reacting to new leisure demands: 'We in rugby league have got to formulate ourselves as part of the new society – by playing a game that is suitable to our way of life.'

The talk of a Super League threatened a major 'civil war' within the game. Fearing what would happen if they broke away, clubs agreed to change the levy system and hand more money to the top clubs. Some Second Division clubs voted in favour even though they would be financially penalised because they 'thought it was fair, and just, and needed'. David Oxley had worked to negotiate a compromise that he believed would suit both sides and encourage new enterprise culture within the game. 'The main central wealth of the League is likely to be produced by a relatively small number of clubs at any one time,' he argued. 'Rather than virtually dividing everything 34 ways, the more that initiative and enterprise is rewarded, the better it is for those successful clubs to continue to generate more central funds.'

Towards the end of the 80s there were growing opportunities for clubs to make money. In 1987, the sport dubbed the Challenge Cup Final between St Helens and Halifax as the 'millionaires' final'. Described by journalists as the 'pot of gold', clubs had negotiated a rise in the collection of gate revenue, meaning that the clubs would now take 15% of the takings. 'The biggest pay-out in the game's history is in store,' wrote one journalist. The organisers had set themselves the symbolic target of grossing over £1m from a single game for much of the season. And when they hit the target, they did so with much fanfare and publicity. The press talked about how each player would be on a £2,000-a-man bonus to win.

It was Halifax who caused an upset by beating St Helens, but it was the organisers and the sponsors Silk Cut who were most happy with the extra publicity it generated. The Challenge Cup Final had now entered the listings of the must-see events in the British sporting calendar. Rugby league journalists in the press box noticed that the main sports writers were joining them for the game. Logistically the RFL had struggled to deal with the huge demand for the match. Hundreds of supporters who had purchased seats were forced to sit in the gangways, and there was an overspill on to the greyhound track. Broadcasters such as Michael Parkinson wrote about the magic of the occasion in contrast to football: 'The rugby league final is a reassuring occasion to those who fear the sporting yobs have made a complete takeover.'

The popularity of the Challenge Cup Final meant that matches were often sold out five months in advance, with just an allocation saved for the teams attending. Increasingly, the Challenge Cup tapped into the rising demand for corporate hospitality. Even the public image of the supporter was changing. When the RFL started a competition to find the most dedicated rugby league supporter in the country, there was much publicity when it was won by a stock exchange trader from Clapham.

Others, however, complained that it was the wrong sort of people attending; the *Open Rugby* columnist by the name of Syd was dismayed to find that cup final tickets had been bought by firms of stockbrokers specialising in 'client entertainment'. After finding out that tickets could be purchased for £120, the columnist argued that the game was fast losing touch with its working-class supporter base: 'Rah-rah-based companies, who are only in it to make money, can get Wembley tickets, and lots of them. They aren't interested in tickets for any other rugby league games.' He coined a new phrase: Yuppie League. 'Yuppie League is here for all those chappies who wouldn't normally go across the road to support our game. It's just a shame that genuine people who want to help rugby league and who organise trips on behalf of true supporters to many other league matches in the north can't get tickets.'

* * *

Maurice Lindsay and Wigan watched as St Helens and Halifax fought it out in the 'millionaires' final' and wondered whether his club could find a way of making more money. Having built the most expensive squad in the history of the game, Lindsay had watched as his Wigan team were defeated in the Challenge Cup at Oldham. The lack of a Wembley appearance was financially costly. With a rising wage bill and record transfer fees being broken each season, the club sought different revenue sources. The club had developed a taste for big events in 1986 when they had been chosen to host the first game of the returning Kangaroos.

Dubbed the 'unofficial fourth Test', Lindsay had thrown everything the club had into marketing to signal that Wigan were back in the big time. He told the media that it was the hottest sporting ticket in the country: 'We have had applications for tickets from all over the place ... South Wales, London, Scotland, Northumberland, Cumbria, Yorkshire and the Midlands.' The phrase 'Dare you miss this one?' was the slogan that was used and the club worked with Harry Edgar to produce a series of posters that were put up in pubs. One fan asked the club why they had not produced more and sold them off for 50p a go: 'These posters will become collectors' items in years to come.' Instead, fans resorted to stealing them from pub toilets.

The promotion paid off. In 1982, less than 13,000 spectators had turned up to watch the game between Wigan and Australia at Central Park. Just four years later, the crowd had swelled past 30,000. It was not only Wigan's biggest attendance since the 1960s but also the biggest crowd for a club match against the tourists. The sheer scale of money involved put Lindsay on the radar of the Australian administrators. And when he came up with an idea to have Wigan play the Australian champions Manly in a one-offer 'winner-take-all' match, people wondered if he had gone too far. His gambler's instinct had pushed him towards offering Ken Arthurson, the ARL chairman, the profits and gate receipts if they came over and won.

The deal for the match between Wigan and Manly was struck without the backing of the RFL, meaning it was dubbed the 'Unofficial' World Club Challenge. There was a significant cost involved in staging the game. As Paul Wilson alluded to in *The Independent* on the morning of the game: 'If the supporters fail to show, Wigan have some explaining to do to the bank manager.' The game would be costly. 'Wigan stand to lose money if the crowd is under 30,000,' a break-even point that was double the average Central Park attendance.

However, being an 'unofficial challenge' meant that Lindsay had what he had always wanted: complete control of events. He could market the game however he wished and he immediately set about finding a different type of sponsor. In the 1980s, rugby league had picked up money from brewing companies such as Whitbread, Trophy and Stones Bitter, which was the drinking choice of the audience it was aimed at. Lindsay could have reached out to a local firm such as JJB Sports or Heinz to sponsor the match. But he sensed that there was an opportunity to appeal to the rising influence of Australia.

Britain's drinking habits were changing. In the late 1960s, lager had represented just 3% of beer consumption in the country, equating to about five pints per head each year. But by the mid-1980s, lager had exploded in the British pub scene. The rise was fuelled by a huge investment in marketing and advertising that caught the attention of the general public. In the 80s, lager was a major player in the creative industry. 'The creative standards in this market are very high indeed,' said the account director on Castlemaine XXXX at Saatchi and Saatchi. But one drink appeared to capture the imagination more than any other.

Foster's was intent on cracking the British market by appealing to young drinkers who were no longer interested in bitter and ale. It became extremely popular on the back of Australian-style marketing campaigns in Britain as the unexpected success of the film *Crocodile Dundee* introduced Australian culture to the British audience. Foster's had signed up the actor Paul Hogan to sell the lager to the British public and the advertisements were regarded as the best in the industry.

As Fosters became ever more popular, the advertisers saw sport as the perfect vehicle to develop its brand even further. They tried to get the FA Cup renamed as the Foster's Cup and made a proposal to rename the Oval cricket ground. The chairman of Foster's told the *Daily Mail* that he wanted to make his lager into 'the Coca-Cola of beers' after he had achieved the 'Fosterisation of the UK.' All of which made rugby league an attractive market to Foster's. After a brief negotiation, the lager agreed to sponsor the World Club Challenge and stump up some prize money for the victors. Lindsay demanded that the players participate in promotional publicity with the brewery. Dressed in an official suit and club tie, the players were photographed holding cans of

Foster's. The deal was described by Lindsay as 'the most generous and impressive deal ever for Wigan'.

The Foster's World Club Challenge marked a significant moment for the Wigan club and their ambitions to become an elite professional club. For the *Wigan Observer*, it was the realisation that, once again, Wigan was the centre of the rugby league world: 'Such is the importance of the game that Wigan supporters are interrupting holidays and travelling from all over the country to be able to say those immortal words: "I was there."' All that was needed was a match to meet the pre-match publicity. It had been nine years since a British side had beaten an Australian one. But over 80 minutes, Wigan proved how far they had come since relegation just seven years earlier. Over 37,000 people packed into the ground to witness 'The Game of the Century' as Wigan shocked the world with an 8-2 victory.

The biggest impact the Foster's World Club Challenge had was on those who were watching the sport for the first time. Despite their attempts to secure television coverage, no British broadcaster had been interested. The benefit meant that anyone who wanted to experience the match had to make their way to Central Park. People who had never watched a league game in their lives descended on the town to cover the game. Chris Ducker of the *Bristol Evening Post* was a rugby union writer who was sent to the north to report on the action. He came away with a lasting memory of 'the undiluted commitment and speed of the match'. The tackling, Ducker found, was superb, and the ball handling 'quite brilliant'.

The Wigan and Manly match, with its ferocious competitiveness, had opened people's eyes to the way the sport could be played. A few days later, the *Sunday Times* decided to run a feature on 'the revolution in the professional code'. David Lawrenson and Stephen Jones believed they had just witnessed 'the most significant evening in Rugby League history'. This was, they argued, the moment where a new rugby league era had been forged. 'The cloth cap is now hung, forgotten, on its hook. Rugby League in the 1970s was moribund in its playing standards, in its music-hall joke image, and in its commercial prospects. Today, the transformation is profound. There is a furious urgency as the game works to improve its appeal and its presentation.'

It was after the Manly game that people began to talk about Maurice Lindsay as a potential future successor to David Oxley. The BBC commentator Ray French claimed that Lindsay had put on a spectacular show that 'oozed quality'. The pre-match dinner had seen sponsors and business owners mingle with past players, officials and the media. French stated, 'The impressions of the Wigan club taken away by the many influential guests can only do good for the club and the league code in the future.' And for one young person in the crowd, it offered a glimpse into what rugby league could now offer a young, urban, professional athlete.

* * *

Martin Offiah had only played a handful of rugby league games when he stood in the crowd and watched Wigan defeat Manly. Born in Hackney, Offiah was as far removed from the rugby league heartlands as could be. He won a scholarship to Woolverstone Hall School in a village outside Suffolk where he competed at cricket, football and fencing. He was not very athletic nor very academic and lived in the shadow of his older brother. But those who watched Offiah play for Rosslyn Park as a teenager immediately sensed that he was a unique talent. On his debut as a 19-year-old, the writer for the *Richmond Times* noted how he did things that made people sit up and take notice: 'Offiah then sprinted for a try that was still being talked about on Monday morning.'

By December 1986, Simon Hughes referenced Offiah in the national press for the first time. In *The Independent* he had observed how Offiah had a unique running style that made him almost impossible to pin down: 'Offiah should play rugby to the music of Chubby Checker's "Let's Twist Again", such is his exceptional ability to roll, weave or wriggle out of tackles.' Over pints one Saturday night at Windle Bowling Club in St Helens, Ray French bumped into one of his ex-students who had seen Offiah playing for Rosslyn Park. French encouraged St Helens to have a look at him, but they weren't interested. Defensively he looked weak, and his attack was not very structured. One of the scouts reportedly called him an 'uncoordinated buffoon'. But French kept telling people to keep an eye on him and almost 12 months later someone finally listened.

Dougie Laughton appeared to be yesterday's man coaching yesterday's club. A quality loose forward in the 1960s and 70s with North West giants Widnes, Wigan and St Helens, he had emerged as one of the brightest young British coaches in the game after he took Widnes to Wembley three times. But as the influence of the Australian coaches had gripped hold of the British clubs, Laughton's methods seemed out of date. 'Widnes are something of an enigma in sporting terms,' he wrote. 'We are a members' club run by a committee in a smallish town in a high unemployment area. We haven't the right to compete with the Wigans and Saints of this world.'

Laughton was competitive and looked at what Wigan had done with envy. He knew he couldn't break the bank to sign the top British rugby league players. Instead he decided to look at rugby union players. Laughton met with Offiah over a pint in an east London pub. He warned him that England rugby union was probably not ready to pick a black winger but that he could go far in league. 'You might be 27 before you get one,' he said about an

England cap. 'By then, you would be well on the way to being a millionaire in our game – if you are good enough.'

The prospect of becoming a millionaire looked like a distant dream as Offiah arrived at Runcorn station in the summer of 1986. He looked at the landscape around him and almost jumped on the first train back to London. As the sports writer Peter Corrigan once wrote, 'There are times when it is difficult to suppress the mischievous thought that Widnes was originally called Wilderness.' As you arrived, the first image that hit you was the sight of the giant cooling towers of the power stations. Widnes had carved out a niche as the home of the chemical industry that was central to its rise in the 19th century. John Hutchinson built his first factory in 1847 on land between the Sankey Canal and the railway, which became known as Spike Island. His factory used a revolutionary new technique called the 'Leblanc process' to make alkali. Widnes was ideally located as materials could be shipped in by rail and waterways and then moved anywhere else in the country or abroad.

Entrepreneurs soon built further chemical factories nearby and Widnes grew its rugby league team around the rise in housing that was built for the factory workers. In addition to the manufacturing of products such as soap and bleaching powder, there were other industries such as iron and copper works. But the town became heavily polluted with smoke and chemical emissions. As one journalist noted, the smell had been so 'readily absorbed into the everyday life of Widnes, only strangers seem to consider it worth mentioning'.

Offiah's first impression was not of the smell but of the rows and rows of cobbled streets and terraced houses that reminded him of *Coronation Street*. He wondered what he had let himself in for. When Laughton's assistant met him off the train to give him a guided tour of the area, Offiah questioned whether he had made the right decision. Offiah couldn't drive so would often take the bus around the town to get an understanding of what the town looked like. He was surprised when people would just come up to him and start talking.

The rough image of the town, however, was nothing compared to the roughness he received on the field when he made his first few appearances for Widnes. He was clobbered, battered and hit high every time he touched the ball. He admitted that he was not a 'violent man' and wore shoulder pads to help him out physically. He found a much higher level of violence than in rugby union. But he quickly learned he had to duck as he went into a tackle to avoid being hit.

As a southern-speaking black player, he stood out on the rugby pitch and was inevitably a target for the northern forwards who wanted to teach him a lesson. And for the first few games, Offiah and Laughton wondered if the gamble would pay off. Ten minutes into his debut, he was so tired that he prayed for half-time. For the next few games he couldn't find a way over the line. At half-time against lowly Runcorn in the Lancashire Cup, Laughton gave him a rub down and told him that things needed to change: 'You can't buy a try-scoring winger who doesn't score tries.'

But even though he hadn't scored in his first few games, Offiah remained confident that he would start to. He kept getting chances, which indicated that he was finding the space. And then, in the second half against Runcorn, he scored his very first rugby league try. The floodgates opened and Offiah went on a run of 15 games in which he scored in every one. It didn't take long for supporters to realise that Offiah was an extraordinary winger with pace to burn and an ability to score spectacular tries. 'People are starting to compare Martin Offiah with Brian Bevan and Tom van Vollenhoven, which gives me a warm glow,' wrote Dougie Laughton in his weekly newspaper column.

After just a few matches, Offiah was quickly anointed as a star by the legends of yesteryear. Keith Fielding was impressed by his 'insatiable hunger and fierce determination' to score tries in any situation. Billy Boston said he was a 'tremendous crowd-puller' with 'that indefinable charisma which the great wingers have'. Meanwhile, Alan Smith, the dominant British winger of the 1970s for Leeds, had stopped watching the sport after retiring but had been drawn back in: 'I'd travel to Widnes to watch him anytime.'

Supporters at Widnes responded to his natural enthusiasm for the game. Like Henderson Gill and Des Drummond who came before him, Offiah was a crowd pleaser who thrived on the energy of the fans and the atmosphere. Offiah had an outward confidence that was rare to see in rugby league. For all the talk of change within the image of the sport, league remained a conservative game with stars who remained humble about what they achieved. When players scored tries, they often shook hands with team-mates or punched the air with delight. In the 1960s, the people running the game had been so concerned about supporters complaining about players kissing each other when they scored that they issued a warning. 'If you want to congratulate a team-mate scoring a try, you can pat him on the back or shake his hand,' an official said. 'But kissing and hugging are out.'

At the same time, rugby league fans were more expressive than rugby union supporters and Offiah thrived off the energy in his new code. As he took the game by storm in his first season, Offiah's centre partner Darren Wright noted how he became more and more confident in the game and that the celebrations became more exuberant. Offiah would often begin celebrating before he had even put the ball down. He developed a tactic where he would run past defenders and then jokingly hold out the ball to give them a chance to get it back. Fans responded by running on to the pitch to congratulate him. 'I know the crowd enjoy it', admitted Offiah.

'And I enjoy it, so we both have a good time.' Sometimes spectators would stand in the in-goal area before he had even reached the line, ready to jump on top of him in celebration.

It was not long before people began to criticise his exuberance and the 'showboating' antics. Throughout his first season, supporters would write to the *Rugby Leaguer* each week to express their concern at his behaviour. One supporter feared it would provoke violence in opponents at some point: 'He is in danger of being seriously injured.' After Offiah scored a try and sat on the wall of the crowd, the St Helens coach Alex Murphy remarked that he was pushing things too far. 'Jumping up on the wall after scoring a try isn't really advisable,' argued Murphy. 'Being a showman is one thing, but taking the Mickey out of your fellow professionals is another.' Legends from the 1960s such as Billy Boston couldn't understand why he had to taunt opponents after scoring a try.

Alex Murphy had missed out on signing Martin Offiah as St Helens coach and appeared to have a personal grudge against Offiah. 'I can't believe that we've got players now who have scored a try and done a great thing and can't just go back for the kick-off.' Murphy would often use his *Daily Mirror* column to bemoan how there were no characters in the game anymore. At the same time he was outraged that Offiah 'did a little dance' when he scored. 'We'll have them going out with handbags next!'

Part of his style was his personality. But at the same time, Offiah was trying to work out the best way to survive on a rugby league pitch. In the early 1980s, Ellery Hanley had decided that he would face up to racial taunts and abuse through toughness and discipline on the pitch. Offiah, by contrast, responded to racism through embarrassment. 'There's no greater hurt than embarrassment. It debilitates, it intimidates, it humiliates – and it puts even the thugs in their place,' he later revealed to the *Daily Mirror*. When Offiah got punched in the head or knocked in the teeth he would simply bide his time and humiliate them with his pace. 'There's nothing better than that,' he added. 'Nothing shuts up a violent player more completely.' As he built a name for himself, he could 'see the fear of embarrassment building up in the eyes of some players who just wanted to be violent. That gives me tremendous satisfaction.'

At the end of the 1987/88 campaign, Offiah capped off a remarkable first season by winning the Man of Steel award and was praised for the way he had brought personality to the game. But still there were those urging him to change his style. In one interview with BBC *Sportsnight*, days after he won the award, Eddie Hemmings remarked that his behaviour was unusual. 'It's not normal in this game,' he observed. 'They don't go to the crowd in quite the same manner.'

Because Offiah was not steeped in rugby league traditions he had little time for those who told him how to behave. Offiah understood that rugby league was lacking in national profile and had, himself, stereotyped the game before he had played it. Having viewed the sport 'as a game with a northern, cloth cap image', he was shocked to find 'the game is played by intelligent, superbly fit athletes, and standards are improving each year'. But he was surprised to see how little cut-through the game had in the media compared to other sports: 'Sadly, the message does not seem to have got across to the national public and that's the great tragedy.'

Offiah took it upon himself to change that. He had only been in the game a few months, but he had decided that if nobody else was going to do it, then it would have to be him. 'I am prepared to act as a personality for the crowd if it gives the game a higher profile,' he revealed in his *Rugby Leaguer Review* column. He sensed that it was down to him to help change it: 'We need stars for the kids to identify with, and we need personalities for the media to focus on.' Media opportunities soon came his way. Offiah appealed to producers at *Question of Sport* as well as magazines such as *City Life*. Mike Barnett, who had run the feature on Hanley in 1986, now did a follow-up with Offiah. 'Offiah is the embodiment of the modern rugby league player,' he concluded. 'He's young ... handsome and successful.'

Offiah's image greatly appealed to magazine editors who wanted to write about young, successful professionals. New publications such as *Arena* and *The Face* focused on culture, politics, sport, fashion and other high-end consumer habits to appeal to the new Yuppie. *For Him* magazine was launched in the late 1980s and was distributed initially through men's fashion outlets. Distribution was expanded to newsagents as a quarterly in the spring of 1987 and it later became known as *FHM*. Offiah was the first rugby league player to feature, after the journalist Francis Cottam identified him as one of the more marketable rugby league players. After interviewing him, Cottam presented him as an exciting athlete playing the kind of sport that should appeal to the people who were interested in fashion as much as sport.

Chapter 9

Going North

WHEN MARTIN Offiah moved north he understood that he was giving up on the chance to fulfil a lifelong ambition to play at Twickenham for England. 'At the moment I still feel that missing that England cap has left a big gap in my life,' he told the *Daily Mail*.

'After all, if you have had your heart set on something since the age of 11 it's difficult to forget it just like that.'

At the same time, the prospect of playing for Great Britain against Australia held massive appeal. As Offiah moved around the sports world, appearing on *Question of Sport*, he noticed how fellow athletes such as Ian Botham weren't really interested in club rugby league. But they always watched the Great Britain side.

The 1988 Ashes series in Australia was Great Britain's moment to sell its new team to the world. The Australians spoke about a potential £1m gate by selling out the 40,000-capacity Sydney Football Stadium for the 100th Test between the two countries: 'The Aussies have not forgotten how well the 50th Wembley Final was presented in 1985 and with Britain's cooperation they'd like the Centenary Test to have the same appeal,' revealed one organiser. Back home, the British media promised to cover the tour like never before. For the first time in history, the BBC agreed to show the matches in full, relayed by satellite, just minutes after the game had finished.

More broadly, the 1988 tour to Australia came at a time when British businesses were increasingly confident on the global stage. Mrs Thatcher began talking about the 'global village' and the need for British businesses to export to the world: 'All of it is a global village and the trade is much more interconnected, interrelated. Our standard of living depends upon having much more, freer trade.' Australia had been identified as a potential market for companies to export to by the end of the decade and rugby league officials wanted to be part of it.

In 1988, Brisbane in Australia was host to a world exposition that brought the business community to the city. The first exposition was held in London in 1851, devised as a celebration of 'industry and human achievement'. World Expo 88 was on the theme of 'Leisure in the Age of Technology' and was opened by the Queen. David Howes met with Expo 88 authorities to arrange appearances by the players at the British Pavilion. 'We'll make our presence felt, just like we did 200 years ago,' Howes said. Howes' advance promotional trip was the first of its kind by a British league official. For the first time, a merchandising company produced and sold Great Britain merchandise to supporters. A Sydney-based sports agency was also given a contract to handle areas of promotion and public appearances to maximise profit and profile.

After all the preparation, however, the tour quickly turned into a disaster for Howes and the British organisers. Ashes tours were notoriously long and drawn-out. The players were subject to an 18-match tour that took them to the far corners of the country. They started in Papua New Guinea and then moved from Cairns to Tamworth to places such as Rockhampton, Toowoomba and Orange. The British players struggled to capture the imagination of the Australian crowds. The team were soon decimated by injuries as stars such as Shaun Edwards and Garry Schofield flew home early. And while Great Britain gave the Australians a contest in the Centenary Test, organisers were shocked by the low attendance. The British blamed the high ticket prices while the Australians said it was a tough sell. Defeat in the second Test at Brisbane then killed any hope that it could be a competitive finale.

By the time of the third Test in Sydney, the team appeared to be at rock bottom. Eleven players from the original selection were unavailable. A Sydney bookmaker offered a handicap of 29 points and Ray French had compiled his research on the biggest defeats ever suffered by a Great Britain side. John Hogan of *The Australian* remarked that it would not be a Test match at all: 'This match is a sham. The Lions are simply not good enough and will be forced to field a team which is not in the same class as their awesome opposition.' Great Britain had lost 15 games in a row against the Aussies and there was little chance they would end it. Only 15,994 people were in the ground, which was the lowest-ever attendance for an Ashes match.

Those tuning in to the BBC breakfast coverage of the game found Harry Gration, an injured Shaun Edwards and Peter Fox tasked with narrating the coverage to the public from the studio. Fox had been the coach the last time Great Britain had beaten Australia in 1978. 'Technically I'd say we have no chance,' opened Fox. But over 80 minutes, Great Britain pulled off a miraculous victory that would again thrust the sport into the national consciousness. The image of Henderson Gill racing away for a try and 'dancing a boogie' was topped only by the effort of Mike Gregory, who outran the Australians to seal a victory in the final stages of the match.

For those involved in the long slog to turn the game around, it marked a moment of rare triumph in a decade of disappointments against Australia. Shaun Edwards admitted that he was disappointed to be watching it from a studio and not playing, 'I think it's one of the best days in Great Britain rugby league history.' In the BBC studio, Gration apologised for 'milking' the victory by repeatedly asking the producers to show the Gill and Gregory tries again. 'Why shouldn't we? It doesn't happen very often that we beat the Australians.' The morning after, the rugby union journalist Stephen Jones told *Sunday Times* readers that 'a long-forgotten team burst back into sporting consciousness'. He argued that the victory was 'the sensation of the year in sport', which had 'interrupted the depressing sequence of defeats suffered by our national teams in most of the other major sports'.

The pre-match talk about injuries and record defeats had created a narrative that tapped into the British psyche. The Great Britain coach Malcolm Reilly put it down to the 'Bulldog spirit' in the camp and the desire to win it for their country, 'There's nothing more dangerous than an Englishman with his back against the wall.' Mythology around 'Dunkirk spirit' and 'Rorke's Drift' inevitably gripped the public imagination. When the BBC *Nine O'Clock News* led with the victory, the image of Henderson Gill was beamed into millions of homes across the country.

In the days following the victory, the journalist David Lawrenson found no end for people who wanted to talk to him about the game. At the offices of *The Times*, he saw people who had never shown an interest in the sport saying, 'What a result – isn't this fantastic!' He received a message from a friend who had been out of the country for a few years and was amazed at the British handling skills and support play: 'Is all rugby league played like this now?'

* * *

Jonathan Davies watched on as Great Britain won the plaudits of the nation and wondered whether he, too, should have been part of the spectacle. Davies was the pride of Welsh rugby union and the biggest name in either code in the summer of 1988. At the time, Davies was profiled in the newspapers as the saviour of the Welsh game and a genius who appeared to possess once-in-a-generation talents. 'Every now and again a god is born in the Welsh valleys,' ran one profile in *The Times*. 'And for 20 years or so, he grows up like any normal human being. But the word spreads that he can perform magic and superhuman skill with an oval ball, and the people come to see, and they recognise that he is the saviour for whom they have been waiting.'

The rugby union press believed that Davies could become 'rugby's first global entertainer' when he burst on to the scene in 1986. And he seemed eager to reject any advances of turning professional. He once claimed to have turned down £100,000 to move north. 'It's nice to be offered so much, but I have a lot to lose down here in South Wales,' he admitted. But by the late 1980s, cracks were beginning to appear in rugby union's amateur ethos. The sport had maintained its pretence of amateurism by banning players from accepting awards from businesses and 'commercial firms', which was seen as contrary to the principles of the game. Over the 1970s, the rules were relaxed as teams began to secure sponsorship deals for boots and equipment. But there was still more money to be made as an individual by playing rugby league.

Davies was just the latest in a long line of Welsh players who piqued the interest of the rugby league scouts. Since 1895, when the rugby codes split into two, Welsh players had made the journey to the north of England in search of fame and fortune. In addition to the greats such as Billy Boston and Clive Sullivan, there were British Lions such as David Watkins. In 1967, Watkins shocked the world when he 'turned professional' to join an ambitious Salford in a world-record £16,000 deal. 'Obviously, the reason I turned professional was from the financial point of view,' he told a BBC documentary in the 1960s. 'I think everybody has to secure themselves for life.'

'Going north', as it was called, carried emotional overtones in Wales. As one Welsh journalist said, 'To switch to the professional code of rugby league is to defect: not only from amateur rugby union itself, but from your roots.' The decision to play rugby league could isolate a person from their community for life. In the fictional ITV drama *Fallen Hero,* the central character, Gareth Hopkins, had decided to 'go north' in the 60s to set himself up financially. But he pays a price. His family refuses to speak to him, and he is ostracised. He's banned from drinking or even entering the local rugby club and can't even coach a local rugby union side.

Fallen Hero tapped into the long-standing efforts of rugby union to prevent its players from moving north to play league. Once you stepped over the line and played a game of rugby league, you were banned from ever playing rugby union again. In the 1980s the government had prided itself in eradicating a range of what were called 'restrictive practices' in industry. Mrs Thatcher had broken up employment legislation in the early 1980s to make it easier to 'hire and fire'. Yet rugby union still operated a closed shop with its rules and regulations. This was increasingly brought to the attention of MPs.

David Hinchliffe was a rugby league man who had supported Wakefield Trinity his entire life. His claim to fame had been that he was in the crowd the day that *This Sporting Life* had been filmed at the ground. In 1987 he was part of a new generation of Labour politicians who entered the Commons with little background in Westminster politics. He knew few people in Parliament but soon found that people were interested in talking to him about rugby league. In a House of Commons still dominated by the Conservatives and the public schools, there was a prevailing orthodoxy that league was a 'dirty' code. Over beers in the Strangers' bar, Hinchliffe was shocked to discover how many MPs had been 'brought up to genuinely believe that playing league is, more or less, on a par with some sort of criminal activity'.

Harry Edgar had long used *Open Rugby* to outline the hidden structural problems that the league faced in its battles with rugby union. As early as 1984, he argued that the game needed to pressure the government to change legislation to end discrimination: 'In this day and age, where there are laws against sporting clubs refusing membership to individuals on the grounds of race or religion, it is still rugby union policy to deny membership to anybody who has played "any other form of rugby".' The word apartheid was often used to describe the way in which rugby union had gripped hold of the people running the government and businesses to keep league at bay. Those players that did dip their toe in rugby league water did so under the cloak of anonymity. Players who were trialling would be listed in the programme under the name A.N. Other.

But by the 80s, with technological changes and video and newspaper reporting of every game, this was becoming much harder. One of the people who was caught was a Welsh amateur called Steve Ford. Ford made the mistake of playing a game of rugby league for Leeds, scoring two tries and winning man of the match in the process.

He was made an offer to move to rugby league, but he changed his mind at the last moment to pursue a dream of playing rugby union for Wales. Unfortunately for him, a secretary of the Welsh Rugby Union (WRU) was sent a news cutting which showed Ford playing league. The WRU had no option but to ban him for life.

Such practices seemed increasingly at odds with the new economy that the Thatcher government had created. People no longer had jobs for life and were encouraged to reskill, move to new areas and seek as many different opportunities as possible. 'Freedom' was the buzzword of the age. But when it came to the divide between league and union there was still a massive restriction of trade. League began to lobby for change and caught the attention of the BBC. Jonathan Dimbleby's current affairs show *First Tuesday* decided to put together a special documentary on Ford's case as they outlined the 'bitter divide' between the two philosophies. Dimbleby wanted to show that the divide between the two codes was 'not just an academic one' but 'has victims'.

The documentary brought together a range of administrators and politicians who believed that the law needed to change. David Oxley announced that league would support a legal challenge by Ford to allow him to return to union. 'The rugby union's attitude can no longer be tolerated,' he said. Other figures such as Labour's Merlyn Rees, who had been a Cabinet minister in the 1970s, framed it as a human rights issue first and foremost: 'Human rights and natural justice is a growing aspect of the law in the last 20 years.'

Oxley branded rugby union 'hypocritical' and argued on *First Tuesday* that the laws banning players from switching codes were 'discriminatory, against public policy and not operable in law'. In response leaders of the WRU said they were wedded to the structures that remained: 'Every sports organisation is perfectly entitled to make whatever rules and regulations and wishes provided it doesn't act against natural justice.'

It wasn't just rugby league officials who believed that the rugby union establishment needed to change. The RFU had refused to allow former players such as Bill Beaumont – the former England captain – to return to the game after he had been accused of 'professionalising' himself by writing a memoir. The England winger Derek Wyatt argued for greater transparency in union circles and began to write for *Open Rugby* in the 1980s about the discrepancy between the two codes. He recounted how after one club game he had played in front of a capacity crowd; he had seen the car park full, the programmes sold out and the bars packed: 'Where, I pondered, was the money going?'

David Hinchliffe believed that as an MP he could use Parliament to force the issue and try to lobby for change. He struck up a friendship with the Labour MP Ian McCartney who had become hooked on league after he became the MP for Wigan in the 80s. McCartney was shocked by how the sport was treated in the media and other institutions and urged fellow MPs to set up an All-Party Parliamentary Group (APPG) to lobby for change. He wrote to every MP with a side in their constituency and asked them to be part of the group.

In March 1988, the first meeting of the Rugby League APPG was held in Westminster. The group found that there were lots of issues to lobby against. In addition to ending the ban on players moving freely between the two codes, the group found there was deep-rooted structural discrimination against the game. Hinchliffe noted how, after the Falklands war in 1982, working-class people from rugby league towns who had signed up to the forces had been unable to play league as it was banned. Their first campaign centred around introducing it in the armed forces.

As Hinchliffe and McCartney began to lobby for change, they found allies in the most unusual places. Michael Jopling was seen as a 'true blue' Thatcherite who was Minister for Agriculture, Fisheries and Food. As Chief Whip in the early part of the 80s, he had been responsible for trying to implement Thatcher's policies when she was deeply unpopular. But in the 50s, Jopling had been a Conservative candidate in Wakefield. To the surprise of the APPG he attended one of the meetings, where he revealed a story that emphasised the divide between the two codes.

Hinchliffe recounted in his memoir *Class War* how, at the 1959 general election, Jopling had been invited to Wakefield's Belle Vue to kick off a match against Hunslet as part of the campaign. 'Following the match, I found that I was deemed to have professionalised myself by taking part,' he revealed. Hinchliffe was shocked as Jopling went on to say, 'How ridiculous such a situation was then,' and 'How sad that such stupidity was still occurring nowadays.'

* * *

While the politicians looked to challenge some of the structural problems in the game, Jonathan Davies was increasingly frustrated by the lack of ambition within rugby union. *Sportsweek* magazine secured a major profile of Davies ahead of the Five Nations Championship, where he was announced as the new captain of his country. The tournament remained the dominant sporting contest in rugby union and was guaranteed to attract attention on the BBC.

Over the course of the interview, Davies toured Neath's working men's clubs and explained why rugby union needed to respond to what was happening in rugby league. Davies said union was his first love and he would happily stay in the game. But he expected to be paid what his market value was. His biggest fear was turning down rugby league and ending up with nothing to show for it: 'I do feel that you should have some financial reward at the end of your career after putting so much in.' For ambitious working-class athletes like Davies, rugby league now offered a route to financial security. Davies then delivered the bombshell news that he was '99%' certain that one day he would turn to rugby league if things didn't change. 'I love South Wales, and I love the people,' he admitted. 'But I have a dream about life – I would like one day to own a nice big house with some land and security for my family.'

Davies had been around rugby union circles long enough to see that it was a short career for little financial reward. Unlike the people who played rugby union for England, the Welsh lads had less opportunity to maximise their earnings in the private sector with jobs in the corporate world. The jobs market was changing and it was becoming harder to mix work with playing part-time. And financially the rewards were in rugby league.

One only had to compare the fortunes of Davies with a rugby league star like Shaun Edwards. Like Edwards, Davies had known hardship when he had lost his father at a young age. Edwards's ambition had been to buy a house for his mum and dad, which he had been able to do after just a few years in the game. Davies, by contrast, still worked for a living and had to be satisfied with the pride he had in putting on a Welsh jersey. But in the new age of Thatcherism, Davies recognised that he was in control of his own destiny: 'Eventually you have to do what is best for yourself,' he admitted. 'I know it sounds selfish but nobody else will look after you. I know which I would rather have, between 50 caps and £100,000,' he revealed.

The hard work that rugby league had put in to reward the players who packed the terraces out and pushed forward with standards was obvious: 'Davies's philosophy is closely linked to the League idiom,' concluded the *Sportsweek* piece. Rugby league aspired to be the best it could be and reward the players who achieved excellence. 'There is a more professional attitude in rugby league,' Davies said. 'And that sort of attitude suits me because when I play, I want to be the best.' The Davies interview was a signal to the rugby union world that players wanted to be paid their market value. 'Everyone treats us like professionals, yet we do it all for nothing. At the end of the day, you sit down and think, "Is it worth it?"' For the WRU, however, Davies's interview was a betrayal of everything the sport believed in.

* * *

The *Sportsweek* magazine drew much publicity and the owners placed adverts in newspapers in the north to encourage rugby league supporters to read the 'sensational world exclusive' interview. The WRU general committee immediately investigated whether Davies had 'professionalised' himself and he later revealed in his book *Code Breakers* how he had to 'grovel for his survival'. Barely a week would pass without Leeds, St Helens, Wigan or Widnes floating the idea in the media that they would sign him. In the end it was Dougie Laughton who eventually persuaded Davies to pack up his bags and move north.

The story that Jonathan Davies had switched codes catapulted the game into the national spotlight and rapidly became the biggest transfer story in a generation. Over January 1989, the rugby union press openly mourned the loss of their 'prince', talking about him in the past tense as if he had died. 'Davies joins the professionals,' ran *The Times*, while the *Daily Mirror* dedicated a back page to the huge sums of money involved: 'Oh Boyo!: Welsh skipper in £300,000 swoop'. Davies admitted that he was 'very sorry to be leaving this area' but that it was 'going to be a lifestyle that will secure me and my family'.

Davies mania gripped the sport ahead of his debut as newspaper columnists debated how he would fare in the new code. Ray French concluded in the *Rugby Leaguer* that his capture amounted to 'the biggest nationwide publicity event for any event in rugby league's history'. The scale of the transfer moved Davies from the sports pages to the front pages. Ahead of his debut, the *Daily Mirror* secured an exclusive interview and profile with the famous 'lifestyle' interviewer Noreen Taylor. For much of the 1980s, Taylor had travelled the world interviewing figures such as Jacqueline Kennedy, Paul McCartney and sports stars from Muhammad Ali to John McEnroe. Over a double-page spread, she introduced Davies to the world as 'the rugby genius' hoping to become the face of his new code. 'There's a whole world out there waiting to sponsor the boy,' revealed one business expert. Davies was open about his ambitions: 'I'm working class with a wife and son. I'm not like other players who have degrees and professions.'

One marketing agent revealed that Davies would have the chance to make millions in rugby league: 'He doesn't realise his true worth yet, because there's never been a marketable rugby star.' Even before he had stepped on a rugby league pitch there was talk of clothing deals, toiletry endorsements, video documentaries and book contracts off the back of it. Davies was the rare talent of someone who had a profile beyond the traditional sports pages. The hope was that he could help take the game from the sports pages to the lifestyle pages of the press.

* * *

It wasn't long before Davies' ex-team-mates were looking at him and wondering whether they too should switch codes. Laughton developed an attractive Widnes side around a core group of ex-rugby union players. Alan Tait from Scotland soon joined Davies, Offiah and Paul Moriarty in the side. Other clubs soon recognised the potential of a big-name convert in terms of media exposure and increased attendance figures. Jonathan Griffiths became the big key signing for a revived St Helens side and he immediately twisted the knife into union. 'Rugby league is the game of the 1990s,' he declared. 'That's where I wanted to be.' The Welsh prop forward Dai Young moved to Leeds and spoke about how appealing the game was: 'The skill, tackling and speed make it exciting: defence one minute and attack the next.'

There were enough warning signs to prompt those running the game in Wales to call for changes. 'It is crippling parochialism, pettiness and a lack of realism that has brought Welsh rugby to its knees,' wrote one journalist in *The Independent*. Robert Jones, the new Welsh captain, admitted in an interview for BBC *Sportsnight* that the rules around payments needed to change. 'When you consider the money coming into the game,' he said, 'there have got to be ways to reap the rewards.' The Wales coach Ron Waldron believed that the rules were a cap on the ambitions of people who wanted to get on in Thatcher's Britain: 'More working-class people are coming into the game who tend to be susceptible to a decent offer.'

After Jonathan Davies, attention within rugby league circles switched towards the ultimate 'code breaker'. Of all the players that were linked to a move up north in the 1980s, it was Jeremy Guscott who was subject to the most media attention. Guscott caught the eye of league scouts as the centre who made history in 1989 when scoring a hat-trick on debut. Guscott was attractive, articulate and seen as the perfect player to symbolise the change that rugby league wanted to project. Signing him became seen as the 'holy grail' for some clubs. Each year they won the Challenge Cup, Wigan would send Guscott a video of the Wembley highlights to show him what he was missing out on. As one *Daily Telegraph* study on him argued, it seemed to only be a matter of time before Guscott switched: 'As rugby league's profile soars the attractions must get even greater.'

However, the clubs had much more difficulty in signing top English players who were middle class and had business interests in London. League officials had always sensed that the English players who went to public school were out of reach for them. In the BBC documentary *The Game That Got Away* that was broadcast in the 60s, the Wigan directors admitted that it was usually 'a working-class type of fella' that took the bait. They said they would not look at any player who was educated at Oxford and

Cambridge. But by the 1980s, there was a belief that league was able to match the money that people made in the private sector. At one point Huddersfield resorted to finding Jeremy Guscott a modelling contract to try and tempt him to Yorkshire and offset any business losses. Others such as Will Carling, the England captain, were constantly linked to league clubs at the end of the decade. He told the *Daily Mail* that he would never consider a switch because league didn't 'have the same network of contacts which exists in union'.

The prospect of Guscott or Carling switching codes became central to the sport, creating media stories and free publicity for itself. Clubs were getting a better grasp of how the new media landscape operated. A rugby league club would tell the media that they were interested in a player, which would fuel days of news and comment pieces about whether a player would give up their amateur status. Stephen Jones felt that rugby union was being manipulated purely to boost the image of rugby league clubs: 'The whole thing is a promotion, a part of rugby league's current drive to market and glamorise its image,' he wrote in one *Sunday Times* column.

'It's called a PR machine,' said Guscott in his memoir. 'And once it clicked into gear, it was almost impossible to stop.'

Offers of £1m in the 1990s were still not enough to tempt him to switch codes. The scale of the money involved did, however, cut through into the national consciousness. *Drop the Dead Donkey* was a BBC sitcom, set in a television newsroom, which satirised the media industry. Each week the show inserted topical jokes from the week to give it the sense that it was 'live' and contemporary. In a week that Guscott turned down another offer, they led with the joke about how 'England's Jeremy Guscott has turned down £1 million to turn pro and decided to stay on as a PR officer for British Gas. Well, he's obviously got his head screwed on.'

* * *

After struggling to lure the big-name English players over, attention soon turned to another country that was wrestling with the divide between professional and amateur status. For all the talk of the professionalisation of rugby league and the interest in the Kangaroo tours, it was the All Blacks who still held a mythological power over the British sports press. In the late 1980s, John Gallagher was a dominant figure in an All Blacks side that lifted the first Rugby World Cup. The sense of Gallagher's importance to the game can be seen in the title of his autobiography: *The World's Greatest Rugby Player*. But just as the players were winning everything before them, they too were having similar conversations about their market value.

Leeds were a club that had struggled for much of the 1980s in the shadow of Hull, Widnes and Wigan in terms of winning trophies. But the club always had an eye for a big-name signing. In the 1950s, Leeds shook the rugby union establishment when they signed Lewis Jones for £5,000 – an amount of money that could buy three houses in Leeds at the time. In the 1980s they continued to buy the best British talent such as Garry Schofield and Lee Crooks, whilst bringing over Australians such as Andrew Ettingshausen to keep spectators happy.

John Gallagher was seen as the latest big-name player that Leeds wanted to join the club and when they made him an offer, Gallagher admitted that it was too good to refuse. Dubbed the 'half a million pound man', his signature was so big that it ran as the main sports story on ITV News ahead of the announcement of Bobby Robson's England World Cup squad for Italia 90. 'We've even knocked Leeds United and Yorkshire cricket off the back pages of the local papers,' added chief executive Alf Davies. 'And that has not happened for nearly three decades.' Gallagher's open ambition to become a professional rocked the All Blacks and there was much discussion about a new wave of talent switching codes. He informed the media that other team-mates would seriously consider an offer: 'There is a natural frustration at knowing the rewards you can get in league when playing in a top sports side who are very professional in their attitude.'

The signing prompted much soul-searching in the rugby union press. In the *Daily Telegraph*, Simon Turnbull equated Gallagher's acquisition to Maradona signing for Leeds United or the New Zealand cricketer Richard Hadlee 'breaking into the closed ranks of Yorkshire cricket'. The chairman of the New Zealand RFU, Eddie Tonks, admitted that the sport could do nothing to stop the flow. 'I am very disappointed,' he told the *Daily Mail.* Tonks wondered if the game could do anything to turn it around. 'The money these young men are taking is far in excess of what they could ever earn through a relaxation of the amateur regulations.'

The signing of Davies and Gallagher in quick succession showed how rugby league was open to those who wanted to be professional and maximise their market value. David Howes announced in *The Independent* that there was now a lot to be optimistic about. 'We see the All Blacks as a new source of talent for the game,' Howes admitted. 'They recognise that rugby league is entering a new era where players have a high profile and are rewarded for their efforts. It is their chance to make a living in an open and honest atmosphere.'

There was a confidence that emanated from the clubs down towards the terraces. In the first season after the 1988 Ashes series and the arrival of Jonathan Davies, gates rose by 25 per cent on average. Since the 'streamlining' of the top division from 16 to 14 clubs, the figures were 50 per cent up as a total of 1,327,192 people passed through the turnstiles of the First Division. Wigan's average of 14,543 was the highest of any team since the 1960s. Every club in the First Division, bar Warrington, increased their attendance.

It was not just that clubs had increased their attendance gradually: they had done so in many cases by 2,000 people.

League increasingly saw itself as part of the big event sports culture and the entertainment industry. Officials began to take more games such as the Charity Shield, the Premiership Final and Challenge Cup semi-finals to football grounds where they encouraged attendance records to be broken. For Widnes, in particular, the signing of Davies moved them into the 'elite' club bracket. In 1989, when Widnes took on Canberra at Old Trafford in the now 'Official' World Club Challenge, not only did Foster's return to fund the event, but the BBC had agreed to broadcast it live. Over 80 minutes, the nation watched as former union players Jonathan Davies and Martin Offiah led Widnes to a famous victory.

In 1987, Wigan defeated Manly through their defensive intensity. Widnes, by contrast, drew Canberra into an attacking conflict. Offiah was the Widnes hero with two tries, while Davies braved violent attacks to the head to score a try on the Old Trafford pitch. For Paul Wilson at *The Independent*, it was evidence that the game had risen to match the standards of the Kangaroos: 'The best of British can live with the best of Australia, and Widnes are a team of immense character.'

The performance of Davies and Offiah on the national stage, and the way in which Welsh rugby union had been raided, prompted rugby union officials to fight back.

In 1990 *The People* ran an exclusive story on the new battle plan to reverse the trend. 'Rugby union is ready to declare all-out war on rugby league,' revealed one 'battle plan'. On the agenda was an amnesty for rugby league players who had made the switch to allow them to return. The amnesty pleased Eddie Tonks in New Zealand, who said that the game in Britain needed to change: 'We must hit back at rugby league.'

Eventually the WRU allowed Steve Ford to return to rugby union and relaxed the rules around players trialling for rugby league clubs. The Ford case was seen as a significant victory for David Oxley and the RL APPG, who had gambled that they could win the case. One journalist remarked that it represented 'a breach in a frontier, erected a century ago between union and league, which everyone had grown up to believe to be impenetrable'. The relaxation of the rules did little to change the perception that rugby league was fast becoming the dominant code of rugby in Britain. For decades, league supporters had bemoaned how the BBC had used rugby union people to talk about rugby league. Now people such as Jonathan Davies were being asked to comment on the Five Nations while playing for Widnes.

The shift was enough to encourage the political journalist Alan Watkins to attend his first rugby league game since the end of the Second World War. Watkins was a British political columnist and an expert rugby union writer. In his column for *The Independent*, Watkins admitted that rugby union administrators should ask themselves what league had got right: 'Why is it that league can organise an altogether happier, more exciting event than they seem able to lay on?' he asked. He looked at league and saw how families were in attendance with young children. 'My impression was that league had replaced soccer as Saturday entertainment.'

When the football writer Hunter Davies was sent to a Five Nations match, he declared it boring: 'For the outsider, rugby league is much better to watch.' He estimated that half of a rugby union game was stoppages. Other rugby league supporters began to emerge in the most unlikely places. Jimmy Greaves was arguably the most famous football pundit in the country as the presenter of *Saint and Greavsie* on ITV. One afternoon he waded into the debate about the two codes. 'I confess to being a closet rugby league fan,' said Greaves, as he questioned whether Davies would have 'the physique to withstand the hard-as-nails tacklers in rugby league'. But Greaves was in no doubt that Davies had made the right decision: 'The 13-a-side version will become the undisputed king of rugby soon.'

Margaret Thatcher arrives at Downing Street following the Conservative victory in the 1979 general election.

OPEN RUGBY

A BI-MONTHLY NEWS-SHEET OF COMMENT & OPINION FOR ALL RUGBY LEAGUE PEOPLE

Introduction

TOURS SHOULD STAY

The first issue of Open Rugby drew on inspiration from the punk movement to give rugby league a new voice.

David Oxley and David Howes were the men tasked with turning the sport around. But many critics thought it was a lost cause.

Rugby league arrived in London in a blaze of media publicity but it soon faded away.

At a time of heated national debate about the children of the Windrush generation, Des Drummond emerged as a superstar.

People protested against unemployment as it reached the dreaded three million mark in the early 1980s.

Featherstone Rovers arrived back in their pit village to scenes of jubilation. But the miners' strike would soon have players fighting to feed their families each week.

Mal Meninga was a short-term and expensive signing for St Helens. But he radically changed the fortunes of the team and the town.

Shaun Edwards couldn't believe he was playing at Wembley aged 17. He said he 'got all the luck my father didn't get'.

Keith Bell stopped fundraising for his testimonial as the miners' strike took hold.

The 1985 Challenge Cup Final was immediately seen as the greatest of all time as Kenny and Sterling fought their own personal battle in front of millions of TV viewers.

Julia Lee challenged the male-dominated rugby league traditions to become a referee.

Ellery Hanley understood the power of image. He projected a very different type of 'fashionable' rugby league star to what had come before.

Harry Edgar used his magazine to push the boundaries of debate at Open Rugby.

Rugby league expanded to new areas like never before. But life in the Second Division was tough financially and crowds were dire.

Clubs increasingly looked to America and Australia to create the 'razzmatazz' of the live event.

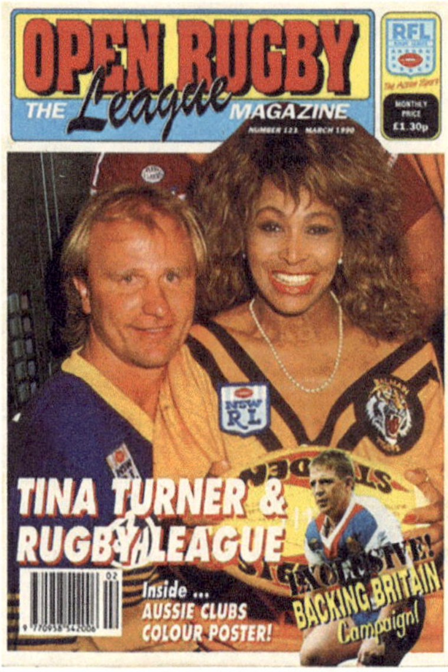

Tina Turner changed the face of rugby league in Australia with a radical advertising campaign.

Britain's leisure and consumer habits were changing and rugby league had to compete for attention.

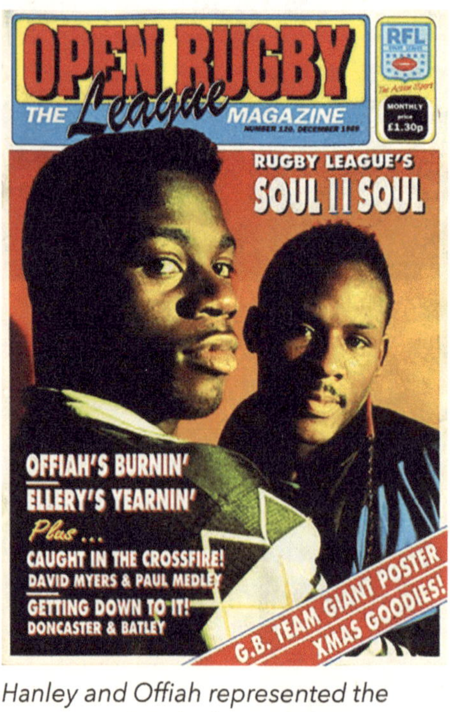

Hanley and Offiah represented the aspirational rugby league player at a time of changing youth culture in Britain.

The dramatic promotional image of Offiah captured the hype around international rugby league in 1992.

Black Wednesday and the recession reopened debates about 'streamlining' the sport in the Major years.

BSkyB revolutionised the way the sport was covered and began to promote it in a different way.

The role of women in rugby league was changing from the pitch to the boardroom.

Jonathan Davies said that playing for Wales at rugby union was an 'ambition' but making it for Great Britain was an 'achievement'.

The resistance to mergers reopened deep wounds from the miners' strike - but this time the people won.

Maurice Lindsay and Ellery Hanley had changed the image of the game beyond recognition. But their meeting at the 1995 final marked the end of an era.

Chapter 10

Enterprise

WHILE BRITISH rugby league continued to grow towards the end of the 1980s, rivals in Australia moved even faster. In the 1970s, the game down under had been mired in violence, with organisers pressured to clean up its image and make it more attractive to new viewers. A crisis moment had come in 1981, when a semi-final at the Sydney Cricket Ground erupted into an all-in brawl after just a few minutes. It prompted a radical change which would change the way the sport marketed itself. Severe punishments were handed out for violence, attacking play was promoted and the arrival of State of Origin turned it into a major television product for broadcasters.

Central to the economic boom was a partnership with Winfield cigarettes. But at the same time, those running the game knew that they were still selling the game to a male, working-class audience. And while the cigarette money was helpful, there was a feeling that it no longer fitted the image of the modern rugby league player. 'The Winfield sponsorship, for all its longevity and mutual benefits to game and company, does not sit too comfortably with many of the health-conscious and intelligent players who populate Rugby League in the 1990s,' reported one journalist.

The concept of the 'rebrand' dominated the big business world as firms looked to compete in an ever-more hostile and aggressive marketplace. In the ongoing battle between Coca-Cola and Pepsi, the two companies had looked at different ways they could reach the new youth market. With the expansion of media and advertising agencies, the power of a brand lay not just in marketing a product but in creating a relationship with the audience.

Celebrity endorsement was an increasingly lucrative way to do so. In 1984, the pop star Michael Jackson was paid $5 million to become the face of Pepsi to help them in their battle with Coca-Cola. Crucially, Pepsi made Jackson the centrepiece of a bespoke 'new generation' campaign that was more than selling a soft drink. Reworking the lyrics of 'Billie Jean' to 'We're the Pepsi generation', the advert proved to be hugely profitable for the company. Although Coca-Cola remained the world's best-selling soft drink, Pepsi continued to gain market share, prompting them into their own rebrand. In 1985 they introduced New Coke to the world in a blaze of publicity, with a new recipe, new name and new design to take the battle to Pepsi. But it alienated the core audience and within a few months it was ditched.

There was one other person used by Pepsi to draw in new consumers in the late 1980s. The pop star Tina Turner had been recruited by Pepsi to bring 'sex appeal' to their adverts. 'The taste for living' was a multi-million-pound advertising campaign that saw Turner front an advert, record a song and have her world tour sponsored by Pepsi. Her success and popularity had people in Australia wondering if one of her songs might help do the same. 'What You Get Is What You See' was a song released on Turner's 1986 album that barely charted in the UK, the USA or Australia. But when executives heard it, they wanted it to be part of a new campaign to 'contemporise and make the game appealing to women, white-collar workers and younger men'.

Initially the marketing department wanted to buy the rights to the song but as they discussed what the advert would look like, they came to the conclusion that they should reach out to her instead. Turner would not come cheap. There were rumours that she would charge $500,000 for a morning's work and that the cost of running an advert through the season, rather than at the beginning, would cost millions. Moreover, there was a fear amongst some of the Sydney clubs as to whether a black woman from America could connect with their traditional rugby league supporters. 'We're not looking at the converted; we're looking at a completely different market,' admitted John Quayle in the *Australian Financial Review.*

The news coverage of Turner's involvement added millions of pounds' worth of extra publicity before it had even been released. The central premise was the idea that 'sex sells', which was a phrase that had come to dominate advertising in the 1980s. 'We want to present these guys as we really believe they are,' explained John Quayle, the head of the league, 'and that is dynamic, that is sexy. They're physical – and they're smart.' When the promotion was finally unveiled, it was clear that this was a radically different advert than anything that had come before it. The video did not portray the players as tough and hard as it would have done in the 70s. Instead, it focused on the community aspect of the game. Supporters were filmed walking to the match, while players ran topless on the beaches of Sydney. Brisbane's Alfie Langer was filmed signing autographs for air hostesses while Manly prop Noel Cleal was seen picking up a child.

'What You Get Is What You See' turned out to be a major hit with the Australian public. The New South Wales Rugby League reported an immediate increase of 21.5 per cent in females watching televised rugby league. 'The Tina Turner campaign was not directed at our converted people, it was directed at a younger audience and the female viewer,' said Quayle. He said that the sport now had 300,000 more female viewers watching on television over 12 months. And when the game repeated the trick to the song 'Simply the Best' the next season, news of Turner's involvement made the pages of the British tabloids. The *Sunday Mirror* revealed exclusive photographs of the video that had cost $500,000 to make: 'BEACH that! Singing sex-bomb Tina Turner makes waves wherever she goes. And she made a real splash with this line-up of hunky Australian rugby players working out on sun-kissed Bondi Beach.'

* * *

The idea of making rugby league 'sexy' and more 'fashionable' became a huge discussion point within the British game. Harry Edgar argued that the challenge for the sport in the 1990s was to 'go out and create their own promotional effect ... Achieve that national credibility ... We've got to bury parochialism once and for all. We need our own Tina Turner and more!' The game had bigger sponsorship than ever before with Silk Cut cigarettes pumping over £900,000 into the Challenge Cup to become its primary sponsor. The game also secured a record deal with Stones Bitter to sponsor the First Division. Meanwhile, JPS had been associated with the cup for so long that people began to forget it was a cigarette brand. Imperial Tobacco pumped in another £850,000 but asked for the tournament to be renamed the Regal Trophy instead.

At club level, Wigan had fully embraced the opportunities that the 1980s had offered them. Maurice Lindsay was always keen to emphasise how important brands and marketing were to their standing in the game. When the *Sunday Times* magazine ran a feature on the revival of the Wigan club, money and sponsorship drew the journalist Sally Vincent's attention: 'Everywhere you look – on the front of their shirts, the back of their shirts, up the walls and down the hoardings it says Norweb.' And as Vincent walked around Central Park, she was taken in by the diversity of sponsors. 'And look around the other boxes. Heinz, NatWest, Whitbread – quite upmarket, don't you think?'

By the beginning of the 90s, Wigan were not just selling a rugby league team to the town; they were helping to refashion its identity. After the closure of the coal mines, Wigan had transitioned to the services and leisure industry that was booming in Thatcher's Britain. The local council noticed how people began to come from across the country to watch the rugby league side and offered 'tourist weekends' where you could watch the team play and visit the town's tourist hot spots. The council took out stalls at travel conferences and put together a package that allowed tourists to visit the club, meet the players and take photographs on the pitch. 'Whenever we've been promoting Wigan at travel fairs and exhibitions, it's been clear from talking to tour operators and members of the public that we could sell rugby league weekends,' said a member of the Wigan Leisure marketing department.

Central to Wigan RL's turnaround was developing the business side of the club to generate extra revenue. One of their first steps had been to purchase a house outside Central Park at the end of the street to serve as a souvenir shop. Lindsay had been sick of the 'spivs' selling unofficial, cheap-quality merchandise outside the ground on matchday and decided that the club was missing an opportunity to make money. The club's marketing went well beyond what most other clubs were doing and attempted to sell the players as 'aspirational' figures. When a new hotel opened in the town, the Wigan players were recruited to promote it as the place to go after the game for a drink. The marketing campaign featured players in suits drinking wine in contrast to other clubs who still used working men's clubs to hold functions.

Lindsay urged other clubs to adopt a more aggressive mindset when it came to raising money but he remained disenchanted with the way that it was run. Lindsay had studied the NFL and marvelled at how they had created money and a market out of nothing. Lindsay looked at what the NFL had done with merchandising and felt

Britain had been asleep. 'The NFL have been laughing their socks off at this country,' he observed. After putting the game on Channel 4, they understood they could sell sports merchandise despite needing a foothold in the area. 'Every kid in every town seems to have a Chicago Bears T-shirt,' he concluded. Lindsay calculated that the NFL must have made several million pounds. By contrast, the RFL turnover for merchandising in 1988/89 was just £16,000.

By the end of the 1980s the word 'enterprise' had entered the national debate and had become central to Mrs Thatcher's politics. In the early 80s the Chancellor Nigel Lawson had been committed to creating 'enterprise' zones to foster the spirit of urban renewal in towns and cities. Barely an interview or speech went by when Mrs Thatcher didn't link her political philosophy to enterprise. 'A country is not wealthy according to its natural resources,' she argued. 'It is wealthy according to the spirit of enterprise of its people.' When a project began to revive Canary Wharf, she praised the 'new spirit of enterprise' emanating from London which could spread across the country. In her New Year's address to welcome in the 1990s she reflected how 'our policies of freedom and enterprise have produced a decade of solid achievement'.

Rugby league had struggled to adopt the spirit of 'enterprise'. Bar cigarette and alcohol sponsorship – which was often handed over above market rate because of the negative connotations involved – the game struggled to attract enough money from sponsors. The sport was not alone in taking money from tobacco companies in the decade. In 1965 the government had banned cigarette advertising on television, forcing them to put money into sports instead. Prior to the ban, tobacco sponsorship was around £1m across the sports industry. By early 1983 it had reached £100m and that had doubled again by the end of the decade.

In 1989 the RL Council decided that it needed a dedicated department focused on bringing in extra commercial revenue.

And in the spirit of the age they named it Rugby League Enterprises. When they opened up advertising for a new marketing executive, people were surprised at the number of high-quality applicants. Over 160 people from across business applied and in the end the job went to a 43-year-old sales director with Puma called Michael Turner. Turner had been at the forefront of the battle to establish Puma as a major sports brand in Britain in the 1980s, where he had been head of sales. He talked about how he had helped 'oversee an increase in turnover from £500,000 to £60m' and had ambitions for league. Turner immediately examined how NFL clubs had marketed themselves and spoke with Manchester United about how they had developed their brand and opened a huge souvenir shop at Old Trafford. Most importantly for those running the game, Turner promised to bring a competitive edge to sales: 'I am not used to failing. I like to win at everything I do.'

Central to the development of Rugby League Enterprises was the creation of a distinct rugby league brand and logo. At *Open Rugby*, Harry Edgar had tried to develop one along the lines of the NFL logo which helped turn rugby league into the Rugby Football League (RFL). But Edgar's logo was restricted to adverts in magazines to sell a small range of T-shirts and baseball caps. Turner believed that the game needed a new logo that emphasised how much it had changed over the decade. 'The key to the project will be a modern new logo through which the game can be identified at a glance,' he revealed in *Rugby Leaguer Review* magazine.

Politically the Labour Party had reached the same conclusion when they swapped their red flag for a red rose under the guidance of Peter Mandelson. There had been outrage when delegates arrived at the party's annual conference to see that the word 'party' had been dropped from the logo while documents were handed out in salmon-pink folders rather than the traditional red. Rugby league clubs were less open to changing their image. Clubs often retained their local area's traditional coat of arms and the mottos accompanying them.

In an attempt to create a logo fit for the 1990s, Turner introduced the idea of the unique selling point (USP) for the sport. When he studied every other sport he realised that rugby league was the only one with 13 players on each side. 'We stopped anybody in the street between the ages of 18 and 25 wearing sportswear and asked them their opinion.' The logo would then be placed on any number of products that were licensed by the RFL. These ranged from jerseys, boots and equipment to stationery, toys and videos. Turner wanted people to be able to see the logo and immediately identify it as a rugby league product. He wanted the game to embrace the market to endorse its own beer, soft drinks, toiletries, calendars, diaries and luggage: 'Rugby league has not taken a penny out of these things until now. We have not even begun to scratch the surface of the game's potential.'

Britain's consumer habits were changing rapidly during the decade. Rising disposable incomes had been boosted by the loosening of rules around lending, which gave rise to the credit card. Shopping malls were opening across the country and were replacing sport as a leisure activity at the weekend for young people. In the week that Hull hosted Australia on Humberside in 1990, eyes were turned at the new multiplex cinema that was opening at St Andrew's Quay. The cinema opened with a 'fabulous fireworks fiesta' and promised to offer everything that the Boulevard did not. It had free car parking, air conditioning, eight mega screens and '1,678 luxury seats'. The owners, UCI, promised a 'cinema revolution' in Hull with 'Choice, Convenience and Comfort' at the centre of it.

Rugby league officials attempted to draw young people back into the game through merchandise sales. Turner advocated for a shop to be opened at the rebuilt Rugby League headquarters in Chapeltown to sell the new merchandise. He even had a special Rugby League Enterprises bus built that would advertise the new logo and the brand around the country. 'We have especially catered for the fashion-conscious young people because we want to present the right kind of image to the outside world,' he told the *Rugby Leaguer Review*.

Under the strapline 'It's getting harder to tell the players from the fans', the Great Britain fashion range was launched with Umbro to tap into the sports leisure market. The launch came at a time when the relationship between sports and fashion was changing. In the USA traditional sports brands such as Nike had revolutionised how young people thought about clothing through their 'Just Do It' campaign. The campaign linked Nike with success, and made consumers believe they could be successful just by wearing Nike products. At the RFL, supporters could buy a range of products made with the X13 logo on it, from American-style bomber jackets and printed T-shirts, drill jackets, shell suits and windbreakers. At £64.99, the shell suit amounted to a significant outlay for supporters. But the game believed that its fans wanted more choice and were willing to pay for it.

The launch of the new product range was the signal that rugby league was willing to embrace the 'enterprise' culture of the 80s. And to communicate it to the public, they turned to the person who had done so much to help revitalise the image of the north. As a TV presenter, nightclub owner and founder of Factory Records, Tony Wilson was intrinsically linked to the cultural life of Manchester. Wilson believed in enterprise for Manchester and the revival of a cultural spirit around its arts scene. In 1983 he opened the Hacienda nightclub to give Mancunians a space to be proud of like New York, Berlin and Chicago had. A fierce advocate for the North West, he refused to move to London. And at the end of the 80s he was increasingly interested in the way that rugby league was confidently expressing itself to the world.

In an *NME* interview Wilson admitted that the ITV highlights show *Scrumdown* was amongst his favourite television shows. At the same time, rugby league players were increasingly spotted at the Hacienda and made their way into the gossip pages of the *Manchester Evening News* each week. The summer of 1988 was dubbed the second 'summer of love' as house music and the rave scene arrived in Britain. The impact of deindustrialisation had brought the UK's manufacturing industry to a halt, with factories and warehouses abandoned. Industrial sites and empty wasteland became the key sites for raves. The Hacienda tapped into the scene to become the most popular night out in the UK.

Martin Offiah and Ellery Hanley had toured together in 1988 and returned to the UK as the second summer of love took hold. Hanley was the first person to take Offiah to the Hacienda, opening Offiah's eyes to the world of celebrity that being a top-line rugby league player could bring. He soon entered a Manchester music scene where they were jumping to the front of queues, getting in clubs for free and rubbing shoulders with celebrities such as Boy George, Mark Moore from S'Express, Mike Pickering from M People and Mick Hucknall from Simply Red.

Henderson Gill, meanwhile, was creating house music of his own. Gill released a single with the band Plus One, 'The Song Will Always Be the Same', published by MCA Records. As Gilly G, he talked about emulating MC Hammer, who was 'in a world of his own'. Unlike John Barnes's rap or Paul Gascoigne's 'Fog on the Tyne', Gill was serious about the music. This was a house track: 'I'm not doing a Gazza!' he told the *Rugby Leaguer Review*, ahead of its release.

The links between the rave scene and rugby league were apparent to Harry Edgar at *Open Rugby*, who wanted to project his cover stars like celebrities. In 1989 he sourced a rare picture of Hanley and Offiah that had been part of a photoshoot with Andrew Varley in Australia. The image was striking and conveyed the feeling that the pair were at the cutting edge of popular culture. He placed the image on the cover of *Open Rugby* under the heading 'Soul II Soul' in reference to the band that had taken the music industry by storm with their track 'Back to Life'.

As the boundaries between rugby league and pop culture became increasingly blurred, an opportunity arose for the sport to launch its new merchandise range on one of Tony Wilson's television programmes. *The Other Side of Midnight* was a late-night cultural arts show that focused in on things happening in the north. It was seen as Wilson's attempt to create a Manchester equivalent of *The South Bank Show*. 'Not one edition of the show goes by without some nepotistic plug for Factory, Ikon, Hacienda or one of Wilson's other financial interests,' said one critic in the *NME*. It was also the place where young bands such as The Stone Roses were given their breaks.

In June 1989, rugby league featured on the programme as part of its attempt to revolutionise that image. Shots of action taken from *Scrumdown* were intertwined with an analysis of how the game was now marketing itself to a different audience. The feature outlined how the new enterprise department was looking to appeal to young people in the cities. Wilson showcased the new leisure range that that chimed with the new 'baggy' fashion that was impacting the Manchester music scene. The producers even managed to link an interview with Mike Turner with Tina Turner's promotion in Australia. One fan admitted that it was 'the most exciting, stylish, downright trendy presentation of league on TV that I have ever witnessed'. Wilson described the sport as one of the north's best-kept secrets. He told viewers that it was 'an exciting, tough and physically impressive action sport' and urged viewers to change their preconceived ideas about it.

* * *

The emergence of Rugby League Enterprises came at a time when there was a clear window of opportunity for the game to capture the public attention. The game decided that the next bold step was to take the first Test of the 1990 Ashes series to Wembley. This was immediately seen by some as a gamble too far. By 1990 the London experiment had well and truly fizzled out as Fulham had been forced to move from their ground due to lack of support. They moved to Central London Stadium in Chiswick, where attendance was less than 1,000. By the time they had moved to Crystal Palace in 1990, their hardcore support was just 500 people.

There were long memories within the game of what had happened in 1973 when Great Britain faced Australia at Wembley. After inviting the Prime Minister Edward Heath along as a guest of honour, organisers had been dismayed when just 9,874 people spread across an eerily empty Wembley. 'It was a case of spot the spectator in that big stadium,' said Bob McCarthy, who played in the second row that day. 'I hope it works out for the British League, but if it doesn't, there will be no atmosphere.' Widnes coach Dougie Laughton admitted in his *Open Rugby* column that he had 'doubts about the wisdom of taking a Test match to Wembley'. 'I can only hope the English League have done sufficient research into the project and have convincing evidence that the Test will be a big draw card,' said Ken Arthurson. 'We certainly weren't consulted about such a radical move.' Organisers, however, were convinced that rugby league was now big enough to compete in the elite sports event marketplace. In the bid to make it easier for southern supporters to attend, they could, for the first time, purchase tickets from Virgin Megastore in Oxford Street.

Part of their ambition for the tour was just how much Australian culture had become part and parcel of everyday British life. Apart from England football's quarter- and semi-final matches at Italia 90, there was no more watched event on British screens in 1990 than the Australian soap opera *Neighbours*. Kylie Minogue and Jason Donovan became household names in the UK off the back of it. 'Its success has been attributed to its wide-ranging appeal to all age groups – from granny down to pre-school-age children, in fact almost anyone who can sit in front of a television set!' reported the *Daily Mirror*. And studies by the Broadcasters' Audience Research Board showed that it was immensely popular with young people. Over 80% of people aged 12–15 and 16–24 said they watched the show weekly.

The show was owned by Channel 10, who were constantly thinking about how they could grow *Neighbours* in the UK. In 1990, as the Australian players arrived for the Kangaroo tour, Channel 10's producer of league and sport, Alan Catt, revealed the strategy was aimed at making the televised tour 'the most exciting ever' by summoning the cast over to the UK to help promote the match at Wembley. 'The association between Australian television stars and rugby league in England is natural,' he said. News of the tie-up soon reached the British tabloids, who were always eager for any *Neighbours* content. Gill Pringle, the entertainment columnist in the *Daily Mirror*, announced that 'The entire cast of Ramsay Street will move to London in October' to publicise the match.

When the Kangaroos were invited to Wembley to shoot some promotional and marketing material with Jason Donovan, it drew interest from people who had rarely watched a rugby league game. Meninga was called upon to lift Donovan, to the delight of the 50 'popular newspaper photographers and television crews snapping and whirring away'. The use of Donovan helped generate extra publicity for a game that had already caught the public imagination. The press interest in the series had reached levels unimaginable just a few years earlier. In the *Sunday Mirror* magazine, Martin Offiah was profiled as the most exciting player on the planet. Offiah revealed that he was more than willing to do any publicity the game required to ensure that the match was a success: 'It's all part of being a professional rugby league player anyway in 1990.'

Meanwhile, Ellery Hanley was using his image to promote the Test in ways that no other player would have been able to. Herbert Ritts Jr. was an American fashion photographer and director known for photographing celebrities, models and other cultural figures throughout the 1980s and 90s. His work concentrated on black and white photography and portraits, often in classical Greek sculpture. On the eve of the first Test, he combined with Ellery Hanley to launch a new advertising campaign from Gap. On the pages of the *Sunday Times*, Hanley was pictured in a Gap hooded T-shirt priced at £19. The most revealing aspect of the ad campaign was who could actually purchase the clothes. In 1990, Gap only had stores on Oxford Street and Covent Garden, Guildford, and in Richmond, Hampstead and Croydon.

* * *

All the talk in the pre-match build-up was about how the Australians would handle the pressure and aura surrounding Wembley. No player in the Kangaroos squad had touched a ball on the turf. The young Australian half-back Ricky Stuart admitted that he was nervous just thinking about it. For Mal Meninga, he said that the first Test would be a significant milestone in his career. 'Playing at Wembley has always been one of my dreams,' he told the *Sydney Morning Herald*. Meninga predicted that the atmosphere would be incredible. 'The British will be all fired up,' he said. 'We are stepping into the lion's den.'

British organisers believed that they had to find every single possible edge that they could to unsettle the Australian team. Throughout the 1980s, Meninga's side had been unfazed by everything the British game had thrown at them. They had experienced the arctic conditions of Odsal and Watersheddings, the abuse from the threepenny stand at the Boulevard to the 'white hot' atmosphere of the mega crowds at Central Park and Headingley. Each time they had overcome the British side and gone on to win the Ashes with ease.

The aura of Wembley was seen as Britain's trump card. In the run-up to the game, people talked about the need to engage in 'psychological warfare'. People running the game had noticed how Australians had crumbled under the pressure of the Challenge Cup Final in the 80s. Most memorably, in 1989, St Helens had flown in Michael O'Connor and Paul Vautin and watched in horror as the magnitude of the occasion had got to them. For those who believed in the power of Wembley, the crucial moments would come in the last quarter of an hour before kick-off as the teams got ready to stand in the Wembley tunnel and walk slowly out from the darkness into the noise. The tunnel had acquired a mythology of its own. Phil Larder used to argue that the occasion of Wembley could count as much as 25% of what you do on the pitch. He had players doing 'mental rehearsals' and 'visualisations' to neutralise the nerves.

Alongside the long wait in the tunnel ran another rugby league tradition. 'Community singing' before big matches was a tradition that the sport had prided itself on. Before each cup final, the game would hire a celebrity such as Ken Dodd or Bernard Cribbins to lead the singing of various songs such as 'Congratulations', 'On Ilkla Moor Baht 'at', 'You'll Never Walk Alone' and 'She's a Lassie from Lancashire'. The most important of these was 'Abide with Me'. It was first sung before the 1927 FA Cup Final and adopted by rugby league a few years later. To some, it stirred images of miners' solidarity and, accompanied by a brass band, would often bring the crowd to tears. Before one cup final, BBC presenter Des Lynam argued that it captured the essence of what the game was about: 'There are plenty of occasions here at Wembley where you don't get community singing.' But the tradition added to a 'splendid' party-like atmosphere.

But as the first Test approached, organisers wondered whether it would be able to unsettle the Australian players. Desperate to create a hostile environment, organisers decided to do something different. Throughout the 1980s, the song 'Land of Hope and Glory' was integral to the image that the Conservative Party had wanted to project. In 1979, campaign organisers had played the music through speakers as journalists waited at press conferences, to remind them of former glories. By 1983 it had been revived as a symbol of British victory in the Falklands and was used along with the *Dambusters* music and 'Rule Britannia' to emphasise Mrs Thatcher's war-like leadership. As the decade progressed, each party conference would become more enthusiastic about singing along to it. Delegates would wave their flags as if it were the *Last Night of the Proms*.

When the rugby league journalist Dave Hadfield heard that organisers were planning to use the music to intimidate the Australians at Wembley, it sounded like one of the game's more 'dubious' ideas. People didn't use music when players walked on to the pitch, preferring to allow the players to hear the crowd instead. But Oxley, Howes and the marketing people at the RFL wondered if it might just add to the spectacle of the occasion. The game was aiming for a record crowd for a Test match and was confident that it could reach it. And as the sides walked out of the tunnel and into the light, the sound of the music chimed with the supporters to unleash a giant spontaneous roar. As he walked out, Garry Schofield felt immense pride. 'The singing of "Land of Hope and Glory" as we came out of the tunnel was a nice touch and it lifted us. We knew what a victory would mean to the fans,' he told the media.

Dave Hadfield watched as the Great Britain players' chests 'visibly swelled' as they faced out to the crowd. On the BBC Ray French noted how the roar from the stands was drowning out the choir. Even the veteran writer Jack Winstanley, who had been covering the game for decades, admitted that he had been 'caught up in the tide of emotion' as the players walked out: 'I cannot think that Sir Edward Elgar, in 1901, ever imagined how inspirational that particular section of Pomp and Circumstance would turn out to be.'

The huge press pack of Australians had never really experienced anything like it either. Adrian McGregor noted in his book of the tour, *Simply the Best*, that he found himself overcome by emotion: 'One of the most moving moments of any football match I've ever attended.'

The chorus of 'Land of Hope and Glory' that rang out around the ground unnerved the Australians. When the match kicked off, they did something they rarely did and dropped the ball on the first set. And over the course of 80 minutes, Great Britain came up with a performance that finally matched the pre-game hype to deliver a 19-12 victory.

The match at Wembley, in front of a record Test crowd of 54,569, was above all a personal moment of triumph for Ellery Hanley. 'If ever a man showed his true greatness, in his country's hour of need, it was Ellery in a quite majestic performance,' concluded Martin Offiah in his *Rugby Leaguer Review* column. There had been an expectation that Britain would become exhausted or lose focus as the game entered its final stages but Hanley led the team from the front with several runs and tackles that left the Australians shell-shocked. 'The memory of Hanley,' wrote the Australian writer Neil Cadigan, 'will live forever.' A defeated Mal

Meninga admitted to the press that on that performance Hanley was 'the best player in the world'.

As the sports pages were cleared to deal with the magnitude of the victory, the *Daily Mail* again asked the rugby union journalist Terry O'Connor to come out of retirement to cover the game. And it was Hanley that stood out above anything he'd ever seen: 'Hanley's vast array of talents not only inspired Britain to their historic victory. They also ranked him as one of the finest rugby footballers I have seen since the war … in any code.'

For Harry Edgar it was a moment that he had been working towards for much of the decade: 'It was the day our game put itself on the national stage and brought the house down.' Celebrations on and off the pitch were emotional. But underpinning it all was a feeling that rugby league had finally entered the mainstream of British sport. To Stephen Jones at the *Sunday Times*, the sheer scale of the event put the game in the 'mega-crowd division normally inhabited by soccer, rugby union and Bruce Springsteen'. And as Hanley walked off the field with a Union Jack around his shoulders, nobody could be in any doubt that they were the best that the British had to offer.

* * *

Over four million people watched the first Test at Wembley, which put it in line with the ratings for major sporting events in the UK. 'Those are very good figures,' said *Grandstand* editor John Phillips. 'The days of double figures for football and snooker on television are over,' he declared. 'These figures for rugby league compare favourably with most major sports events on the programme.' Phillips admitted to *Open Rugby* that the game was attractive to broadcasters, 'People are beginning to watch rugby league who haven't watched it before. The sheer quality of the game is making them stop and watch.'

The BBC were again on hand to capture the second Test of the series at Old Trafford as the top sports writers arrived to see whether history could be made. After the euphoria of Wembley, there was astonishment at the level of drama as Australia snatched victory in the dying seconds. The contest was immediately judged to be the greatest ever between the two countries and gave the sport the headline coverage it had always dreamed of. The *Sunday Times* put the match on the front page of its sports section under the heading 'Australia last-gasp try seals it'.

Jeff Powell was the chief sports writer at the *Daily Mail* and had been to one of his first rugby league games. 'The physical impact of the conflict was barbarian, the spirit of the contest Herculean, the speed of the challenge utterly relentless.' Powell admitted to his untrained southern eye, 'The northern man's game when played to this high order is a dazzling spectacle.' The headline on his feature was unavoidable because the power dynamic between the two codes was shifting. This was 'Rugby to make the All Blacks shiver'.

David Oxley heralded the series as the culmination of all the game's work over the 1980s. 'Never before has the attention of the nation been so firmly fixed on our game,' he wrote a few weeks later. He sensed that the sport's 'skill, athleticism, tactical brilliance, courage, fitness, commitment and sportsmanship' was recognised nationally. British Coal, the sponsors, said that the game 'had never looked in better shape'.

But one thing remained the same. Australia took the Ashes in the third Test at Elland Road without even conceding a try. Organisers were disappointed with the way that it ended but understood that things appeared to be shifting in their direction. The 1990 Ashes tour was the biggest and most profitable in the game's history. The three Tests had grossed over £1.1m in revenue, and the popularity of the Australians meant that an average crowd of over 20,000 spectators had been to each tour game. The figures eclipsed the record set in the golden age of the 1940s. The Great Britain 'brand' was now well and truly established in the national sporting consciousness. Over the Christmas of 1990, the RFL reported that sales of the replica jersey had been unable to keep up with production. Umbro told the league that stocks would be 'extremely limited'.

* * *

As the British public were enthralled by the Ashes series over the autumn of 1990, the people in Westminster were enjoying their own political thriller. In November 1990 the BBC premiered a new drama series called *House of Cards*. It told the story of the dramatic rise to power of the Machiavellian Chief Whip of the Conservative Party, Francis Urquhart. In the very first scene, he is at his desk looking at a framed photo of Mrs Thatcher. 'Nothing lasts forever,' he says, before turning it face down to reveal that she was no longer the Prime Minister.

After 11 and a half years in power, Thatcher had shown no signs of stepping back as Prime Minister. At the Conservative Party conference in October, delegates had chanted that they wanted her to continue on for 'Four more years!!' But after a divisive summer where she had faced riots over the Poll Tax, divisions over Europe and an economic dispute that saw her Chancellor resign, she ran out of support. MPs began to fear that she would lose the next election. In the end, her downfall was as shocking as it was quick. The last Prime Minister to be forced out of office by a political party was Neville Chamberlain in 1940.

As the Kangaroo tourists trained in Leigh ahead of the match, they were told the news that Thatcher had resigned. The first concern of the players was that the news might affect the pound and give them a worse exchange rate. The Australian full-back Gary Belcher joked that she didn't want to still be Prime Minister when the Aussies recaptured the Ashes. The new Conservative leader John Major promised to offer a different type of leadership to what had come before him. On the steps of Number 10 he said that he wanted to 'build a new country that is at ease with itself'. After the battles of the 1980s, he argued that Britain needed to move into a phase of reconciliation: 'A country that is confident and a country that is prepared and willing to make the changes necessary to provide the quality of life for all our citizens.' As the country hurtled towards the 21st century, rugby league was increasingly confident that it could play a major part in selling Britain to the world.

PART THREE:
THE RECKONING

Chapter 11

Television

TOWARDS THE end of 1990, the best of British sport were at the BBC for the annual Sports Personality of the Year awards. Rugby league had had a fractious relationship with the show ever since it had begun in the 1950s. Each year supporters would increasingly monitor how much airtime the show received. And each year they would watch as rugby union received more focus and awards. In 1987, the year that Ellery Hanley broke try-scoring records for Wigan, won the World Club Challenge and became the captain of Great Britain, the sport was given just 16 seconds of coverage in a round-up that was added on to an extensive union feature.

Players were rarely invited to attend the awards and they were never interviewed as part of the broadcast. They had virtually no chance of picking up any silverware. In 1990, however, things were beginning to change. The biggest draw of the night was Paul Gascoigne, who was awarded the top prize for his efforts to try and win the World Cup. At the same time, there was a recognition of the titanic Ashes battle that had just taken place over the autumn. Mal Meninga, due to the tours of 1982, 1986 and 1990, had become a household name in Britain and as recognisable to the sporting public as the domestic players. And in 1990 he became the first rugby league player to be honoured at the awards when he lifted the Overseas Personality of the Year. From a dressing room in France, he accepted the award and told the nation that he looked forward to coming back to England again one day to play.

The success of the Ashes tour had given the game a real confidence that it could kick on and become a truly national game in John Major's Britain. But while many basked in the glow of unprecedented success, Maurice Lindsay was moving on to the next battle: 'The Ashes series was a great one, but it's gone. There is no point in looking back at it, we've got to look ahead.' And when he looked ahead he sensed that television would be the next one. 'I'm totally convinced that the only way to extend the game is through the TV screen,' he argued. 'People are not going to come to games just on the say so of their mates in a bar, but they might come if they can see it for themselves.'

In the late 1980s, Lindsay had been appointed to a secondary role on top of his Wigan position as the director of marketing and television at the RFL. Lindsay had been seen as the ideal person to help the sport push itself through television. As well as being a bookmaker and a businessman, Lindsay prided himself on being a networker. At Wigan he had taken it upon himself to build a range of contacts across the television industry to help promote the club and offer them access to the Wigan side. His sheer force of personality had made him an attractive figure to producers. The BBC documentary *Up and Under* was a million miles away from the portrayal of Doncaster at the start of the decade. Lindsay injected himself into the centre of the storyline by agreeing to be filmed while going about his business. Lindsay had also emerged as a prominent figure in the controversial book *Blood, Mud and Glory* by Neil Hanson.

Supporters increasingly wanted access to the players and technological advancement was changing the way that fans interacted with players and clubs. The 1980s had seen the emergence of the club telephone information service following the deregulation of the industry. ClubCall allowed fans to listen to a telephone news service dedicated purely to their team, keeping them up to date with transfer gossip, training news and exclusive interviews with players and coaches. Clubs encouraged the access as they received a percentage of income from the calls to their official information line.

In the late 1980s, the newspaper industry had been revolutionised by *The Independent* newspaper's arrival, which offered daily high-quality sports reporting. Developments in technology and printing ushered in a plethora of new magazines across Britain. And *Open Rugby* was no longer alone in its commitment to rugby league writing. In 1988 a new magazine called the *Rugby Leaguer Review* emerged as a rival. At the same time, a weekly newspaper called the *League Express* was launched. Meanwhile, *Open Rugby* was evolving and responding to increased readership and advertising revenue by bringing in more colour photographs and more pages to attract young people to the magazine: 'The sparkling colour action has been a big hit with younger fans ... and THEY are the future of rugby league.'

But it was television that people continually came back to as holding the key to future success. Maurice Lindsay often made the case that the future of the sport rested upon both how it was perceived on television and how it could draw maximum value for the product that it had. The 1980s had ushered in a new battle for television rights, which began when ITV secured the rights to domestic athletics in 1984. It was a significant moment when a major sport had been prised away independently from the BBC for money. And despite its mounting image problems, football benefited from the battle between the two companies to broadcast the domestic league. In 1988, ITV shocked the industry by putting up £55m for a five-year deal to show First Division matches. ITV also secured the rights to the 1991 Rugby World Cup, which marked another significant coup for the RFU.

Rugby league was not involved in any bidding wars. 'We do not yet have a competition that compares with the Five Nations in terms of prestige and structure, and therefore you can't make comparisons,' Lindsay admitted. For much of the 80s, supporters had wondered why Channel 4 had not been interested in acquiring the rights to highlights packages. Rugby league had an equally difficult relationship with ITV in the early 1980s over its highlight show *RL Action*. Launched in 1981, it had arrived with much fanfare and was seen as a way to bring new people into the game. But it proved to be a major ratings flop, and Granada and Yorkshire TV moved it around their schedules until it was broadcast at 12.15am. In an age where VCRs were still a rarity the spectators complained that they had to stay up too late to watch.

By the end of the decade, however, the relationship with ITV had radically improved. *Scrumdown* became the most popular show amongst supporters after Granada acquired the rights to domestic matches and highlights of the regular season. A young commentator called Clive Tyldesley was brought on board to front the coverage and he was immediately praised for his passion and enthusiasm for the sport. He admitted in interviews that he was 'an amateur league fan' when he was appointed to the role. But Tyldesley treated his task as a professional and watched games on video and sat in the stands with coaches to get a feel for the action. As an outsider, he told the *League Express* that he was 'conscious' that his commentary style was 'a little different to anything that's gone before in rugby league'.

Tyldesley understood what a casual football fan might want from the coverage of the sport. Viewers in Morecambe, Middlewich and Blackburn wouldn't enjoy a 'Blood and Thunder' rugby league match: 'We try and make the programme two hours of entertainment, a dramatic and educational experience for the viewers.' In contrast to the BBC, ITV spent a large amount of time focusing on the intricacies of the game. They brought in Phil Larder to explain various aspects of it and chose the Australian coach Brian Smith to co-commentate with Tyldesley. Smith believed that it was important for coaches to get involved in the broadcasting of games to give 'an inside view of the game and hopefully help educate the public about what's happening on the field and what the players are doing'.

'The quality of media coverage can make or break a sport,' Smith wrote in his monthly *Open Rugby* column. Smith urged the English game to do more in persuading the key people in television, print and radio to take the game seriously, stating, 'We've got to present our game with quality and high standards, to make us attractive to these decision-makers.' He argued that it was producers, as much as players and coaches, that could determine how popular a sport can become: 'Right down to the backing music they choose, if a sport is produced in the right kind of up-market, up-beat manner, television presentation is an instant attention grabber.'

* * *

During Mrs Thatcher's first term, television policy had largely focused on the establishment of Channel 4 as the government sought to break up the monopoly of the BBC and ITV. Pay TV had been introduced in the US, but experts believed that it would never take off in the UK. The satellite age didn't really begin until 1989 when Rupert Murdoch's Sky television went head to head against BSB to see who could establish a foothold within the country. As millions and millions of pounds were spent on advertising, the race was dubbed 'Star Wars' as Sky and BSB battled for the best talent, marketing agents, sales teams and news presenters. Murdoch launched first with Sky One, Sky News and Eurosport. But it was his blockbuster movie channel, Sky Movies, that was expected to be the trump card in his battle. By contrast, BSB focused on its sports coverage and when producers were looking for cheap sports to help boost their scheduling, they found themselves drawn to rugby league.

Announcing an agreement to cover domestic games and overseas tours, BSB believed that they could turn the Sunday afternoon slot into a rugby league one. 'We think young people especially will welcome live sport at that time of day,' announced BSB head of sport Andrew Croker. For the rugby league supporters who had been used to half an hour a week on the BBC and ITV, BSB promised to offer a remarkable increase in exposure. 'Initially,' wrote Dave Hadfield in *The Independent*, 'half a million people will be able to tune into BSB on cable TV', with plans to allow pubs and clubs to show sports. Most importantly BSB promised to feature rugby league in its four half-hour sports bulletins daily.

The producer Jon Davis had big ideas for what BSB could do for rugby league. Working on athletics, he revolutionised coverage by installing a camera that followed athletes around the track. His ambition was to do the same for rugby league. 'If a player races 80 yards for a try, I want the viewer to be able to go with him,' Davis said. 'And if he gets stopped along the way, I want the cameras to pick up the thud and the impact of the tackle, too. This game has a hell of a lot going for it, and we should illustrate that.'

In the 1980s, Oxley and Howes had worked hard to win over the tabloid newspapers but the revival of international rugby league has sparked the broadsheets into covering the sport. When the journalist Chris Irvine arrived at *The Times* sports desk in the early 1990s hoping to write about rugby league, he found that they were interested in what had happened at Wigan and with Great Britain.

Irvine was unique in rugby league circles in that he had done his apprenticeship in the 80s as a 'serious' news journalist who covered everything from the Gulf War to the politics of the age.

In his early years, he had been a correspondent at the *Warrington Guardian*, where he had grown to love the sport. But he was an outsider. Irvine came from Coventry and had few contacts in the game. But when an opportunity arose to write some pieces for *The Times,* he sensed that the sport was on the cusp of breaking into the mainstream. Irvine's editor told him he didn't know much about the game but wanted to learn more. Irvine was given a licence to run news stories. But most importantly, *The Times* wanted more features on players and what made them different from other athletes in Britain.

It was not long before Irvine was writing lengthy profiles about the players and the coaches alongside daily reports on the battle for the game's future. Irvine was constantly looking for features that told the game's story and such was the popularity and knowledge of the game, he could spend his time on something other than introducing the characters to the public. His first profile for *The Times* outlined the new type of journalism the game was subject to: 'There is precious little glamour at Fartown. Through the rusting shoal of barracuda guarding the entrance – the club used to be known as the Barracudas – past the pavilion, the cinder track leads to the back of an ancient wooden stand. Alex Murphy is ensconced in a Portakabin underneath, headquarters of Huddersfield rugby club. "Welcome to Steptoe's yard," he said.'

An example of how far the game had travelled was seen by the decision of John Major to attend the 1992 Challenge Cup Final. Margaret Thatcher had been to only one rugby league game in her life, when she attended the 1976 Challenge Cup Final as Leader of the Opposition. She had been booed as she arrived to greet the players and meet each one before the game. In 1992, Major was not the guest of honour, nor did he give the winning Wigan side the trophy. He was there just to watch. And in the media afterwards, he admitted that he had been enthralled by the action. Describing the match as 'an enjoyable occasion with a wonderful atmosphere', Major said that 'the physical level was amazing'. He told the press that 'the main thing is the attitude of the players on the field, which was beyond reproach'. Major had been a football fan all his life but admitted that rugby league's changes over the 1980s had repositioned it in the public imagination: 'It is the way sport should be played.'

The new image of the game that had been carried forward by Ellery Hanley was drawing the attention of other sports. American football was increasingly popular in Britain in the 90s, and when there was a push to create a European football league, there was a belief that the game needed to do something spectacular to promote it. American TV pumped $49m into a new world league, and the London Monarchs were one of the top franchise clubs. And one way in which they looked to secure maximum publicity for their venture was to bring Ellery Hanley on board. In March 1991, the *Daily Mirror* landed the exclusive story and dedicated page after page to the news that Hanley would be dipping his toes in. 'I may not make it,' he admitted to Ted Macauley. 'But I've got to give myself this chance to prove that I can be right at the top in another sort of challenge.'

Dubbed the $10m man, Hanley posed in London Monarchs kit and was splashed all over the media for weeks. Hanley even ended up on the *Jonathan Ross Show* to discuss the move. Jon Smith, the chief executive of Wembley Stadium, admitted that Hanley was central to the fortunes of the venture. 'Ellery Hanley on his own could half-fill Wembley,' he argued. Part of the rationale was that Hanley could make American football popular in the north. Most significantly the organisers admitted that the money for

Hanley was not going to come out of a playing budget but out of the marketing budget of $2m. 'If Ellery comes through, most of that money will be his,' Smith told *The Independent*. In the end, it proved to be a false dawn as Hanley never played for the Monarchs. Critics said it was purely a publicity stunt by the game to raise awareness of the new venture. But it worked, as the Monarchs began to play in front of large crowds in their inaugural season.

* * *

As the battle between BSB and Sky heated up, the rugby league coverage was soon beset by problems. Producers found that the new innovations, such as a motorised buggy that ran up and down the sidelines to capture the action, were not made for rugby league grounds that were small, undeveloped and with pitches that were covered in mud. Journalists, who had been expecting a revolution in terms of coverage due to the advertising and marketing hype, soon had reasons to criticise it. 'Viewers who regard BBC's sports coverage as the yardstick of traditional quality need not concern themselves about the standards to which British Satellite Broadcasting aspires,' concluded one TV critic in *The Independent*. The bigger problem for BSB was that nowhere near enough people had taken up subscriptions to justify the costs: 'The problem, if you have not noticed, is that – despite £1.3 billion investment in the company – BSB satellite dishes are even harder to find today than defenders of the poll tax.' The joke around the industry was that satellite broadcasting for both Sky and BSB was a licence to lose money.

Murdoch had staked his entire media empire on Sky succeeding. In 1990 he was losing around £2 million a week and was desperately seeking support to refinance the debt. With neither Sky nor BSB able to lose more money, a long-anticipated merger between the two broadcasters was put forward. British Sky

Broadcasting (BSkyB) was launched towards the end of 1990. 'The price will be less competition and less choice for viewers,' concluded the BBC News coverage of the merger. In the battle to establish Pay TV, the two firms had spent roughly £1.25bn and only just reached 1% of the UK television audience. As Sam Chisholm, Murdoch's top executive, suggested, in the book *Sky High,* it had been an expensive venture: 'The truth was that both businesses were conceptual failures … It hadn't just been a failure. It had been a conceptual failure.'

Just as experts had predicted, sport proved a difficult sell in the battle to establish Pay TV in Britain. Rugby league administrators worried that rugby league would be the first to go in the wake of the merger. Viewing figures had not been great and there had been rumours that the take-up had disappointed BSB. But when Sky Sports was launched in 1990 as part of the new service, league found that it had a strong ally at the very heart of the Murdoch organisation. David Hill was an Australian who had worked on rugby league coverage down under in the 1980s as Kerry Packer and Rupert Murdoch began a battle over the rights to television coverage.

Hill's reputation was built on the way that he had radically changed coverage by importing American production techniques to change the speed and tempo of the broadcast. Hill had revolutionised cricket through his philosophy of 'slick and cutting-edge' production aligned with top-name pundits and presenters. His most controversial innovation was the development of an animated duck, which waddled across the television screen when a batsman was dismissed for nought, to illustrate that they had been 'out for a duck'. It provoked much anger in a sport with conservative traditions and structures. Ian Woolridge, the sports columnist for the *Daily Mail* said, 'Bloody ducks ruined cricket for me. Hilly is totally, absolutely mad. Bonkers.'

In the late 1980s, Rupert Murdoch tempted Hill away from Nine. 'The Nine Network was always our competition and Hill was a legendary figure in Sydney,' Murdoch recalled in the *New York Times*. Hill quickly adapted the tools of American sports TV for Sky Sports by using more cameras, developing better instant replays, enhancing graphics and encouraging more controversial punditry and analysis than the BBC would provide. Hill struck up a relationship with Maurice Lindsay and the pair soon realised that they wanted the same things for the game. The pair were ambitious about broadcasting and sensed that the game could benefit from a radical change in its coverage. Some believed the game was taking a huge gamble by backing the Murdoch project and taking matches away from Granada and Yorkshire TV. But Lindsay believed it was a gamble worth taking. 'BSkyB are a fledgling company but there is no better time to join an expansionist movement than at the start.'

Most significantly the tie-in with BSkyB finally put the sport on a par with others in the market. Rugby league was now being marketed on full-page adverts in Murdoch newspapers alongside cricket, tennis, F1, athletics and golf as 'The best sport in the world'. An advertising campaign in club programmes offered supporters deals to watch the action: 'When it comes to covering all the sporting action, you'll find that Sky Sports is in a different league.'

Maurice Lindsay was rapidly moving beyond his position at Wigan and used any opportunity he had to advocate for television, challenging anybody who believed pay television was not the game's future. 'Let's be honest,' he argued in the *League Express*, 'they are making the effort to explain the game and promote it.' In an attack on the 'traditionalists', he called for a shift in mindset, saying, 'I want people to stop bleating about free TV and realise that we are in the modern world – even the BBC won't be free forever.'

BSkyB signalled their intent by appointing Neville Smith as producer and rebadging the Championship as the Big League in order to try and rebrand the coverage and take it to new audiences.

The most controversial idea that was put forward was to try and crack the Friday evening slot. Popular in Australia, sport was rarely played on a Friday night in Britain and was seen as a huge gamble. But the decision gave the sport the opportunity to frame itself as modern and dynamic. The announcement was billed as 'a first for any sport and any British TV channel'. And to give it the feel of a Friday night audience, it was edgier than the coverage that supporters were used to on the BBC. Television shows such as *The Word* on Channel 4 proved popular because of how they made 'ordinary' members of the public stars of the show. On Big League, young journalist Bill Arthur was tasked with interviewing supporters outside the ground to bring the voice of the spectators into the coverage.

Those watching Big League soon realised that this was a very different type of production than that which had come before. Coverage benefited from the development in on-screen graphics that David Hill had created in Australia a few years earlier. Whereas cricket had introduced the cartoon duck, rugby league developed graphics that moved across the screen for the sin bin, red cards and concussion injuries. In the pre-game build-up, the show ran a crossword and quizzes across the screen to keep the audience occupied and engaged during the advertising breaks.

The most radical move initiated by Sky Sports was the decision to introduce a soundtrack that symbolised how league was bigger and bolder than ever before. Sports soundtracks had rarely changed over the 1980s. The *Grandstand*, *Match of the Day*, *Ski Sunday* and *Rugby Special* themes were universally known and put together through orchestras and brass bands. Coverage of the Big League, however, wanted to connect with a younger audience. Each week coverage opened with a boxing-style introduction which announced that this coverage was 'taking rugby into a different league'. 'BSkyB's coverage attempts to reflect the new modernity of rugby league,' argued *The Independent* TV critic Stan Hey. 'In every sense, the programme title *Big League* is deserved.' The use of the track 'Carpe Diem' by the acid house duo Edrenalin was cut to various shots of stars such as Ellery Hanley, Jonathan Davies and Martin Offiah busting tackles and scoring tries.

Not everybody was enthusiastic about the aggressive up-tempo style that David Hill and Neville Smith had initiated. Some supporters wrote letters to the *League Express* asking why fans 'had to suffer four or five replays every time a try is scored', why they were 'trying to be clever with a trace on the screen showing how the try occurred', as well as introducing 'intrusive background music'. Yet as Hey argued in *The Independent*, the sound immediately changed perceptions about the image of rugby league. 'In tone a deep, no-Northern voice as the titles roll, not to colliery brass-band Hovis-ad themes but to thoroughly energising rave music.'

* * *

For much of the post-war years, rugby league commentary had been dominated by just two people: Eddie Waring and Ray French. While regional broadcasters such as John Holdsworth, Keith Macklin and Alan McGuinness commentated on radio and on video subscription channels, the dominance of the BBC meant that the game was associated with its main commentator. When BSB were first setting up their rugby league coverage, however, they had been drawn to two young broadcasters who had started out in football. Clive Tyldesley had proved popular on ITV while Eddie Hemmings had become a popular figure in rugby league in the 1980s thanks to his coverage of the game on BBC Radio 2.

Hemmings had first come to the attention of Harry Edgar in 1986 when he gave an interview with *Open Rugby* supporting the decision to take the first Test to Old Trafford. 'You have to make strong decisions to achieve progress. You can go on and on putting things off.' Over the course of the decade, Hemmings struck up relationships with people like Maurice Lindsay, who were eager for the sport to be communicated in a different way. He proved himself to be a strong advocate for the game on a show called *Sportsround* which was produced in Manchester. When the show was launched, Hemmings admitted that 'rugby league should have a big say because of its importance to the region'. League would be entitled to around six minutes per week which amounted to a quarter of the programme. 'I don't think the sport has ever had that kind of exposure before and fills a great gap in the North West sports coverage.' Hemmings encouraged those running the sport to provide 'personality features' to boost its profile.

In a close-fought contest, BSB recruited Hemmings over Tyldesley but struggled to find someone to commentate with him. St Helens scrum-half Neil Holding was renowned in the game as a 'character' for his comedic performances and impressions of people such as Frank Spencer on the training ground. But he didn't work as an analyst. Others offered up for a trial run were former Great Britain hooker Terry Flanagan as well as the Salford coach Kevin Ashcroft. Even Gary Hetherington worked on a Yorkshire Cup Final with Hemmings. But the chemistry was not there. When BSB agreed to cover the 1990 Ashes series they wanted a pundit with knowledge of the Australian game to help educate the public. One afternoon Hemmings was reading a copy of the Australian *Big League* magazine when he saw an advert for a supporters' tour hosted by Mike Stephenson. He immediately knew that he had to find a way to get him on board at BSB.

Mike Stephenson had been a member of Great Britain's 1972 World Cup-winning side where he scored a try against Australia in the final. But like many of the best players in the 1970s, he had been part of the exodus to Sydney. He eventually settled in Penrith where he became a pundit following his retirement. As the British voice in the Sydney media, 'Stevo' had various columns in tabloid newspapers as well as radio work for the ABC. But the nature of the coverage was changing. Towards the end of the 80s, producers wondered if he was out of touch with the modern game and the new pundits. He quickly lost his newspapers and radio work and found himself scrabbling round Sydney to find any job just to make ends meet. He had just taken a job digging holes in the ground in Sydney when BSB made a call.

Hemmings encouraged BSB to bring him on board for their coverage of the 1990 Ashes tour and the pair quickly formed a double act that impressed both the broadcaster and the subscribers. Becoming 'Eddie and Stevo' they were elevated to a central position in the marketing of the coverage once BSkyB developed the Big League. Eddie and Stevo differed from Waring and French because they knew they were operating in a more competitive marketplace. At the BBC, Waring and French had taken up the view that they needed to 'educate' the casual listener who may be tuning in to watch a game for the first time. This often led to criticism that they were living up to stereotypes of the north that the BBC had created for them. By contrast, Hemmings knew that whenever he picked up the microphone, he was competing with *Eastenders* and *Coronation Street* for attention. They needed to sell the drama of the sport each week to keep people watching and parting with their money.

While the game had always wanted higher viewing figures to help negotiations with the BBC, it didn't matter how well the BBC sold the game. The Challenge Cup was going to be broadcast whether it captured the public imagination or not. Eddie and Stevo, by contrast, had to develop narratives and storylines so that viewers were interested in the players. They had columns in rugby league newspapers where they introduced talking points each week. They would then use the magazine show, *Boots N All*, to become a platform for the game to debate issues and promote people within the game.

When Great Britain had beaten Australia in 1990 on the BBC, Ray French and co-commentator John Monie had remained impartial in their commentary. Two years later, when the Ashes tour was broadcast 'exclusively' live on Sky Sports, Eddie and Stevo had a free rein to commentate as supporters of the British side. As Great Britain pulled off a remarkable victory in Melbourne, viewers back home watching over breakfast heard Stevo cheer them on. 'Gee, but it's great to be a Pommie!!' And when Offiah touched down for a try in the final moments, Stevo couldn't contain his delight at the win: 'I think this pass was a mile forward – but I don't care!!'

* * *

The Big League coverage radically changed how the sport was presented in Britain and administrators believed that it could finally turn rugby league into a national sport. The end-of-season Premiership Final was fast becoming one of the best-attended events in the rugby league calendar at Old Trafford to rival the Challenge Cup Final at Wembley. The sponsors, Stones Bitter, commissioned a special rugby league advertisement to sell the final to the wider public. The advert was intended to be the British answer to the Tina Turner promotion. Shot over four days at Tong

Hall in Yorkshire, Garry Schofield took on the role of weightlifter in the gym while the Leeds hooker Colin Maskill was filmed topless working out on an exercise machine. The film then moved to Wigan's Joe Lydon and Denis Betts running through the fields in vests to show their muscles. It then cut to Martin Offiah and Shaun Edwards sat in a red sports car. It was heavily promoted as 'rugby league's first tailor-made television advertisement on the ITV network'.

The advert, coupled with the arrival of BSkyB, presented rugby league players as aspirational with a focus on their individuality. Creating stars was central to what David Hill and Neville Smith were trying to do at Sky Sports. And in 1992, no star shone brighter than Martin 'Chariots' Offiah. It was Dave Hadfield who observed the subtle changes that had occurred to the game at the beginning of the 1990s that showed just how big Offiah had become. One morning he was reading over the cricket pages, and he noticed that a rugby league player had been used as a metaphor by another sports writer writing about their sport. The cricket writer Simon Hughes was commenting on David Gower's absence from the England side. Hughes argued that any expectation that Gower could perform his way back into the side through county cricket 'would be like expecting Martin Offiah to perform on a quagmire'.

In the early 1990s, Martin Offiah cemented his place as the most famous and marketable player in the British game when Wigan signed him for a world-record fee to replace Ellery Hanley, who had moved to Leeds. After scoring two tries on his club debut at Wembley, in the Challenge Cup Final against Castleford, Prime Minister John Major told Offiah that he was 'quicker than a camera shutter'. Those watching Offiah understood that they were watching a 'once in a lifetime' player. After Offiah scored ten tries in one match against Leeds, Dave Hadfield admitted that he didn't just want to interview him, he wanted to go over and thank him: 'As long as people watch this game, they will ask their elders whether they were there the day Offiah went mad.'

Offiah was the closest thing that the game had to a major celebrity. In the early 90s he was a regular on sports television programmes. In contrast to Ellery Hanley, he engaged with the tabloid media in order to maximise his profile. As Wigan continued to dominate the sport, journalists continued to write about Offiah. In 1992 he would often write columns in the *Daily Mirror* to promote matches and be photographed in various locations. 'I'm in the mood to become the first man to score a hat-trick of tries in a Wembley final,' he argued, which became the dominant news story in the run-up.

His profile meant that others wanted to knock him down. Alex Murphy wrote that Offiah was 'the best of a bad bunch of wingers' who was 'finished' after a short run of injuries. 'The cruel truth is that he scares nobody nowadays. I think he has lost his bottle and some of his crucial speed.'

Offiah was unusual in that he actively embraced the criticism that came his way. 'I wouldn't expect to win many prizes in a rugby league popularity poll among my fellow professionals,' he wrote in one *Daily Mirror* column. 'You just can't play the game the way I do without making enemies along the way.' It meant that he was a national media star the like of which had been rarely seen in league circles for much of the post-war period. And when Wembley was chosen as the venue for the one-off match between Great Britain and Australia to determine the winners of the World Cup, organisers sensed that it was time to cash in on his profile in the country. The RFL decided that it would put up to £30,000 into a poster and publicity campaign to sell the World Cup Final to the nation. They promised it would be the biggest in the history of the British game. The aim was not just to sell tickets but to enhance the perception that rugby league was a major sport capable of putting on events in the capital.

By the early 90s, rugby league was confident about marketing itself around the image of one individual star. In the 1990 Test series, the RFL had used an image of Wally Lewis and Ellery Hanley to market the game. But the image was static, featuring the usual headshot of each player. For the 1992 final, an advertising agency was encouraged to create something much more impressionable and eye-catching. The agency spent the afternoon with Offiah as they photographed him running through flames. The use of pyrotechnics and a studio emphasised how seriously the sport wanted to market the game. The title chimed with the marketing and advertising ethos of the age. Commuters heading into central London were asked the question: 'Will the Aussies catch Offiah at Wembley?'

David Howes briefed the media saying, 'Offiah was chosen because he is the greatest personality in the game. He has a London background and great showbiz appeal. Like goalscorers in soccer, the great try scorers are the heroes and the personalities.' In *The Times*, Chris Irvine examined how even the name Offiah was a construct to help sell his image to the wider public. Offiah's name was Nigerian and pronounced Off-ear rather than Of-fire. 'It still niggles him that he is more usually called "Of-fire",' wrote Irvine, ' except that it sounds good, makes a good headline and is exceedingly good marketing sense.'

The story of the poster captured the attention of the media which made the image a story in its own right. This was the type of marketing campaign that Margaret Thatcher had pioneered with Saatchi and Saatchi in the late 1970s when the 'Labour isn't Working' poster had created such controversy in the media that it had amounted to millions of extra pounds' free advertising. The Offiah poster was picked up by the *Daily Mirror* as a serious news story. In September, a month before the final, the paper reprinted a full-page poster of Offiah in their 'picture power' section: 'This is the sight all British rugby league fans will want to see.' Signalling that the game was taking over the capital, the paper advertised how 'this dramatic poster of the most exciting talent in the game has gone up at more than 1,000 sites alongside escalators at London's main tube stations'.

The starkness of the image even prompted people to write into the public opinion letters pages: 'The great new poster of Martin Offiah burning up the Wembley turf is as dazzling as his play.' The BBC had secured the rights to the final and encouraged broadcasters to talk about the Offiah poster. It was discussed on BBC Radio through Simon Mayo and Steve Wright as well as on the children's television show *Going Live!* League was now in the unusual position of having a player that had name recognition. The marketing campaign didn't need to explain the sport, the rivalry or what was at stake. All they had to do was encourage them to come and watch Offiah: 'If you can get this kind of publicity, your advertising needs only awareness and back-up,' said David Howes. The poster led to an immediate 40% increase in ticket sales from people in the south and organisers could announce a world-record Test attendance with a week to go before the match.

The scale of the 1992 World Cup Final, in terms of public interest, was unlike anything that the game had ever experienced. Not only had organisers managed to run a successful promotion campaign, it had major sports brands helping to market the sport. In the 1970s, Nike had struggled to crack the new aerobics market in America and was rapidly losing out to its rival, Reebok. When Nike first ventured into rugby league in the 1980s they struck up a deal with perennial First Division strugglers Oldham. Nike created innovative adverts to promote their deal to supply the club with boots and training gear. One of the posters, set in the classic white and black block print, asked: 'Who's screwed every stud in the Oldham team?'

Nike's fortunes changed in the middle of the decade when they began sponsoring Michael Jordan in the NBA. By the 1990s they were operating in a very different marketplace, selling a lifestyle as much as a trainer. Sports advertising was seen as a way to sell Nike products to young people for leisure as much as exercise.

As the journalist Jim White observed in the early 1990s, 'Hyperbole became Nike's trademark – the strategy: sign up top athletes and promote them as supermen.'

Nike wasn't interested in traditions. They wanted to sign people who were different. In the 1980s, they signed up the tennis player John McEnroe and argued that they sold more shoes every time he caused controversy. They continually signed deals with players who had attitude and style and captured the public's imagination. Ian Wright became intrinsically linked to Nike at Arsenal. 'Most of the people buying Nike are not going to wear them to play sport,' argued White. 'So Nike tends to go for sportsmen its younger buyers think are cool.'

Not everybody within the sports world approved of their methods. In the early 90s, Nike ran a marketing campaign with the England rugby union team around the slogan, 'These men are dangerous. Do not attempt to tackle them', with four of the squad mocked up with police mugshots. For a sport trying to move away from its violent image, the RFU was furious at the way that they had been portrayed. 'We do not wish for advertisements of this type which bring the game into disrepute.' The RFU threatened to end its agreement with Nike, warning that 'they are bad for the image of the game'.

Rugby league, by contrast, appealed to Nike because of its speed and its athleticism. Offiah was exactly the sort of character and personality who appealed to Nike's ethos. Ahead of the 1992 World

Cup Final, Offiah was featured on a major national advertising campaign which showcased the best athletes that Britain had to offer. On billboards, magazines and on tube posters there were pictures of Martin Offiah running, with the caption 'The hand can't catch what the eye can't see'. The campaign not only elevated Offiah to the elite of British sport, it ensured that rugby league would have Nike sponsorship for the final. As the spectators took their seats at Wembley, Nike had taken out sponsorship across the electronic advertising hoardings.

The country had bought into the idea that this was the 'Offiah final'. On the morning of the game, the *Daily Mirror* dedicated its back page to Offiah: 'London's Burning. HOT-SHOT winger Martin Offiah will provide the fireworks at Wembley today when he takes on the Aussie World Cup holders.' The *Daily Mail* ran on the idea that this was the biggest game in the history of the sport. Under the heading 'Eyes of the world on Wembley showdown', the paper told its readers that 'A GLOBAL audience will watch Great Britain and Australia fight it out', with the match being beamed across Australia, Asia and South Africa. Chris Irvine of *The Times* sensed that victory might just tip league into the national consciousness for good. Maurice Lindsay briefed the media that a win 'could represent an acceleration of about ten years' development in 80 minutes'.

From a marketing perspective, the game had been proven right in selling the game around their superstar as over 70,000 people packed into Wembley to see whether Offiah could break the Australian dominance. But all the hype and the pressure around Offiah proved to be too much. Within a few minutes, people realised that this was not going to be a game for wingers like Offiah. It turned into a tough, defensive battle with neither side wanting to make the error that would cost them the World Cup. Those that had come to watch Offiah were hugely disappointed when he had one of the quietest games of his career. And in what was becoming a familiar pattern, Great Britain and Australia took their rivalry to another level, but, in the end, it was the Kangaroos who left with the trophy.

Martin Offiah was the rare sort of rugby league player that thought about how history would judge him even as he was playing. He had sensed that the 1992 World Cup Final had been his moment to immortalise himself for his country and at Wembley.

He knew that this had been his final. He thought of all the great iconic players who had created great moments and realised that he had yet to create one. In the immediate aftermath, he felt like he had squandered a golden opportunity for both himself and the game. 'I took that more personally than any defeat I had ever experienced in the game,' he admitted to his biographer David Lawrenson in the book *A Blaze of Glory*. 'I could imagine a lot of people new to rugby league, who had got caught up in the whole marketing thing, thinking "What was all the fuss about?"'

Offiah was devastated by the way things had turned out at Wembley. In the aftermath, the media concentrated on how poorly he had performed and how the game had focused on defence rather than attack. When the Australians lifted the World Cup, Offiah was criticised for not joining his team-mates in a lap of honour at the end of the game. 'There's no need for a lap of honour when you lose!' he told the press. But while he may have been personally disappointed with the way things had turned out, the sponsors believed that league was now in the big time. To celebrate the record-breaking attendance, Stones Bitter took out an advert to express their pride in their links with the game. In full distinct orange print, a poster was placed in several tabloid newspapers. 'There's always a good crowd where there's Stones. A record 73,631 people were at Wembley for the Stones Rugby League World Cup Final.'

Chapter 12

Boom and Bust

THE FULL house at Wembley, and the record crowd, stood as a testament to the revival of the international game that had occurred in the 80s and early 90s. Rugby league was now operating in the elite sports event marketplace, competing with rock concerts and football matches for commercial revenue. David Oxley had always known that 1992 would be the year that he would have to give it all up. It had been stipulated in the job advertisement in 1974 that nobody over the age of 55 could work in the role. Oxley was now one of the most-respected administrators in sports business and interviewed for a major role at the FA. It was a mark of his longevity that newspapers ran full-length profiles on him alongside Offiah in the run-up to the final.

As he reflected on his period running the game, he remembered the dark days of the mid-1970s when people had advised him not to give up a career in education to run the RFL. As Alan Fraser wrote in the *Daily Mail*, 'It was a prophecy as wide of the mark as the weekly predictions of Armageddon from the man with the sandwich board in Oxford Street.' Oxley was far too modest to suggest that he had saved the game but the outpouring of tributes emphasised how well he had kept the sport together during a period of radical change.

Of all the people who bought into Oxley's ideas to change and professionalise the image of the game in the 1980s, it was Maurice Lindsay who had benefited the most. The respect between the two men was mutual. Oxley believed that the standards set at Wigan now needed to be replicated across the entire sport. They had, he argued, changed everything. 'It can't be over-estimated what Wigan's tremendous example has done for the public perception, nationally and internationally, of rugby league as a great game – entertaining, exciting, stirring – played by outstanding athletes.' Lindsay admitted that Oxley had been the best in his field during the 80s: 'David Oxley has been the most articulate and presentable administrator in any sport in the country.'

Rugby league rarely changed the person who was running the game. Since the great split from rugby union, the sport had only had four chairmen, in Joseph Platt, John Wilson, Bill Fallowfield and Oxley. It seemed inevitable that Maurice Lindsay would be the person to replace Oxley as the chief executive of the sport in 1992. Having slowly gained more influence over the sport and increasingly using the media to advocate for change, he had long held ambitions beyond his Wigan brief. When he announced that he was applying for the role there was little value in interviewing anyone else.

Everybody knew that it was going to be a very different style of leadership. When John Major had replaced Mrs Thatcher in autumn 1990, he had succeeded in framing his leadership as a distinct break with the past. After all the 'pomp' of the Thatcher Years, Major wanted to show that he was a very different type of Prime Minister. In his opening speech to the country he had promised to lead a nation 'more at ease with itself' after the division of the Thatcher decade. Internally he promoted people with different political views to him and was quickly renowned for holding lengthy cabinet meetings.

The sense of being 'ordinary' in contrast to Thatcher underpinned his well-crafted image. He quickly mastered the art of the photo opportunity, which at all times was to put himself in 'ordinary' situations to 'show it was possible to be Prime Minister and remain a human being'. He ate at Happy Eater cafes and went to cricket, football and rugby matches. The media, eager to find new ways of reporting on politics, bought into it too. By 1992, a *Sunday Times* profile entitled 'The Importance of Being Ordinary' sold Major to the voters as 'an ordinary man in an extraordinary position'. The party even played on his humble roots for a famous political poster that asked the question: 'What does the Conservative Party offer a working class kid from Brixton? They made him Prime Minister.'

David Oxley had been like John Major in temperament. He used his collegiate and schoolteacher manner to bring the rugby league community together to face the challenges of the 1980s. He had pushed for expansion but rarely at the expense of the smaller clubs. For a rugby league administrator, he was liked by people across the game. The changes had, in many ways, been revolutionary. But he was far too modest to frame it as such. Speaking with Dave Hadfield in *The Independent* about his time at the top, he refused to say that the game would have died without him, 'It wouldn't have died – there were too many good people involved to let it die – but it was in trouble.' He instead put the revival down to the players themselves. 'We are so lucky with our players,' he said. 'One thing I hope as I leave is that they realise the esteem in which I hold them.'

Lindsay, by contrast, was more like Mrs Thatcher. He believed in creating narratives and placing himself at the centre of events. When he became the chief executive of the sport, he talked about how he had saved the Wigan club from terminal decline and would bring the same drive and determination to pull the sport up to that level. The mythology and aura around his personality, often self-made by himself in the numerous media profiles that he organised, were framed around the idea that he was a successful businessman bringing those practices to an out-of-touch sport: 'My business background means that I am bound to approach the job in a different way.' In *The Times*, Chris Irvine acknowledged that Lindsay would 'bring a more abrasive business edge' in contrast to 'Oxley's diplomatic stealth and quiet persuasion'. Lindsay believed that the administrators needed to be visible and open to the media at all times: 'We need to explain the corporate affairs and background to the decisions, not just the personalities and the people that play the game.' With the sport having made significant changes to match the Australians' playing standards, there was a feeling that new leadership would maximise new business opportunities. Oxley endorsed the Lindsay appointment, declaring that his time had come. He even urged Lindsay to take on the job in a different manner to him, using his 'characteristic dynamism and energy' to take the game forward into the next century.

* * *

Maurice Lindsay was never going to stop and bask in the success of Oxley's leadership for too long. But people within the game were surprised at how quickly he started to create the narrative of crisis and decline. Within days of taking over he talked about the need for 'serious self-examination' before 'we can determine in which direction our game should be heading' as the new millennium approached. Lindsay said that the sport had been 'drifting along with no one prepared to take the game by the scruff of the neck and act positively'. In the wake of Hillsborough and the Taylor Report into standards at sporting stadia, Lindsay knew that there would be a huge battle for resources. And he wasn't the sort of person that would let others determine the nature of that debate. Of primary concern was the dramatic increase in transfer fees and wages across the game. 'Players must have thought the gold rush had arrived,' he said. But it had been an illusion. 'Few people took the trouble to look beneath the surface; had they done so, they would have seen a number of problems.'

The dilemma facing Lindsay as he articulated 'the way ahead' was that most people within the game held him entirely responsible for the 'gold rush'. It was Lindsay who had ushered in the age of the free market at Wigan where he had consistently argued that players should be paid their true value. At Wigan, Lindsay had spent money on top-line international talent in the hope that revenue would increase through sponsorship and gate receipts. Players were offered eye-watering win bonuses to incentivise them to keep winning the key matches. By 1992, Wigan had won five Challenge Cups in a row and were dominating every aspect of the game. Part of it was down to Lindsay's foresight and ambition. But it was also about getting a headstart on the rest of the game.

Widnes had tried to copy the Lindsay business model by bringing in top stars from rugby union. The two clubs had been engaged in a competitive arms race to find the best talent from around Britain and the world. But the boom of the early Offiah/Davies years had given way to stagnation as the club struggled to bring in the commercial sponsors to pay for them. The long impact of industrial change meant that there was still high unemployment in the area and less money to go around. Almost 3,000 supporters had drifted away, which left them on the brink of financial catastrophe. As Dave Hadfield put it, 'If any club can be said to have experienced a season that was a microcosm of British rugby league in the 1990s, that club was Widnes.'

What shocked most people within the game was how, when the club managed to sell Martin Offiah for £440,000, it didn't seem to alter their fortunes. It should have been a tidy profit on a player they had unearthed for nothing just a few years earlier. But the bank took up most of the money to pay off a large overdraft. For Jonathan Davies, there was an added criticism that he was in part to blame for the financial situation the club found themselves in. After finding himself a target, he agreed to do an interview with Dave Hadfield where he outlined his concerns for the future of the sport. Photographed on the banks of the River Mersey, Davies revealed that he was struggling to understand the criticism: 'There are times when you need the backing of rugby league people. They could be more open-minded and supportive.'

In the same interview, Davies acknowledged that he wouldn't be playing league if it hadn't been for the financial boom that had come into the game in the late 1980s:

'You wouldn't take the risk. It would be like leaving *The Independent* to work for the *Widnes Weekly News*. You wouldn't do it, would you?' With Widnes on the brink of a financial reckoning, Davies argued that the game now needed to attract the corporate sponsors and the television contracts to ensure that it would survive into the 21st century: 'We talk about rugby league being the greatest game in the world, but if a club like Widnes can't survive, the sport is going to lose a lot of respect.'

* * *

There may have been a new Prime Minister in 1990, but the impact of Thatcher's changes were still being felt. John Major had won the 1992 election by warning that Labour could not be trusted on the economy. To the shock of the pollsters and the bookmakers, Major pulled off a surprise victory. Winning more votes than any political party in history – over 14 million – he could, in the end, feel hard done by that his majority was just 21. But his premiership was soon hit by economic problems. In September 1992, Black Wednesday saw Britain suffer a huge loss as it exited the Exchange

Rate Mechanism, causing a huge run on the pound. The recession was very different from the one that had occurred in the 1980s. This time it hit homeowners in the south and London just as hard as it hit those in the north. The aspiration of homeownership – the idea on which Thatcherism had been largely built – came under threat from spiralling interest rates and record numbers of house repossessions. The term 'negative equity' became the buzzword of the age, as voters became trapped in properties they could no longer afford.

With little disposable cash around, the wider economy took a massive hammering. The drinks industry announced sales were down in pubs, clubs and hotel bars. People were said to be doing less DIY, while the Confederation of British Industry noted how people were continually shopping for bargain deals in supermarkets. And as unemployment edged towards the dreaded three million mark again, the police warned of a disturbing increase in street robbery due to social inequalities. Two of Labour's most popular politicians, John Smith and Gordon Brown, made a case for Britain being at the foot of every table: 'The Tories claim criticism is talking Britain down. But it's they who are letting Britain down,' they argued.

Nobody expected rugby league clubs and their supporters to be immune from the recession. Maurice Lindsay warned the clubs they had to offer a good product to keep people coming through the turnstiles at the end of each working week. Lindsay ordered referees to speed up the play and clamp down on those lying on in the tackle to slow down the play and the ball. 'We are part of the entertainment business,' he argued. 'It is essential in these times of recession that we give the spectators full value for money.' The *League Express* sounded an ominous warning for the clubs when it observed that credit was becoming far tighter after the boom of the 1980s 'when bank managers almost seemed to be competing with club directors in extravagance'.

There were wider changes happening in society that emphasised that the changes initiated in the 80s had not yet reached their conclusion. In the aftermath of the 1984/85 strike, there had been a slow and steady reduction in coal mines, with certain areas developing 'super-pits' to save costs and increase production. In less than 50 years, the number of miners working in Britain had declined from around 700,000 in 1947 to around 45,000. But the government still subsidised the industry by £100m a month. And with coal available at lower prices abroad, there was an economic incentive to cut the industry further.

Just a few days before Great Britain faced Australia in the 'Offiah' final, the Major government announced plans for another round of cuts that would see 30,000 miners lose their jobs and effectively finish the coal industry for good. The difference between 1984 and 1992, however, was that these miners had been the ones who had supported Thatcher's plans. 'It is dreadful, but it is right,' argued Michael Heseltine, who was tasked with delivering the plan. 'A whole range of industries that helped defend us are finding that demand for their product has gone.'

Less than a decade earlier, Featherstone Rovers had won the Challenge Cup with a team and a community that was centred around the pit. Now the presence of mining had all but disappeared from the game. When Doncaster's Kevin Parkhouse was playing in the 1980s, he often arrived at training still covered in coal dust from his shift at Askern Colliery. But when the closures came he had seen the community break up. At one point, he calculated that 80% of the Doncaster team had worked down the mines. But by the 90s, there was just one player. 'Rugby is an escape for many miners in places like Doncaster and Castleford,' he argued. Pit life had suited those players who wanted to play part-time. But the changes in the nature of work impacted their ability to play. 'The training involved, even for a third division club these days, would cost a bloke a lot in missed overtime, and some people might need to travel around to get contract work.'

There were other immediate problems the coal cuts had on the game. British Coal, who had sponsored Great Britain in the moment of their greatest exposure in 1990 and 1992, admitted they would pull the plug on sponsorship. They also announced that they would no longer sponsor Wakefield Trinity. There had been an expectation that mining would have to be cut to balance the books, but to the surprise of the Major government, there was an unprecedented backlash. And the 1992 World Cup Final became a battleground for protest. On Wembley Way and in the pubs around the ground, supporters debated what the cuts to the industry would do for the game and the country. 'Many came to Wembley dressed in the national side's red, white and blue shirts, and most had mutilated the British Coal logo with TUC stickers,' reported one journalist.

The guest of honour was Douglas Hurd, who was the Foreign Secretary and had been a central figure in the Thatcher government in the 80s. Boos rang out around the stadium whenever Hurd's name was mentioned. In the crowd that afternoon was the *Daily Mirror* political editor Alastair Campbell, who later used his weekly column to talk about the 'politically charged' atmosphere at Wembley, adding, 'There was also some inspirational chanting, some of it obscene but much of it witty, too.' He urged football fans to take up rugby league's lead and make 'Tory betrayal echo around every stadium in the country'.

Not everybody was happy with how commentators had latched on to the political angle. Andy Wilson of the *League Express* didn't appreciate stereotyping rugby league fans with the declining coal industry: 'Southern-based journalists arriving at probably their only League match of the year were determined to exploit the link between the British Coal-backed northern game and the British

Coal-sacked northern workers,' he wrote. Wilson observed how the demographic of rugby league supporters had changed dramatically over the course of the 1980s which meant that there were as many schoolteachers, social workers and private sector workers as there were miners in the crowd: 'Off the field, at least, this was rugby league 1990's style – but you wouldn't expect southern-based journalists to tell their readers that, would you?'

* * *

The cuts to the coal industry were another blow for the people in Featherstone who had continued to fight through the industrial changes. At the end of the miners' strike in 1984/85, the community had slowly and steadily broken up. From being a virtual one-industry area, people had begun finding new jobs as labourers and taxi drivers. The idea of one job, one trade union, one social life, one club had been smashed. And economically, the town still experienced high levels of unemployment. The writer Ian Clayton had been a striking miner during the dispute and was a popular historian of Featherstone Rovers. Always eager to link the sport to wider politics, he had a weekly column in the club programme, often focusing on the club's identity.

Clayton remained a defender of Featherstone's 'people before product philosophy', arguing that he was sick of the 'greed, greed, greed mentality' of clubs like Wigan. In the late 1980s, as privatisation became a buzzword, he joked that when Wigan had heard about the sale of water, sewage and electricity, the club had asked whether they could play in the front row together.

Clayton had noticed a lot of changes in the area. He often remembered how, at the beginning of the decade, he would wake up and look out of his living room to find 'three pit-head gears' in the distance. 'Almost overnight, they disappeared in the pit closure plan.' And he watched a succession of banks, building societies and well-established businesses being boarded up and broken into. Crime, which had never been a factor in the town's day-to-day life, was on the increase: 'For the first time to my knowledge, I've known Featherstone folk pinching off one another.' The local media wrote about a rise in alcohol and drug addiction amongst unemployed teenagers.

The aftershocks of deindustrialisation and the welfare dependency that often came with it were becoming increasingly prevalent beyond rugby league towns. In the early 1990s, there was a moral panic about the rise in antisocial behaviour across the country. At the beginning of 1993, the tabloids focused on what looked like the new 'lawless' Britain, where young people turned to violent crime. *The Sun*, who had heavily backed Thatcher for over a decade, were beginning to write about the breakdown in law and order. In a special feature on 'Violent Britain', the paper outlined how the 'beatings, battering and rapes' of pensioners were now 'commonplace' and the streets resembled 'the lawless days of the Wild West'. The Labour Shadow Home Secretary Tony Blair was one person who was linking it to a breakdown in moral values in society. He talked about how town centres were now 'no-go' areas at night, 'Old people afraid to live within their home, never mind go out on the streets.'

Ian Clayton believed that rugby league was the glue that held communities together in the face of long-term unemployment and economic hardship. For his book *When Push Comes To Shove*, Clayton pulled together a series of short fan stories to emphasise just how the sport was different from other forms of the entertainment industry: 'Rugby league goes beyond mere physical exercise – it means birth right, and opposition to an increasingly systemised world where everything is pigeonholed and organised like a day out to the local theme park.'

But it was clear that even in places like Featherstone, where Clayton wanted to preserve that sense of place and working-class identity, that it too was changing. To the surprise of everybody in the game, Featherstone had fought back against the odds to develop another solid side in the early 1990s. The club managed to sustain itself and maintained a solid core of support of around 4,000 spectators, which was, remarkably, at the same level as it had been in the early 1980s. And the club still provided a pathway for young people in the area. By the early 1990s, Featherstone remained a hotbed of talent for the game and provided opportunities for working-class children that other outlets had left behind.

Ikram Butt was one of the players that Featherstone had picked up from neighbours Leeds in the 1980s to help rebuild its side. After the emergence of Hanley, Drummond and Gill in the early part of the decade, there was much talk about how the game could also expand into Asian communities in Yorkshire. 'The Butt brothers, Kurshid and Ikram are the exceptions to one of the rules of British sport,' opened Dave Hadfield in *Rugby League Week*. 'Asians don't take up body contact sports, least of all rugby league, the story goes.' Asian players were not just a rarity in league but in most sports in the early 1990s. There were no professional footballers from Asian backgrounds nor had anybody made it into the England cricket side. Ikram Butt admitted that in the Pakistani community there were barriers in place to make it for Yorkshire cricket which put people off playing sport at all, 'They tend to think that if they can't make it at cricket, which is part of our culture, what chance do they have at anything else?'

When *The Independent* ran a feature on some of these obstacles, reasons ranged from their diet being unsuitable, to people not liking 'open changing rooms' and 'the physical element' to the prejudiced 'some of them refuse to take off their turbans'.Butt, however, proved to be a revelation at Featherstone, quickly developing under the guidance of the legendary coach Peter Fox. Like the children of the Windrush generation, he too faced battles with racism both on and off the pitch. 'The majority of this was chanting from opposing supporters, but there were racist comments from opposing players too,' he later admitted to the historian Richard de la Riviere.

Culturally the sport did not initially adapt to and accommodate his religion. When he was 19 years old playing for Great Britain Colts against France, he couldn't eat the players' meal of steak and chips because it was not halal. People were confused when he fasted and he found the dressing-room 'banter' to be intimidating: 'I came across a lot of colonial attitudes – "This is how we've always done it and we're not going to change."'

Butt represented a different type of winger than those who came before him. He used his size and his strength as much as his speed and was part of a changing dynamic where wingers were being used to make yards when coming off the defensive line. By 1995 he was in the England side and was the first Muslim player to represent the country in either code. When Dave Hadfield profiled him ahead of his debut, he found a player that was determined to make it in the game and prove people wrong: 'Butt admits to doubling his efforts to demonstrate that he has the toughness and resilience which many routinely and unthinkingly assume British Asians lack.' He put it down to a dearth of encouragement of people from a young age. 'You aren't expected to have a strong enough interest in rugby league to get very far in it.'

Alongside Ikram Butt in the new Featherstone side was a young player who had ambitions of making it big. Paul Newlove was part of a new generation of Featherstone Rovers players who didn't work down the mines but committed themselves to the game full-time. Born in Cobblers Lane, Newlove was a talented athlete scouted by Sheffield Wednesday in the late 1980s. Newlove was not a crazy rugby league fan like many people in the town. In fact, he had often found the matches boring. 'Occasionally I would go,' he later wrote, 'but I didn't like it as it was freezing cold.' Newlove didn't play the game just because he enjoyed it or because he saw it as an extension of his identity. He played it because it offered him the chance of a better life.

Newlove was part of the first generation of players who could see the riches rugby league could provide. From the streets of Featherstone, he set himself the target of becoming a Great Britain star by age 21. He did it while he was still 18. He then talked openly about making money that would set him up for a good life afterwards. Newlove had ambitions to become rich and famous, 'I'm looking to retire at 30. It would be nice to be a millionaire by then.' Hanley, Davies and Offiah were people that he wanted to emulate: 'I'd like to have a boot and clothing deal like them.'

Newlove arrived just when the idea of 'rugby league millionaires' was becoming a tangible prospect. In Thatcher's Britain, people had become very comfortable talking about amassing wealth. In 1989, the *Sunday Times* had responded to changing public interest by launching their annual *Rich List*. It wasn't long before they were focusing on how different sports stars ranked in comparison with each other. When *Business Age* compiled their list of the 100 wealthiest British sports stars a few year later, it was noticeable that rugby league players were in the mix. Players such as Martin Offiah and Ellery Hanley made the top 50, lodged alongside boxers such as Chris Eubank, the motor-racing driver Damon Hill and snooker player Ray Reardon. One rugby league agent expected there to be many more millionaire rugby league players as the 1990s dawned: 'Rugby league can be a fabulous career for any young player talented enough to represent his country … the millionaire dream is a reality for a growing number of players.'

Featherstone understood they couldn't keep hold of Newlove for too long. The nature of the inflationary transfer system actually favoured them. Others wanted to create a similar model. In 1992 Oldham floated the idea that supporters could buy into a 'syndication' scheme where supporters would be able to donate money to the club to help fund player transfers: 'If, for example, player A is purchased for £20,000 and is sold in three years' time for £40,000, the people who have invested in the player will divide the original sum plus the profit.' Newlove was eventually sold to Bradford for £245,000. 'In the working men's clubs of Featherstone, fans think they have been short-changed,' reported Ian Clayton. But Newlove understood that a rugby league career was short and you had to take opportunities when they arose. 'I'm a working-class lad who left school with no qualifications except to play rugby,' he revealed in one interview with *The Independent.* 'Now', he remarked, 'I'm earning more than them that went to university.'

* * *

Players like Paul Newlove were arriving into a sport that was increasingly committed to professionalism. At Wigan, Andrew Farrell joined the club as a 16-year-old with ambitions to be the next Ellery Hanley. Like Shaun Edwards had done in the early part of the decade, he had set his sights on becoming a professional from a young age. As an 11-year-old he had attended the 1984 Challenge Cup Final and been taken in by the magnitude and spectacle of the big occasion. To make it happen he began to adopt the professional mindset. He started goal-kicking and spent hours practising to make sure that he had an extra skill to offer the club when he finally did make it.

Farrell had been told that players like Ellery Hanley trained on Christmas Day to give them that added edge so he started to do it too. By the time he was in the Wigan side at the age of 16, he already had the physique and skillset of a player that had been playing for over a decade. Whereas Alex Murphy had placed Shaun Edwards on the wing to ease him into the side, Andy Farrell was thrown into the middle of the park. Before the 1993 Challenge Cup Final, Wigan paired Dean Bell, as captain, with the inexperienced Farrell to help him calm the youngster's nerves. In the end it was Bell who was sick with nerves while Farrell was relaxed sat on his bed with his Walkman on. He then turned to Bell and told him not to worry: 'We can beat these guys today, no problem.'

Players like Paul Newlove and Andy Farrell were part of a new generation that could see their life as a professional mapped out in front of them. Other young players such as Phil Clarke, Chris Joynt and Jason Robinson formed the nucleus of a new Great Britain side that could be marketed to the public as the elite athletes for the new century. Top rugby league players were becoming more aspirational and appearing in lifestyle magazines as much as the sports pages. Wigan's success had turned its players into national stars. Before the 1992 Challenge Cup Final, the *Daily Mirror* ran a lifestyle feature on Dean Bell where he talked about why he 'got a kick out of housework': 'I hoover and dust and basically do everything a housewife would.' Before the 1994 Ashes series they focused in on Phil Clarke. Posing topless for a series of modelling photographs in the *Sunday Mirror* magazine, Clarke was sold to the nation as someone who was 'in a league of his own' and easily 'the fittest and smartest forward in British rugby'.

Maurice Lindsay was eager to develop more business opportunities for the game in order to create an elite level of stars at the top level. One of his first ideas was to bring a specific business person on to the RL Council to bring an outsider's view on how they could attract big business. During the 1980s a new type of business celebrity had emerged within popular culture. In America it had been represented by Donald Trump and in the UK there were figures such as James Hanson and James Goldsmith. Goldsmith had been the subject of four biographies over the decade. Other business celebrities such as Alan Sugar of Amstrad and Richard

Branson of Virgin, together with Anita Roddick of the Body Shop, had been seen as the major titans of industry in a way that trade union leaders and chief executives of nationalised firms had in the 1970s.

Lindsay cited British Airways, Marks & Spencer and Norweb as companies with senior league enthusiasts who now needed a route into the sport to offer advice on business development. The Lindsay blueprint involved reducing the number of people making decisions about the game's future. 'A group of 30 or 40 people meeting so regularly cannot run the game properly,' he said. Central to the approach would be to move beyond the sponsors that had bankrolled the game in the 1980s. The problem with rugby league sponsorship in the early 1990s was that it was centred almost entirely around cigarettes and alcohol. In 1991 Imperial Tobacco celebrated a 25-year association with the game by pumping even more money into the sport. They celebrated a silver jubilee which they claimed was the 'longest-running sponsorship of any major British sport'. They were credited with putting £2.5m into the game that could not have elsewhere been sought.

Society, however, was rapidly moving against smoking and the way in which it marketed itself. There had been a push to encourage people to stop smoking through the National No Smoking Day, while campaigners began to unpick the impact it was having on consumers. In a British television documentary made in 1988, a former marketing consultant for tobacco lifted the lid on how the industry targeted people: 'The problem is how do you sell death? How do you sell a poison that kills 350,000 people per year, 1,000 people a day?' The answer, he said, was with advertising.

Politicians were increasingly concerned about the influence of cigarette sponsorship on the game. As early as June 1990, Harriet Harman had announced that any future Labour government would commit itself to a total ban on all cigarette advertising and sponsorship. And although Labour was still in opposition, the new rugby league APPG identified it as a major problem for the sport going forward. David Hinchliffe questioned the idea that it had little impact on the consumer, quoting a Rothmans spokesman who admitted that 'No one hands out big cheques just to get a warm fuzzy feeling.' Ian McCartney concluded that the industry was using rugby league to 'peddle their message of death' while a government-commissioned review found that 'the balance of evidence supports the conclusion that advertising does have a positive impact on consumption.' In response, David Oxley told *The Guardian* that the APPG was being 'spurious and hypocritical'.

Rugby league was in no financial position to turn down money from tobacco companies. And those clubs who sought new and innovative sponsors knew that they would get paid well over the odds to publicise controversial industries. When the television company Continental moved its headquarters from Manchester to Salford in the early 1990s, they sought the support of the rugby side to help publicise the move. The biggest rugby league sponsorship offer in history – a rumoured £1 million – was pitched to the cash- strapped club. The only problem for Salford was that Continental TV was a pornography channel. David Tarry, the Salford chief executive, admitted that the club had to consider the offer, 'But it's like the devil himself wanting to make a pact. We like to think of ourselves as devilish and hot but maybe not quite that hot.'

It was not the first time the club had turned down controversial sponsorship. When Durex approached the club in the late 1970s, they offered up £15,000 to put the condom brand on the front of the shirt: 'At the end of the day though we have 1,200 junior Red Devils who we allow in to each match for free. We're not so hard up that we have to subject children and their families who come along to a rugby match to pushing pornography.'

* * *

The eagerness with which Lindsay wanted to bring more money into the game was heightened by the need to fulfil the obligations of the Taylor Report. After the Bradford fire in 1985, clubs had found millions of pounds to make ground improvements but others were simply forced to close. One of them was Swinton's Station Road which had been seen as a 'destination' stadium for the sport in the 1950s and 60s. Located between the giant clubs in Yorkshire and Lancashire it was, as Keith Macklin outlined, a ground with an 'aura of importance'. But in the 80s it was no longer deemed suitable for major events. With its wooden stands in need of repair, it fell short of new standards. After a lengthy debate about how to modernise it, the club eventually sold it to a property developer for less than £1 million and moved in with Bury Football Club in the hope of turning their fortunes around.

Other clubs followed the same path. Hull KR were forced to leave Craven Park, their home since 1922, after it proved too costly to keep open. Ten years after they had faced the Australian Kangaroos as English champions, Leigh Centurions were also on the verge of bankruptcy. Needing to raise money to pay wage bills, the club entered a court battle that saw them have their ground taken away temporarily. Fundraising boxes were sent around the stands to 'Save Hilton Park'. The players' wages were scraped together by a local business firm. Even the ball boys refused to accept their usual £2 match fee. The general manager, John Stringer, admitted it was a body blow: 'The community has lost everything else and now sees its most precious asset disappearing.'

The emotional impact of the change was something which *The Independent's* Simon Kelner alluded to when he wrote about the sale of Station Road in his book *To Jerusalem and Back*. The ground had been a place for the community, something which had deeper meaning than the action that occurred around it. Kelner articulated how some people had been sitting in the same seat or standing in the same spot for most of their lives. Their ground was, as much as anything else, their home. Kelner found that swiftness of change hard to take. Swinton's sale of Station Road had 'merited only a couple of lines on the Press Association wire service'. But to the people of Swinton who still supported the club it was everything, 'It was a blow as grievous as any except for the closure of the club or the changing of its name.'

At the same time, however, there was a growing feeling amongst the supporters that the game had neglected the fans who turned up in all conditions to watch their side play. When Maurice Lindsay was criticised for wanting to change the way the game was run, he would often say that he was doing it because rugby league supporters would never demand these things themselves. 'They ask for nothing,' he told the Australian journalist Roy Masters. 'For most of the century, all they expected was 80 minutes of good football.' Lindsay put that down to the old spirit of the post-war world where people just got on with things. 'They haven't even asked for cover over their heads. They have stood in most grounds in the pouring rain.'

Standing on the cold terraces in the depths of winter was seen as a badge of honour for supporters. Grounds such as Bradford's Odsal and Oldham's Watersheddings were said to have their own 'micro-climate'. But beyond the weather, there were serious questions being posed in the wake of Hillsborough about the way that spectators were treated. Grounds built in the Victorian era had not had fan comfort in mind. For much of the 1980s, rugby league supporters had had little way of making their voices heard on such issues. Other than writing a letter to a newspaper or attending a fans' forum, there was little that they could do to enact change.

Advances in technology were mobilising supporters to act. After Hillsborough the 'alternative' football media, in fanzines, had lobbied for the governing body to take action. Desktop publishing revolutionised the way that fans could quickly put fanzines together. In rugby league circles, a fanzine scene developed across the country as supporters began to produce their own independent publications. There was Blackpool's *The Tangerine Dream*, Hull KR's *Flag Edge Touch*, Castleford's *Rebel Yell*, and *Wally Lewis is Coming* at Wakefield. One evening the Bradford supporter John Drake came across a radical new Bradford fanzine called the *Steam Pig* outside Odsal. The way in which it was written and produced, and challenged the problems of the club, greatly appealed to him. Drake soon found himself writing for it and selling it outside the ground.

It was, as Drake observed, 'a spit and sawdust' approach to publishing where ideas were tested and things were thrown together. After all the developments within the news media, with the rise of glossy magazines and pay television, supporters were increasingly looking back to the punk movement for inspiration. The fanzine culture helped 'democratise' supporter views and give ordinary people the opportunity to express themselves again. Before long, the network of fanzine editors and writers were meeting up in person to share their ideas about how to change the game. In 1990 they met up in a pub in Cridling Stubbs and decided that they would create a supporters' group to put their words into action. The Rugby League Supporters Association (RLSA) had four aims: to democratically represent the views of all supporters; to strive to have the fans' voice heard on all committees; to promote friendship between supporters; and promote and expand the game.

'Quite frankly, the state of most RL games is appalling,' remarked Bas Kerville in the opening issue of the RLSA magazine

The Greatest Game (*TGG*). In contrast to the 'serious' publication *Open Rugby*, TGG was inspired by new magazines such as *When Saturday Comes* and *Private Eye* which combined fierce editorials and news pieces with satire. *TGG* was radical in its approach to taking the fight to everyone involved in the game: 'The game gets absolutely no help from the national media, from the institutions of government, or, in the long term, from its sponsors.' Underpinning the aims of the RLSA was the idea that supporters should have more say in how the game was run. 'Those who dedicate their time, money and energy to the game should have the final say in how the game is run – anything less is a betrayal of everything that rugby league stands for.'

The RLSA didn't just offer up criticism of the way the game was being run. The group came up with a number of alternative solutions to bring more voices into the sport. A 'Citizens' Charter' was something that had been spoken about on the left of politics for a long time. The prevailing mantra of the Thatcher government had been about offering people 'value for money' from public services, which underpinned their desire to privatise and outsource. But the free market had failed to offer consumer rights and protections. John Major wanted to 'end the excessive focus on financial inputs rather than service output' by introducing a Citizens' Charter that would give people basic rights in relation to a range of consumer goods and services.

In 1990, the RLSA had convened a conference of supporters and put together their own Fans' Charter, which outlined the basic minimum standards that they hoped would be the standard to which clubs could one day aspire to:

1) Decent, dry, non-segregated facilities for all, standing or seated, wherever league is played
2) All clubs to provide family tickets and distribute free tickets to local schools

3) Creche facilities at all grounds, staffed by qualified childminders
4) Full access and quality viewing areas for the disabled at all grounds
5) Clean, hygienic, and plentiful toilets for men, women and children at all grounds
6) Fresh, nutritious and reasonably priced food to be sold at all grounds
7) No to hooliganism, racism and sexism on the terraces
8) A proportion of club proceeds to go back to the development of grounds for non-corporate supporters
9) No to ground-sharing or club moves/mergers without agreement with supporters
10) For democratically elected supporters, representation on the board of directors at each club.

In the wake of Hillsborough the RLSA committed themselves to undertaking a major survey of the rugby league grounds to understand exactly what state they were in. 'To our knowledge, this is the first time in any UK sport that a supporters' organisation has actually inspected the facilities offered to the fans.' A supporter questionnaire was created that addressed 15 various categories around the basic fan experience. Most importantly they decided that they would do it without asking clubs or giving them opportunities to explain themselves. For example, if one of the amenities couldn't be found by looking or asking a steward, the club was marked with a 0 score out of 10.

One of the issues that the group quickly identified was how basic access to toilets in grounds had barely changed over the course of the decade. In the 1980s, supporters had been accustomed to urinating against a brick wall at the side of the stands, which would often trickle down on to the terraces. Women had even less access to toilets and supporters would know, before they even entered the ground, that they would need to go beforehand in a pub or hold it in for 80 minutes. The RLSA demanded that the clubs invest to bring them up to modern standards. They argued that every toilet should have a washbasin, soap, towels and hot and cold running water. They suggested that women's toilets even have sanitary vending machines and that the disabled toilets were fitted with an alarm: 'The practice of calling a wall with a gutter along the bottom a "gents' toilet" should be outlawed.'

Even the RLSA were surprised by the standards at the elite level of the game. Wigan, Warrington, Hull, Castleford, Widnes, Rochdale and Oldham had no facilities for disabled people and many didn't even offer an extra viewing platform for wheelchairs. Six of the top 14 clubs ranked a score of two or less out of ten for the quality of the women's toilets. In the spirit of *Private Eye* magazine, *TGG* issued a special DIY cut-out-your-own portaloo sign that could be stuck on the walls of the toilets on the grounds. 'Voila! Your own authentic RL toilet facility!!!' The RLSA put together a poll of over 2,200 supporters and found that 85% of people were dissatisfied with spectator comfort at grounds.

Rapidly, the RSLA gained media attention, with John Drake and a Hull KR supporter called Tony Collins emerging as the prominent spokespeople for the group.

Collins had been a copywriter at Saatchi and Saatchi and had the ability to generate publicity and media interest at speed through press releases and publicity stunts. Drake admitted that they had 'no resources' but were incredibly 'serious' about what they wanted to achieve. 'We were doing it as volunteers and enthusiasts but we wanted to portray rugby league fans as articulate and intelligent and forward-looking.' They believed that rugby league fans were deserving of a voice.

The RLSA believed that the game was still hierarchical and had, for all the developments at the top level, not opened itself up to scrutiny. Collins and Drake quickly came on the radar of those running the game. In a heated radio exchange between Tony Collins and David Howes, which was reprinted in *TGG*, Howes referred to their work as a 'very, very non-professional survey' and questioned whether the RLSA had got their methodology right: 'The type of question that has been asked here is so basic it's unbelievable.' Howes was protective of the legacy he had cemented in the 80s and dismissed the RLSA as a group with a 'very impressive title' but who 'cannot purport to reflect the whole views of the rugby league spectator'.

On the face of it, both Maurice Lindsay and the RLSA appeared to be in sync over standards and how they needed to change to take the game forward. 'Having established a high-quality package on the field, we need to house it in a welcoming, clean surrounding – and we have not done that generally yet,' Lindsay argued. The modern consumer, Lindsay claimed, wanted a lot more. 'We can no longer expect fans to stand in the rain with a soggy pie or hot dog. We need to invite people to our stadiums for a whole day's entertainment and lay on a variety of food and drink.'

Bradford Northern was one of the clubs who wanted to modernise their ground but found that it was almost impossible to get the funding. Chris Caisley arrived at the club to rebuild the team in the city after a breakdown with the board. But Odsal was turning out to be a big problem: 'People don't want to go out on a wet and windy winter's day and get soaked through,' he revealed. 'Unless some private developer is going to come in and develop Odsal as a sports stadium, the prospects of achieving substantial development are remote.'

In a sport that was increasingly running out of money, Lindsay returned to the ideas of 'streamlining', which had dominated his thinking since the mid-1980s. In March 1993, just six months into Lindsay's tenure, he announced that the game would streamline into two divisions of 16 and that three clubs would be forced to exit the top two leagues to save costs for the game overall. On *Boots N All*, Eddie Hemmings introduced the news as 'the most controversial decision in the rugby league's history', as Lindsay admitted that the game did not have the players or the resources to support more than 32 clubs.

It put Maurice Lindsay on a collision course with the chairman of Chorley Borough, Lindsay Hoyle, who believed that he was now operating beyond his brief in the interests of the elite clubs. A campaign was mobilised to prevent the changes from occurring but Lindsay was in no mood for negotiation and attempted to hammer through the reforms. He claimed that there had been 'many crocodile tears shed, on a subject about which few people know the true facts'. At the RLSA, Collins and Drake began to hear from supporters who believed that Lindsay was operating both undemocratically and without the interests of the smaller clubs. In response to the streamlining proposals, a special edition of *TGG* was put together to address readers' concerns. 'It makes you wonder why bother with rugby league at all. Why waste time and energy promoting a sport which is run by a bunch of complete morons, dead from the neck up?' ran an editorial.

Lindsay claimed it was a break with the traditional small-minded mentality: 'For the first time in years, clubs have allowed their heads to rule their hearts.' The RLSA dubbed the announcement Black Wednesday and referred to Maurice Lindsay as the Norman Lamont of British rugby league. Collins and Drake marked the decision by placing a wreath outside the RFL and inviting a photographer from the *Yorkshire Evening Post* to capture the scale of the anger at the streamlining of the weaker clubs. The message on the flowers simply said 'The Death of the Rugby League Dream'.

Chapter 13

The People

OVER THE summer of 1993, Maurice Lindsay penned a lengthy article for the *Rugby Leaguer* which offered clubs advice on how they could adapt and survive in the new era. With the battle over the two divisions won, he set his sights on his next fight, to improve the day-to-day running of the remaining clubs. Lindsay urged them to analyse everything about their set-up, to 'start at the bottom and assess everything about their home ground'. 'Was it a welcoming place? Were there adequate facilities for disabled fans? Were there ladies' toilets for the new type of supporter?' With customer service demands changing, he wanted clubs to be proactive in communicating with stakeholders: 'There is nothing worse than for the fan to be unable to speak with someone about a query. The fax machine should be switched on for 24 hours per day, 365 days per year.' He asked press officers to supply local journalists with at least one important news item per day. Above all, he concluded, he wanted them to have pride in their surroundings: 'Make it a smart, clean, working environment which makes supporters want to return again and again.'

The last club that Lindsay expected to take up the challenge and meet the change was Keighley. An old mill town that had produced paper, cotton and wool during the Industrial

Revolution, Keighley were one of the oldest clubs in the RFL. But unlike most clubs who had enjoyed brief moments of success, Keighley had been 'minnows' for most of their existence. They had never won the Challenge Cup nor had they won the First Division title. In the 1970s, when a whole range of clubs enjoyed success, they remained rooted to the foot of the rugby league pyramid.

Lindsay's Wigan team had played at Keighley once, when they were both in the Second Division. And while Wigan had enjoyed a decade of success, Keighley had suffered 15 consecutive years in the Second Division by 1991. In the harsh economic climate of the 1980s Keighley had almost gone to the wall numerous times. When one game against expansionist club Mansfield Marksman attracted just 322 spectators, the local paper observed how 'two sides desperate for paying customers gave little value for money'. Bankruptcy and ground sales seemed inevitable. 'End of RL club?' ran the front page of the *Keighley News* in 1987 as they looked to pay off £150,000 worth of debt.

Supporters and sponsors were hard to find. And even the rare sponsors who did put their hand in their pocket were mistreated. In 1987 the club struck up a very small sponsorship deal with a local jewellery firm who agreed to subsidise half the cost of the team's sweatshirts in exchange for a photo session with the players in their store. But after the firm paid for the sweatshirts, the club failed to pay the other half of the fee. They also forgot to send any players to the photo session. 'We've laid out a lot of money for those sweaters,' the owner told the *Keighley News*. 'No one has even come back to me to apologise.'

When Mick O'Neill and Mike Smith were appointed to the board in 1990 they were 'horrified by the lack of facilities and ambition to improve'. Just as Maurice Lindsay had found in 1980 when he arrived at Wigan, there were multiple bank accounts open with hardly any money in any of them. And just as Lindsay had battled against an old board of directors, the pair quickly found that there was a divide between an old and a new generation. When the idea was floated that Keighley needed a new kitchen to cater for hospitality and corporate events, one director resigned in protest.

But Smith and O'Neill were up for a fight. They had been involved in the club in the 1980s as sponsors and directors before spending the decade in the private sector. Between them they brought new business ideas in an attempt to revive the club. Smith believed that nothing short of a complete rebrand would do: 'It needed a complete culture change,' he told *Open Rugby,* with the old club's image stripped away.

In May 1991, the club ran a competition to develop a new nickname. The idea of renaming clubs had been talked about within the game as the popularity of the NFL grew. The Sheffield Eagles, through Kath Hetherington, had employed the same tactic when they had run a competition to find their name. But traditional clubs had found it more difficult to establish a new identity.

Huddersfield rebranded themselves as the Barracudas, and renamed their ground 'Arena 84', to much criticism and derision.

In the end, it was a local schoolboy who came up with the name Cougars and the club ran with it. Keighley Cougars was the symbolic rebrand the side needed to get the town talking about the club again: 'The Cougars want to bring a new dimension to the sport by putting the fun back in.' Smith continually looked around other sports and other industries to see what they did to market themselves. In the 1980s, Maurice Lindsay had looked to Australian rugby league but most of their novel ideas around events and razzmatazz were well known. Smith wanted an edge, to find a new way of doing things and he eventually found it in the place where nobody else in the game was looking.

Wrestling had been popular in the UK in the 1970s via the *World of Sport* programme on ITV. Big Daddy had become a household name to the extent that he filled the Wembley Arena in 1981 for a match against his rival Giant Haystacks. Its popularity with housewives had concerned those running rugby league who struggled to tempt people away from an afternoon's television. But having once reached audiences of 18 million it slowly slipped away and when it suffered a series of negative headlines around how it operated behind the scenes, the show was axed by ITV.

When wrestling returned to British screens it was via a satellite dish. In 1982, Vince McMahon purchased the WWF from his father and rebranded it to tap into the new pay-per-view industry in the US. In 1985, Wrestlemania had turned it into a major entertainment product as characters such as Hulk Hogan, Randy Savage and the Ultimate Warrior became as big as Hollywood movie stars. In the 1990s, it continued to rebrand and expand, creating new storylines, new logos and adapting to the demand for high-suspense drama. It found its way on to Sky and by 1992 it had become hugely popular again in the UK.

The development of the UK market prompted organisers to take the 1992 Summerslam event to Wembley where 80,000 people watched the first major pay-per-view to take place outside of North America. The decision proved to be a masterstroke when it became one of the largest-grossing events in their history. Merchandise sales were soon topping $200 million each year and Bret 'The Hitman' Hart was becoming a household name across the globe. When asked what drew people towards him, a spokesperson said: 'There's some sex appeal there for the women. The kids view him as the coolest thing on two feet. The adult males respect his athletic ability. You roll all that into one and you've got a tremendous amount of charisma.'

Mike Smith admired what the WWF had done with their product in the 90s. 'They withdrew from the market to introduce new characters and identities,' he argued in *Open Rugby*. 'We must introduce a degree of the WWF ideas [to rugby league].' The word 'mania' had become synonymous with fandom in the 80s, used to describe everything from the popularity of the popstars Bros, to the rise of American blockbuster movies each summer. When Hulk Hogan launched a global world tour called 'Hulkamania', Smith and O'Neill set about creating their own version: 'Cougarmania'.

Smith and O'Neill talked about 'Cougarising' the town and creating the 'razzmatazz' that had obsessed rugby league administrators since the arrival of Kent Invicta at the start of the decade. They adopted WWF ideas such as player nicknames, entrance songs and music for each player when they scored a try. They had their own compere on the pitch to generate an atmosphere. More broadly, the Cougars embedded themselves in the community by doing outreach work and visiting schools and hospitals each week and they soon benefited from a boom in media coverage and support. They developed their own education programme at the ground where schoolchildren would do a course in the team where they would play rugby, design jerseys in an art class and learn about the history of the game.

With leisure habits changing, and consumers demanding more choice, Keighley were one of the first clubs to accept that what happened on the pitch over the course of 80 minutes was not going to be enough to tempt people in. One early decision that proved beneficial was when the club invited over 1,000 women to attend a fashion show which would run before the game. Smith identified it as the best marketing the club had done. 'Once you've got the women, you've got the whole family.'

The impact had not gone unnoticed by politicians and councillors in the community. 'The cougars are doing a splendid job,' said the town's crime prevention officer. 'Juvenile delinquency fell by 11% each year and the Cougars are certainly partly responsible.' Attendance radically rose from less than 1,000 to over 4,000 in the space of a few years. And with that came the national newspapers, who were interested in what they had achieved. When the sports writer Owen Slot made his way to the area for a feature in *The Independent*, he observed how 'once a fortnight the town will empty, and an extraordinarily eclectic multitude of men, women and children will follow the white paws'. They presented a modern and dynamic sports community that was open to all and tapped into the young audience: 'They come for their dose of positive vibes,' admitted Smith.

Not everybody was on board with what Keighley were trying to do. In a sport that was still wedded to the idea that the rugby spoke for itself, their WWF-inspired tactics upset the traditionalists. After one match against Swinton, their coach, Tony Barrow, told *The Independent* that Cougarmania was 'very irritating' and that the loud music played at key points in the game affected his players. 'It's not in the spirit of the game and most Second Division clubs think the same.' Others refused to believe that it would bring the crowds in elsewhere. When the Batley chairman asked O'Neill for some advice on how he could turn Batley around, he urged them to think big and rebrand as the Batley Batmen and adopt the *Batman* theme tune as their anthem. 'They thought I was mad,' admitted O'Neill.

Smith believed in Maurice Lindsay's vision for rugby league in the 1990s and spoke the language of business and enterprise that had long been encouraged. Smith, like Lindsay, believed that television was the only possible route to future prosperity for the game. Smith floated the idea of mergers to streamline the game further. Most crucially, he embraced the idea of clubs competing with each other to instigate change. 'We are running a business here so we are in competition and want to beat everybody else.' 'Tradition is a wonderful thing in circumstances,' he argued in *Open Rugby*. 'But however nice that is, tradition does not attract new spectators. The kids who have come down to see our games at Keighley do not care what has happened in the past. We may be interested in the past, but it has not attracted them.'

The club appointed Phil Larder as coach and soon found themselves heading towards promotion to the First Division in 1994/95. But whereas clubs had yo-yoed through the leagues for much of the 1980s and 90s, Keighley wanted to make a statement. As they headed towards promotion, the club announced the signing of Great Britain star Daryl Powell. The club managed to pull off a record £200,000 deal by drawing on supporter donations to a life membership scheme as well as the backing of local sponsors such as Magnet, Whirlpool and Yorkshire Cable. Larder was convinced that Powell would help turn their plan to become 'one of the top four clubs in rugby league' into reality.

* * *

Cougarmania was evidence of what could be achieved in a short space of time with ambitious people with new ideas. But as the game rapidly approached its symbolic centenary season in 1995 there was a feeling that it still hadn't adapted to the demands of the modern sports industry. The finances in the game were still a concern. With Lindsay now at the RFL, Wigan appeared to be heading for the same financial problems that had impacted other clubs in the course of the decade. Wigan's financial model now rested upon them getting to Wembley and winning the Challenge Cup each year, something that they continued to do. Each year they were tested at various stages – away at Halifax, St Helens or Hull – where they would often come within the bounce of a ball of being eliminated. But they always found a way to keep winning. A sign of how dominant the club had been since they turned professional was seen in the trophy cabinet of Shaun Edwards. Between 1985 and 1995, Edwards won eight Championships, nine Challenge Cups, three World Club Challenges, five Lancashire Cups and six Regal Trophies. Edwards admitted that he had 'had all the luck that my father didn't'.

By 1993 the club had a wage bill of over £2 million and were beginning to announce significant losses each year as they too struggled to maintain the upkeep of their ground. As the historian Tony Collins outlines in *Rugby League in Twentieth Century Britain*, the club had, by the 1990s, struggled to build an average attendance beyond the 14,000 figure, 'despite its increasing success and glorious playing style'. But the new chairman, Jack Robinson, admitted that Lindsay's model had left the club in a dangerous position. 'Maurice is a good talker,' he told Paul Wilson in *The Best Years of Our Lives*. 'He used to say there was no player or coach he couldn't persuade to come to Wigan. That made me laugh a bit. It's easy to negotiate deals if you have an unlimited budget.'

The response from the RFL to the economic problems was to bring in the 'experts' again. In the 1970s, the Caine Report had been too controversial to be implemented by the clubs and had become embroiled in a debate about the future of Eddie Waring. This time Stones Bitter were asked to stump up £25,000 worth of sponsorship money to fund a consultancy project that would radically reimagine the sport. Lindsay argued that the findings would produce the ultimate 'State of the Game' document, giving the sport the answers to the questions that it had been too afraid to ask itself. In the 1940s, the Labour Party had created a document called *Facing the Future* which mapped out how the world would need to be rebuilt after the Second World War. *Framing the Future* was rugby league's attempt to come to terms with the settlement of the Thatcher Years. 'The game of rugby league is determined to go forward in an aggressive and business-like manner.'

Framing the Future was eagerly anticipated within the game and the findings were expected to make difficult reading for the clubs. Gary Hulme of Group Strategic Marketing (GSM) was tasked with pulling the findings together and presenting the new blueprint to the clubs: 'I am aware of traditions in the game and why many fans will want to resist change,' he argued. 'But the game is in a financial mess.'

Hulme applied a business mind to his methodology and tried to remove some of the emotion from his conclusions. 'There are too many clubs for the market they serve, they cannot all run as professional outfits because there is not enough money to sustain them,' he announced. He had found the league supporters he had surveyed to be loyal people who loved the sport: 'It is easy to understand their point of view when they have been born into a family which has supported a team for many years.' But he admitted that there would have to be a very 'painful' transition towards a structure that could put the game back on level pegging with Australia.

At the heart of *Framing the Future* was the acknowledgement that Britain's economic landscape had radically altered in the 1980s. At the beginning of the decade, rugby league clubs knew what market it was operating in and how it could reach the people living in their towns. But the opening up of businesses to new markets had made companies more competitive and globalised. The arrival of the single market meant that goods and services could trade more freely between Britain and Europe. The opening of the Channel Tunnel created the prospect of much closer relations with France. When Mrs Thatcher had advocated for the single market in 1988 she had encouraged businesses to embrace the 'market without barriers': 'giving you direct and unhindered access to the purchasing power of over 300 million of the world's wealthiest and most prosperous people.'

The early development of the internet and telecommunications meant that people could access those markets from anywhere in the UK. Rugby league, for all its attempts at expansion, served the same people that it had always served. Lindsay wanted to use *Framing the Future* to address the fact that 60% of all people who attended league games came from just four postal districts along the M62. Rodney Walker, the new chairman of the RFL, set out the problems in stark terms. 'It doesn't take a genius to understand why change is necessary and urgent,' he argued. 'The game is unsustainable; it's only a matter of time before you go bust.'

For much of the 80s there had been talk about creating a breakaway Super League to give the top clubs more power and control. In 1992, the big five football clubs (Arsenal, Tottenham, Manchester United, Liverpool and Everton) showed how it could be done when they had agitated to create a new Premier League. Many had assumed that the sport was beyond saving when Rupert Murdoch's BSkyB paid millions for exclusive rights to it. But within just a few years the image of the game had been radically transformed.

'A whole different ball game' was how Sky Sports had packaged it as producers created a Tina Turner-inspired broadcast to sell the new competition to the public. To the soundtrack of the Simple Minds song 'Alive and Kicking' footballers were seen at home receiving breakfast in bed, playing with their children in the back garden and shaving in the bathroom before exercising in the gym and sharing a shower together. 'There's even a copy of the Canterbury-Bankstown team talk scene,' wrote Andy Wilson in *Open Rugby* magazine, with Peter Reid taking on the role of Chris Anderson instead. When people within the rugby league media asked whether Sky Sports had plans to do the same for their coverage of the Big League, an 'insider' joked that the £500,000 it cost would blow the league budget for the next century. 'So it's down to the RFL themselves to produce a commercial reflecting their view of rugby league's vibrant, new image!' concluded Wilson.

The advent of the Premier League had people within rugby league dreaming of their own 'year zero' symbolic rebrand. Football had quickly tapped into the family market that rugby league had been cultivating for much of the decade. Within the space of a few years the game had attracted a very different audience. A survey undertaken in 1994 suggested that the 'family audience is being won back by the national game'.

Maurice Lindsay began talking about how rugby league needed its own Premier League to match it. Journalists highlighted the need to reflect consumer demands by offering choice and comfort at grounds. Martyn Sadler, a columnist at the *League Express*, found himself thinking about how the sport could create its own 'year zero' moment. Sadler used his columns to float new ideas and argue for radical transformation. He believed that the game needed to move from winter to summer. Outlining his 'blueprint' for the new millennium, Sadler argued that the season needed to begin in April and finish in September with a summer game that could 'tap into the tourist market'. 'League clubs are in the middle of areas with great tourist potential.'

The push towards summer to respond to consumer demands began to gather momentum. Mike 'Stevo' Stephenson argued that the sport was still living in the past.

'We've dabbled at trying to correct our Northern image far too long, we can't live in cuckoo land and believe in fairy stories anymore,' he wrote in his *Rugby Leaguer* column. The changes of the 1980s had altered what people expected. He told readers that he used to go to his local corner shop to buy food, 'now I drive to hypermarkets where comfort is the key'.

At Sheffield Eagles, Kath Hetherington also drew on her own experience as a mother to argue for a change to reflect the realities of modern-day life. Speaking in the *Rugby Leaguers* she recalled how she had once stopped off at IKEA on the way to a match at Warrington.

There she had been shocked to see just how many people were spending their Sunday afternoon shopping. 'There were thousands and thousands of people there.' She compared the crowds in IKEA with the poor crowd at Wilderspool and wondered whether the game was doing enough to attract them in. 'We have a big problem that Sunday shopping is a big draw. It costs nothing to get in there.' By contrast, she had a lot of trouble taking her own daughter to a match, 'She said no, it was cold and the ground we were going to was a dump.'

* * *

Adapting to the demands of the new 'consumer' society became a huge talking point for businesses and political parties in the 1990s. After 15 years in opposition, the Labour Party had reached the conclusion that they needed to appeal to voters as consumers. Having used focus groups and marketing agents to rebrand in the 1980s, the party had, in the early 90s, divided between the 'traditionalists' and people who framed themselves as 'modernisers'. But when Tony Blair replaced John Smith as leader in 1994 he began the final stage of the party's rebrand towards New Labour.

Blair was uniquely placed to reach into those so-called 'no-go' areas. As far back as 1982, when he was the unknown candidate fighting the Beaconsfield by-election, he had worked on ways to frame Labour's message to connect with more affluent, middle-class voters. 'You have millions of people out of work which is costing the country a fortune,' he argued. 'And then you have plant and machines lying idle. It does not add up.'

In the 1980s, as the Conservatives firmly established themselves as the party of the new homeowners and the small investors, Blair still found ways of framing their values as Labour's values. When, in 1988, the investment firm Barlow Clowes was involved in a major 'bond washing' scheme – that impacted ordinary people's savings – Blair demanded the government step in to support them. 'These are not get-rich-quick speculators,' he argued. 'They are Britain's new class of investors, the married couple with an accumulated nest egg, the young couple left a small inheritance, the mineworker or the steelworker left redundant.'

It was an unorthodox approach that soon attracted the attention of Conservative-supporting newspapers. As early as 1990, Blair was already being spoken of in the *Sunday Telegraph* as a potential future leader. 'Blair is a throwback to an earlier type of politician,' Martyn Harris told his Conservative-voting readers. 'To the clear-eyed public schoolboy who came down from Oxbridge brimful of social conscience but unhampered by ideological baggage or practical experience.'

By 1994, Blair was said to be the person who could reach parts of the electorate that other Labour politicians couldn't. Central to the shift was a symbolic decision to remove the party's Clause IV commitment to nationalisation of the 'commanding heights' of the economy which had traditionally meant industries such as coal, steel, telecommunications and railways. The development of New Labour, the new constitution, the new approach to policy and the new ways of campaigning and communicating were signs that the party had adapted to the demands of modern society. It was, Blair argued, a time to bring an end to the class politics of the 20th century: 'I ask in the name of this country's future – forget the past, no more bosses versus workers – we are on the same side, the same team, and Britain united will win!'

Maurice Lindsay watched on and wondered whether rugby league would have its own 'Clause IV' moment. He argued that the sport would get a fairer hearing because of the way that class was becoming more fluid. 'I see people's class attitudes changing,' Lindsay told *The Observer*. He looked at how horse racing, his other passion, had been attracted to new business and new money: 'You couldn't go into certain enclosures unless you were of a certain class. All that has changed.'

In April 1995 the game convened in Wigan to debate a potential switch to summer. For clubs like Oldham who seemed to be forever battling the ice-cold conditions to bring in new fans, the switch seemed the obvious place to begin. 'Summer rugby would, without question, bring vastly increased crowds and with it greater revenue,' argued their chairman Jim Quinn. In contrast, clubs such as Leeds threatened to lose revenue to the Yorkshire cricket club next door. Their chairman Alf Davies promised to fight the switch every step of the way, claiming that 'alternatives for families in the summer far outweighed those on offer in the winter'. The battle over a move to summer looked to be Lindsay's 'high noon'. But just as they came to debate the issues, Maurice Lindsay took a call from Rupert Murdoch. And in an instant, everything changed.

* * *

Maurice Lindsay had actually been expecting a call from Rupert Murdoch for almost a year. For much of 1994 the English game had been keeping its cards close to its chest as the 'Super League War' had broken out down under. After Murdoch had battled BSB in the UK over the birth of satellite TV, he had turned his attentions to winning the fight in Australia. Murdoch's News Ltd and Packer's Optus both identified rugby league as the key to winning the television rights battle and when the ARL signed a record agreement with Optus, Murdoch knew his plans were in trouble.

Rugby league was soon caught in the crossfire of a media fight that spiralled out of its control. Tapping into long-standing grievances between the New South Wales and the Queensland clubs, Murdoch and Broncos executive John Ribot decided to launch a separate, rival competition called the Super League to manufacture a Premier League-style breakaway. The game in Australia rapidly descended into a 'civil war' as different clubs signed up to different leagues. New expansion clubs such as Brisbane and the NZ Warriors quickly aligned themselves with Murdoch's league but many of the traditional Sydney-based clubs did not.

Murdoch's Super League needed to develop a USP to attract players and break the stranglehold of the Sydney clubs. Super League officials sold the concept of a new global product that could sell rugby league to markets in Europe, Asia and the United States. Over the course of the 1980s the British and the Australian clubs had formed closer links due to the success of the World Club Challenge. While Wigan and Manly had lit the fuse in 1987, the match in 1994 between Wigan and Brisbane in Australia offered a glimpse into what a global league might look like. Chris Irvine was part of the press pack that flew down under and found that the Broncos had almost '300 company sponsors, each with executive facilities to make most Premiership football clubs envious'. One thousand press passes were rumoured to have been handed out as Wigan defeated the Broncos in front of 54,220 people. Amongst the attendees was the Denver Broncos coach Wade Phillips, 'Those guys have to be physically and mentally tough – I don't understand how they don't get injured without the padding we have,' he told *Open Rugby*.

Maurice Lindsay's gambler's instinct told him that the English game had a strong card to play if they used it at the right time. Murdoch needed leverage in his battle to win the rights to Australian rugby league and having the English clubs on board would give it credibility. But if they overplayed their hand they could end up with nothing. Worse than that, there was nothing to stop the Australian Super League 'cherry picking' the best English players to play in the new competition. Rodney Walker warned that the game would need to pick a side: 'It is inevitable he [Murdoch] will want to talk to us. If we simply sit back and allow him to cherry pick, there would be the elite and the rest.'

The Times's Chris Irvine was in the press box at Wigan covering a match against Doncaster when Dave Woods from the BBC came over with talk of a 'revolution'. Irvine and his colleagues told him to 'put a sock in it, stuff his daft revolution and carry on preparing for the game'. But within no time there were rumours flying through the press box that Lindsay had been offered a huge sum of money to create a British version of the Super League. Rumours of £10m, £20m, even £30m were speculated as sports editors demanded to know more information about the offer.

Lindsay briefed the media that an offer was now on the table. But if he had learned one thing from his 15 years in the game, it was that rugby league people never came to a decision at speed. When *Framing the Future* had landed in 1994, Lindsay had been powerless to do anything to implement its findings. When it came to the creation of a new Super League, Lindsay was not going to ask Murdoch to give him any time to debate it. He had decided that there was a short window of opportunity to maximise as much money out of Murdoch as possible.

Lindsay returned to the meeting and told the clubs that there was money on the table but that it would be gone within a few days. This was not £5m or £10m or even £20m. It was £77m to wipe the debts of the clubs clean and start again. Before the clubs had even had a chance to think about it, Rupert Murdoch, from New York, declared that an English Super League was evidence that the war in Australia had been won. 'We will have all the British clubs join too, so it will be an international super league,' he declared. The news soon hit Australia where shares in Kerry Packer's publishing group dropped by 4%. One Murdoch newspaper dubbed it, 'The day football changed forever.'

* * *

Less than 24 hours later, Maurice Lindsay, Rodney Walker and Vic Wakeling, the head of Sky Sports, called a press conference at Wigan to unveil plans for a new summer competition called the Super League. The new league would be the game's shot at going global, to match the NFL, the Premier League, cricket and rugby union for sponsorship, revenue and attention: 'The decision paves the way for the future of the sport, not only in Britain but across the globe.' Never one to underplay his hand, Lindsay declared that he had pulled off the deal of a lifetime: 'There is no doubt that this is the most important day in rugby league since 1895.'

What was soon apparent, though, was that this was much bigger than a symbolic rebrand of the game. The sport would indeed switch to summer. But it would also do the thing that Lindsay had been agitating for since he first entered the Wigan boardroom in April 1980. The top tier would be 'streamlined' and consist of 14 clubs, including two from France and one from London. The remaining 11 teams would include five brand-new clubs that merged with each other.

Mergers seemed like the natural conclusion to reflect the changes that had occurred in business during the 1980s, as firms across industries came together to gain a better share of the market they operated in. In the 1970s the Monopolies and Mergers Commission used a range of public interest criteria to judge whether firms could move. But this changed in 1984 when Norman Tebbit announced that acquisitions would be based on the effects on competition. The easy availability of funds made acquisitions more affordable and 'merger mania' became a buzzword in the business world. Merging existing teams and pooling resources would 'encourage people of an entrepreneurial spirit to buy into clubs', argued Lindsay. He likened it to Nigel Lawson's financial 'big bang' of the late 1980s: 'Banks and building societies are amalgamating because they've got branches next to each other after the same customer.'

The new clubs of Calder (Castleford, Featherstone and Wakefield) would join Cheshire (Widnes and Warrington), Cumbria (Barrow, Carlisle, Whitehaven and Workington) with Humberside (Hull and Hull KR), Manchester (Oldham and Salford) and South Yorkshire (Sheffield and Doncaster). The mergers would act as a springboard to bring in extra revenue and extra growth. Then, over time, rugby league would, as the Premier League had done, use its new financial power to expand across Europe. As Chris Irvine concluded in *The Times* the next day, this was the beginning of a very different type of rugby league: 'The small-town game is to be replaced by six hyper-clubs in a 14-team Anglo-French league.' Lindsay agreed: 'We are moving toward a city/large town league,' he declared, with Newcastle, Bristol, the Midlands and London viewed as essential areas for growth.

The expansion would, in time, finally answer the perennial question of 'How can the game become part of life for people not near the M62?' And to the 'giant' clubs such as Wigan, Leeds, St Helens and Bradford who entered the new competition without needing to merge, the opportunities were now endless.

Jack Robinson said that was 'like the Berlin Wall coming down' with the chance to create a truly European brand. This, as Paul Fitzpatrick outlined in *The Guardian* the next day, was just the beginning: 'Now the sport which professionally is played along the M62 corridor is suddenly being linked to Paris, Rome, Cardiff and Glasgow, not to mention North America and South Africa.'

With £77m coming into the game the clubs now had the revenue to do all the things they had talked about in the 1980s. Peter Higham at Warrington had long advocated for reform at the top of the sport. With the Murdoch cash now flooding in, he predicted that rugby league could become bigger than Premier League football in Britain. He predicted that one day even clubs like Wigan and St Helens would have to merge to compete. 'If it takes off like it should, the Super League could become something huge – it will be bigger than football.' Over on Humberside the chairmen of the two Hull clubs recognised that it was a huge opportunity to revive the sport in the region. 'It will bring untold wealth and sporting interest to the city of Hull and Humberside, we must go for it,' said KR chairman Phil Lowe.

For an expansionist club like Sheffield Eagles, the Super League represented an opportunity to invest the money in marketing and promotion. Kath Hetherington emerged as one of the biggest advocates of the move to summer. She believed it would lead to more eyes on the game and greater revenue. 'The cloth-cap-and-whippet image is long gone,' she told Cynthia Bateman in *The Guardian*. 'You are talking about a high-speed contact sport played by finely tuned athletes totally committed to the game.' Central to Hetherington's idea for Super League was the creation of household names that could carry the sport on to the next level: 'Children go for things that are in the media and on television. They want to emulate their heroes.'

Even Featherstone, the club that had prided itself on its deep roots in the community and its traditions, signed up to the mergers plan. The Featherstone chairman Steve Wagner believed that it would be 'suicide' not to merge and make a go of it. In a sideswipe at any potential resistance, he said the Murdoch millions made for 'very exciting times for the game in general but disappointing from a parochial point of view'. Paul Fitzpatrick concluded in *The Guardian* that it was time to break free of the past: 'The game simply could not have gone on much longer as it was doing, a thrilling, ceaselessly rewarding product on the field but in many instances played in dumps and against a background of stark poverty.'

Within just a few hours of the announcement there was speculation about how the Super League would compete with the Premier League for 'eyeballs' and revenue.

With Oldham and Salford due to merge into a new Manchester club, the *Manchester Evening News* compiled a feature on how the venture could halt the rise of Manchester United. John Wilkinson, the Salford chairman, openly talked about the team being 'big enough to take to Old Trafford' and floated the idea of a partnership with United that would radically change the fortunes of the sport in the area: 'We have to put the sport before any parochialism.' 'This gives us the opportunity to join up with a corporation that has a massive international television network,' said Maurice Lindsay. 'And we can take our game into countries where it has never been seen before.'

With an extra £77m on the table it wasn't long before agents were putting players in the shop window. Within the first few days of the announcement, a string of rugby union players speculated that they would jump across and join the new 'megabucks' league. Victor Ubogu, the England prop forward, who was seen as one of the best players in the world, told the press that if £300,000 was put forward he would trade a World Cup appearance for life in league. The *Daily Mail* mocked up a £50m 'super Star Wars' cartoon with price tags on the top union talent, which priced Jason Little at £500,000 and Jonah Lomu at £400,000. At the Sheffield Eagles, Kath Hetherington tried to used £2m of the Murdoch cash to bring Lomu over to league. 'We would have to break our wage structure if we did get him', she admitted. 'We have made an approach and we are still hopeful.'

There was little doubt that the Super League would dramatically change the amount of media coverage that the game received. Tony Lewis, writing in the *Daily Telegraph*, concluded that league had handed over its entire game to Murdoch: 'Television is now the employer of the players, the promoter of the tournament, the marketer and effectively the governing body of the sport.' Lewis was critical of how Murdoch would be able to create his own media ecosystem around his own league: 'You can guarantee the coverage which brings in sponsorship. The newspapers and magazines, in your ownership of course, will publish reports and features that lead to an advertising income.' In the first few days following the announcement rugby league dominated the headlines. The television critic Mark Lawson dedicated his weekly *Independent* column to the news and predicted that the sport would have to get used to this kind of scrutiny. 'One of the potential hidden benefits of this weekend's deal for Mr Murdoch is that rugby league players may now become famous enough to have their private lives turned over on the front pages of the tabloids.'

Maurice Lindsay revelled in being the kingmaker that had brought the deal to the table. He admitted that there would be some 'blood spilt' over the implementation.

But he was adamant that he would see it through. Just as Mrs Thatcher had faced down her Cabinet in the 1980s, there would be no U-turn on the horizon. 'This game was haemorrhaging, alarmingly,' he told *The Times*. 'We have an exhilarating opportunity to expand nationally and internationally. I was fed up with rugby league being treated quaintly, occasionally receiving the odd kind word.'

* * *

One of the teams that had been completely overlooked for the new Super League was the Keighley Cougars. Having secured promotion to the First Division, they had hoped to be included in any plans for a Murdoch league. But they weren't even asked to merge with a team. New rules around promotion and relegation would freeze them out of the top league for at least two years. And it wasn't long before Mick O'Neill was mobilising a resistance to the new competition.

O'Neill appealed to the people within the game to support his cause: 'Tonight the whole of rugby league should be Cougars fans. We are talking about principles, ethics and integrity – the same reasons why the founder members broke away from rugby union 100 years ago.'

There was genuine surprise that Keighley had been overlooked for the new competition. They had developed a model that had redefined community engagement and fan experience while doing all the things that Lindsay had always demanded of clubs. They had been 'enterprising' and 'ambitious' in their approach. But Lindsay was in no mood for a debate. 'Everyone has a soft spot for such an enterprising little club,' he stated in the *Keighley News*. 'But we are planning a Super League, not a Sympathy League.' But if the Cougars weren't going to be part of the Super League, then their ideas would be.

Bradford Northern were the biggest beneficiaries of the new streamlined competition. Not only would the summer conditions allow them to move on from the cold winter nights at Odsal, they were deemed to be big enough to survive without merging with another Yorkshire club. With opportunities now opening for them, the Bradford chairman Chris Caisley emerged as a media outrider for the new plans. 'It can only be the saviour of the game, opening the way to long-term expansion and a worldwide audience that will be drawn to rugby league.'

Caisley had initially been part of some preliminary discussions with Halifax and Huddersfield about a potential merger but the talks never really got anywhere. But one of the discussion points was about naming the club the West Yorkshire Bulls. By 1994, the Chicago Bulls and Michael Jordan had become one of the most successful sports brands in the world. Across the country, Chicago Bulls merchandise was being worn at the expense of English sports clubs. Caisley looked at what Keighley had done with the Cougars and took the Bulls idea to Bradford. 'The name "Northern" has too many connotations with the past and not enough with the future,' argued Caisley. 'Northern' conjured up images of Bradford's historic failings but 'by contrast the name "The Bulls" is synonymous with success', he told *The Guardian*.

By adopting the ideas of Cougarmania, Caisley was the quickest person to embrace the ideas of the new Super League. 'Bradford is a big cosmopolitan city. There is a big Asian community, which has not been introduced to rugby league at all.' He unveiled the blueprint for the new Bulls era that would see the Odsal ground that had been much maligned in the 1980s used to its advantage. 'Our aim is not just to offer spectators rugby league, but a full day's entertainment, particularly from next summer.' Caisley admitted that this was not aimed at those who had supported Northern through the 80s. 'Women and children need to feel welcomed – if they are turned on by the entertainment we provide then they all get the men to come as well.' As became the soundbite of the age for the modernisers, 'Unfortunately tradition doesn't pay the wages.'

* * *

In all the talk on the news channels, in the tabloids and the broadsheets about the Super League, there was one voice missing from those early discussions over a frantic weekend in April 1995. When people began to question why the supporters hadn't been consulted on the radical changes, Maurice Lindsay pointed out that the chairs of each club had ratified it. Those fans who protested in the first few days were portrayed as reactionaries who didn't understand the realities of the economic situation in front of them. But it wasn't long before John Drake and Tony Collins at the RLSA were fielding calls from angry spectators. 'The phones have been melting,' John Drake said. 'The club mergers are going to cause an absolute furore. They already are doing in towns like Featherstone and Castleford. There is going to be blood in the streets there.'

For Ian Clayton, the news that Featherstone Rovers would, within a month, no longer exist came as a body blow that evoked memories of the miners' strike a decade earlier. It reminded him of the day that the NCB announced the closure of the coal mines and how that had dramatically altered the economic lifeblood of his town. 'I've looked out and seen healthy, young ex-coal miners walking up and down in the middle of the day, waiting for the redundancy money to run out,' he wrote in *The Independent*. Without the pit, crime had risen and people had started 'stealing from their own'. He wondered what would happen to the people if they lost their rugby league club too.

Few people celebrated the arrival of Calder and the Murdoch millions in the pubs and clubs of West Yorkshire. In the Jubilee and the Traveller's Rest, fans reflected on all the changes that had occurred in Thatcher's Britain. In 1979 the miners in Featherstone and Castleford had been the most powerful group of workers in the country, able to bring down governments and strike fear into any Prime Minister. Fifteen years on and everything had changed. Behind the bar of the Traveller's Rest was the landlord Tommy Smales, a veteran Great Britain captain in the 1960s. He told the *Yorkshire Evening Post* that Lindsay and Murdoch didn't understand the game. 'These folk have their club's name stamped through them like a stick of rock. It's not just a game, it's a way of life … the chairman and the directors haven't studied what's in people's hearts.'

A few years before the Super League plan was put together, the travel writer Geoffrey Moorhouse had sensed that something like this would happen. In the late 1980s he had feared that the game would be ripped away from its community and forced to merge with rugby union due to market forces. In his influential book *At the George*, Moorhouse explained why he did not believe rugby league needed to expand: 'League has my allegiance … because it is an expression of who I am and where I came from, the history of my people and our ancestral lands. It is the culture from which I spring.'

As the debate about the Super League moved from the boardrooms to the terraces, the struggle tapped into discussions about community. In the 1980s, Mrs Thatcher had been quoted as saying that there was 'no such thing as society'. But for people like Ian Clayton, rugby league was evidence that communities did exist. 'Rugby league fans feel part of their club, whether it be through baking buns for the players to eat after training, offering advice to stars in the chip shop on a Friday night or selling raffle tickets to keep a locally born lad at the club.' Writing in *The Independent*, Clayton emphasised how through a period of change it had remained the one constant for the people: 'If there's nothing else for us to brag about up here, we're still proud.' Another supporter saw it as another attack on their way of life: 'It is ten years since the miners' strike when they took away the pit and killed half the community. If they take away our club they are going to kill the community altogether.'

Simon Kelner was one of the few high-profile editors in the country that had some skin in the game. As assistant editor of *The Independent* he used his own experience as a Swinton fan to explain what differentiated rugby league from other business and industries. 'Globalism runs contrary to the spirit and traditions of rugby league,' he argued. 'Few people want to see their men take on Castleford, their deadly enemies from a few miles down the road. They don't want the clubs to join forces under an artificial banner to take on the world.' Super League had put growth and economics before people and place: 'Identity matters in this post-modern age, whether you live in Barnes or Batley.'

The question of identity and pride of place was something that drew in media attention to places that were thought to have been left behind by the changes of the decade. *Here and Now* was a BBC programme that tackled the major social issues facing Britain in its investigative magazine show. As the battle over Murdoch's league raged on, the team arrived in Featherstone to chronicle the discontent. 'This is a story about the soul of a community,' opened the presenter Juliet Morris. 'What was once a local sport for northern towns will now be beamed to a global audience.'

The programme focused on the role that rugby league played in people's lives. One Featherstone fan spoke about the delayed grief after the death of his father: 'I feel as though I'm losing the club now. And I'm gonna fight. I'm not gonna lose another good friend.' Another supporter talked about how at home she had a role as a mother and a wife but that rugby league was her expression of a different identity: 'Featherstone Rovers is my life. People can't understand what you feel about sport.'

The debate quickly turned in to one about 'the people' versus 'the elite'. Rugby league supporters questioned why they needed to break with local traditions in order to compete in the new global marketplace. One supporter said that his 20-year bond with the game had been broken, 'This sport always belonged to the working man. Now it belongs to the businessman.' And there was no more hated business figure than that of Lindsay: 'If Maurice Lindsay dared to show his face here he'd be lynched – except hanging would be too quick and not painful enough.'

In the battle between the new free market and the traditional rugby league communities, people like Ian Clayton believed that something fundamental would be lost: 'If RL was taken away from us we lose the pivot for all that is good in our towns. Crime would increase, I'm sure, because nobody'd have owt to do. RL gives you somewhere to channel your aggression.' To Clayton, it boiled down to a simple argument between two types of people. 'This game has existed for a hundred years by the generosity, kindness and honesty of good local people with a bit of business acumen.' But now it was to be taken over by the free marketeers. 'Suddenly you've got these so-called visionaries coming in, wanting to take RL into the next century, promote it on a global scale – without even letting us know what they're doing.'

Supporters made protest signs that said 'Bought and Sold for Murdoch's Gold'. The criticism was aimed at an elite group of people who didn't appear to understand the game at all: 'It's a bloody stupid idea. Perhaps if you're in some boardroom in Australia or Leeds it might seem like a good idea.' One fan, speaking at an anti-Calder meeting, said that rugby league is not 'a commodity to be bought and sold by billionaires'. The *Keighley News* dedicated a special front page to what it called the 'betrayal' of the town by Lindsay and Murdoch. Rallies were organised by supporters and meetings were held to begin a legal challenge. The club's community co-ordinator, Mary Calvert, called on every person in the room to use their individual skills to join the campaign. 'We'll frighten the hell out of him [Lindsay], he's underestimated the passion in this town and now we have to harness that passion to prove the commitment of the club, the town and the people.'

Despite the protests, the chairmen of Featherstone and Wakefield were adamant that the mergers would radically alter the fortunes of the areas. The Featherstone vice chairman, Trevor Morris, argued that it would give the club an opportunity to compete with clubs like Leeds and Wigan. The Wakefield chairman believed that over time the local pride and tribalism would disappear from the sport. 'The animosity between some of the fans of the different clubs will, I'm sure, vanish. The truth is, in the First World War, the Tommy Atkins sharing your trench was your friend, especially if he was from the next village or town.'

* * *

League had always prided itself in being a community game with links to the people on the terraces. For Maurice Lindsay, however, survival into the 21st century rested upon it becoming a commodity instead. He talked about how football fans like Alan Sugar and Jack Walker had invested millions into the Premier League and how the Super League could unleash similar opportunities. In the *Daily Telegraph*, Lindsay launched his strongest defence of the 'brave new world'. He claimed that it would encourage 'people of an entrepreneurial spirit to buy into clubs'. 'We have not expanded the game, because we have become regionalised in the north. We have 35 clubs in terrible little tiny areas all competing to get the same sponsors, the same people through the turnstiles, the same players.' 'Nostalgia,' he concluded, 'does not pay the bills.'

The announcements were made just as politicians were taking to the streets to campaign in the local elections. And the areas that were voting that month included Oldham, Salford, Wigan, St Helens, Bradford and Doncaster. MPs and campaign organisers soon found that the mergers were the only thing being raised on the doorstep. One Labour insider told the media that 'people are incensed that their cultural heritage is being sold behind their backs'. At the RL APPG, figures such as McCartney promised to use their resources and networks to fight the change and the group said the game risked becoming 'the first major spectator sport in Britain being sold lock, stock and barrel to a private media interest'.

MPs came out to say that they were astonished that such a critical and controversial decision should be taken in a private and confidential meeting without consultation with shareholders, supporters, players or other interested parties. David Hinchliffe had assumed that the mergers proposal had been a misunderstanding when a journalist informed him of the plans. And it wasn't long before the main political programmes picked up on the story. One morning, listeners of Radio 4 tuned in to the *Today Programme* to hear rugby league's 'betrayal' being discussed on their *Thought for the Day* segment. The journalist Paul Wilson joked in *The Observer* how 'if only rugby league had realised it had so many friends, there would have been no need to jump into bed with Rupert Murdoch'.

Because the Super League proposal had been put on the table with a few weeks to go in the 1994/95 season, the rest of the matches still had to be played. Where mergers had been proposed, the stadiums became a battleground for protest and remembrance. One supporter arrived at Castleford's ground with a wreath of flowers with a message that read 'In loving memory of a great club'. David Hinchliffe attended the final Wakefield match against Leeds and found a ground that was in complete shock. He thought about where his own father had taken him as a boy and wondered what he would make of it all. Hinchliffe had an image frozen in his memory of watching 'an old chap who had sold club programmes for many years quietly weeping on the edge of the field at the end of the match'.

Those expecting fierce confrontation were disappointed. Instead the clubs united in a peaceful protest. Banners in the crowd at the Featherstone and Castleford match acknowledged that they would never get on board with a merger. 'We'd rather be colder in winter than warmer at Calder' remarked one banner. Another read 'Fev is Fev, Cas is Cas. Stick your merger up your ass!' The London-based journalists who descended on the pit town for the first time since the end of the miners' strike found a fighting spirit that had been revived by the prodding of Murdoch and Lindsay. 'Easter uprising' was how Michael Crossley described it in the *Sunday Telegraph*. 'The resulting communal turmoil must surely match that at the time of the historic breakaway from rugby union 100 years ago.'

The scale of the protests and public anger forced Maurice Lindsay into the public eye to defend the mergers. Lindsay was not the sort of person who was going to let people attack him without fighting back. Lindsay resented the idea that he was doing this for money or to destroy the game. He continually reminded supporters that he had 'come from the terraces'. But at the same time he argued that the sport was operating in a deeply competitive marketplace. 'I never wanted to be an ambassador, a diplomat. I just wanted to be a fighter, for an underprivileged sport,' he told Michael Calvin in the *Daily Telegraph*. He reflected on how the game had been discriminated against by government and by rugby union in the 20th century. He talked about the 'bigotry' of the 'Oxbridge' elite who 'want to keep you down with a foot on your neck'.

But in the same sentence, he emphasised how little respect he had for the protestors and the people that attacked him. 'If I'm unpopular with intelligent, reflective, thoughtful people who understand sport as a business and want rugby league to thrive then yes I should worry.' But if he was unpopular with 'loud-mouthed ignorant oafs, why should I?' Lindsay told Simon Kelner, for his book *To Jerusalem and Back*, where he did not need to worry was about people who wrote 'Lindsay is a wanker' on signs where they couldn't spell Lindsay or wanker correctly.

In the battle to defeat the protestors, Lindsay attempted to frame the argument around two types of northern people. The best of the north was represented in the professionals such as Ellery Hanley and Martin Offiah who had carried the sport into the new era. The worst was the people he had felt he had been battling against for most of the decade, 'Those people who whinge represent the worst of northern life. They believe they have a divine right to be the best in the world, without taking their game to the world.' 'The onset of Super League will signal the end of rugby league as we know it,' he claimed. It would be the end of 'playing matches in six feet of mud and wretched weather in decrepit stadia, fighting an endless battle against rising odds just to stay alive'. He defended those who pushed on with mergers, 'It is not a betrayal, treachery or sell-out.' It was, instead, the chance to start again and 'begin with a blank sheet of paper': 'It is the chance of a lifetime.'

* * *

As the game descended on Wembley for the 1995 Challenge Cup Final there was a feeling that it really was the end of an era. It was the *Daily Telegraph* sports writer Paul Hayward who best captured the mood: 'What rose before us in the throbbing crater of Wembley Stadium was an apparition of all that is being left behind.' Within 12 months the game would play in a different season with 'different names, kits, competitions, rivalries, frontiers and a new annual cycle that will render the spring ritual of the Challenge Cup an anachronism'. Yet the final was no cause for celebration.

In the directors' box, Maurice Lindsay sat with Prince Philip who was the guest of honour, and the celebrities consisted of the usual rugby league folk. 'The Prince smiled hugely but not far away rugby league celebs Colin Welland, Michael Parkinson, Jimmy Tarbuck and Bernard Ingham all appeared rather glum,' reported one journalist. On Wembley Way, a group called Rugby League Fans United promised to co-ordinate the resistance to Murdoch's plans. 'Three weeks ago, the so-called representatives autocratically decided to sell our game to a multinational corporation, carve it up, lose several historical clubs in the process, and change from a winter sport to summer. The fans were not consulted.'

In later years Maurice Lindsay would recall how events at Wembley had had a dramatic impact on his thinking. He would often tell a story about how he was confronted by angry supporters who demanded that he stop and listen to them. Lindsay thrived on the heat of confrontation and debate and had been taking on supporters who challenged him in pubs and clubhouses for most of his career. This, however, was a different type of confrontation. As his Jaguar, number plate M1 RFL, exited the ground, a man jumped in front of it and started to shout abuse at him. The Castleford fan pointed at his young son and asked Lindsay, 'Why are you ruining his future?' Lindsay feared that the man would become violent and he only stopped after his wife intervened to pull him away. Lindsay said that it made him realise that he had not communicated his ideas effectively. In reality, there was a growing feeling that it was not delivering for Rupert Murdoch either.

Desperate to resolve the issue to win his battle with Kerry Packer in Australia, Lindsay put forward an alternative proposal that could be ratified much quicker. All of a sudden the grand plans for mergers were ditched, leaving just Paris and London as the expansion clubs. As quick as the initial Super League was announced, a revised format was put together. Yet despite his failure to deliver the mergers, Lindsay still believed the game had a strong hand to play. To ensure that Murdoch had his English Super League, Lindsay asked for another £10m to keep the Second Division clubs happy. And to the surprise of everybody they agreed. Rugby league now had an £87m deal with Sky Sports without the need to lose a single club. In a brief press statement, Lindsay said that he had 'removed the fans' fears over mergers and the loss of the game's traditions'.

The campaign of resistance that was mobilised by supporters over a few weeks in April 1995 was a rare defeat for people like Maurice Lindsay and Rupert Murdoch. The responses by people in post-industrial towns had taken everybody by surprise. The supporters that protested against the mergers wanted the game to succeed. But they wanted to do it on their own terms. For all the desire to expand the game and make it a national sport, they wanted to do it with the clubs that they already had. If Featherstone couldn't compete with Manchester United and Liverpool on their own terms, then what was the point of it all?

For supporters there was a belief that despite everything that happened to their industries and economies in the 1980s, they could one day be part of something again. Had they lost their rugby league identities then it might not happen at all. When Ian Clayton was invited on to the BBC to debate the mergers, he admitted that he dreamed that 'a woman would wake up in Toulouse one morning and turn round to her husband saying, "Do you fancy a weekend in Featherstone?"' Clayton had even printed T-shirts which emphasised the philosophy, urging people to 'Think Global – Act Local'. For everything that had been lost over the course of the Thatcher Years there remained a hope that through rugby league the wider community could thrive.

* * *

Unable to deliver on the mergers, Lindsay quickly reframed the new deal as one that would eventually bring the radical change he thought it required. Lindsay talked about opening new markets in Newcastle, Belfast and Birmingham. While the events of the previous few weeks had made him the most vilified man in the history of the game, he refused to back down. He blamed himself for not selling the mergers to the public. But he believed that he would be on the right side of history. When Simon Kelner interviewed him a few months later he found that he was still in a combative mood. He was quoting Benjamin Disraeli's rebuke: 'You are not listening to me. The day will come when you have to listen to me.'

As rugby league headed towards its 100th anniversary in 1995, it was clear that the game was on the verge of a new era. Britain too was changing and hurtling forward to the new millennium. On the evening of the 1995 Challenge Cup Final, as Wigan and Leeds battled it out in the last final of the winter era, Labour members were sat just a few miles away debating the future of Clause IV. In the build-up to the conference there had been much debate about what it meant for the party to symbolically ditch its commitment to nationalisation. Tony Blair had signalled to the voters that he was going to build on Thatcher's Britain as much as reverse it. 'She was a thoroughly determined person and that is an admirable quality,' said Blair. He told the *Sunday Times* that he believed 'Mrs Thatcher's emphasis on enterprise was right'. On the morning of the vote, Blair was profiled for the *Daily Mail* weekend magazine where he emphasised just how much he wanted to appeal to Conservative voters. The front cover simply read: 'What my Thatcherite father taught me about family values'.

The location for the debate was Central Hall in Westminster, where Clement Attlee had stood 50 years earlier and celebrated the victory that had set Britain on course for the building of the post-war world. In April 1995, Blair called it a 'day of destiny' for the party as they finally removed the clause that had committed them 'to secure for the workers by hand or by brain the full fruits of their industry'. In his speech he emphatically said that he was doing it all with the ambition of government in mind: 'I did not come into the Labour Party to join a pressure group. I didn't become leader of this party to lead a protest movement. Power without principle is barren, but principle without power is futile.'

Just as Lindsay had faced abuse in the streets leaving Wembley, Blair's press secretary Alastair Campbell was met by protesters who labelled him a 'butcher' and a 'traitor' for breaking with the party's traditions. Blair, by contrast, believed he was going to make New Labour the natural political party for people across the country. 'Today politics is moving to our ground. Across the nation, across class, across political boundaries, the Labour Party is once again able to represent all the British people,' Blair had said in his first conference speech. 'We are the mainstream voice in politics today.'

Like New Labour, rugby league had ambitions of entering the mainstream of British life by embracing the opportunities that the new millennium would provide. The ambition was to become as big as Premier League football, to finally cut across class, gender and the divides that had once held it back in a class-ridden nation. Lindsay believed that the sport was heading into a different stratosphere that would one day leave its opponents and its critics behind: 'Super League will represent a dramatic sea change in approach, a quantum leap in thinking. Life is changing. We have to change with it. You can't stop history developing.'

League now had the money and the profile to take its game out into the world. A sense of just how far the game had come in the Thatcher/Major years was seen in the way that the London media now took the sport incredibly seriously. In 1979, just a few weeks before Mrs Thatcher came to power, future Fulham director

Harold Genders had been dismayed by the lack of coverage of the Challenge Cup Final. Nobody in 1995 could accuse the press of ignoring what was happening anymore.

There was a long-standing tradition amongst the rugby league press pack that saw journalists finish their evening in the West End just in time to see the early additions of the newspapers arrive. Each year they would report back to supporters in the north that their 'grand day out' had been totally ignored by the rest of the media. The editor of the *Rugby Leaguer*, Steve Brady, found himself at a street vendor looking at front pages which focused on Blair's victory over Clause IV. 'Which one has got the best rugby league coverage?' he asked. 'Take your pick, mate!'

This year it was not just the sports pages that had covered Wigan's eighth Challenge Cup victory in a row. What caught Brady's eye was the lifestyle magazine *Night & Day* that came free with the *Mail on Sunday*. Each weekend the magazine featured profiles of celebrities that appealed to the people in middle England. To his surprise, Brady picked up a copy to find a picture of Ellery Hanley facing back at him.

And the cover didn't pose a question to its readers but a statement: 'GOOD CLEAN FAMILY FUN. Rugby League: the world game for the 21st Century.'

Acknowledgements

WRITING A book is supposed to be hard but the story of rugby league in Thatcher's Britain is so compelling that the pleasure of revisiting this era was all mine. However, no book could be written without the help of people who gave up their time to bring the story to life. The book wouldn't have happened at all had it not been for the advice of Alywn Turner in putting together a plan and helping to navigate the publishing industry. The same thanks go to Brian Carney for his encouragement in the early days to pick up the pen and keep writing.

Rugby league is a sport that prides itself on access and I appreciate the generosity of everyone who has advised me on research. Thanks to Shaun Edwards, Keith Bell, Jonathan Davies, Julia Lee, David Hinchliffe, Harry Edgar, Paul Mason, Francis Cottam, Marc Kirby, Chris Irvine, Phil Caplan, Mike Barnett and Andrew Varley. They were motivated only by helping the book come to fruition and none of them should be considered to condone the contents of the book or my interpretation of their words.

Alex Du Cross, Jonathan McCombie, Richard de la Riviere, James Oddy, Euan Suanders and Andrew Foster read various aspects of the book and/or offered invaluable advice on aspects from the narrative to the cover design. Phil Tinline's advice on the politics of the 1980s helped shape some of the broader themes.

I'd also like to thank all the staff at the libraries and archives of the People's History Museum, the UK National Archives and the British Library.

I'd like to thank John Barlow for his help with promotion and all the team at Pitch Publishing for bringing this book to fruition. A special extra thanks should also go to Harry Edgar, Keith Bell and Julia Lee for kindly providing photographs for the book.

Like anybody who has written a book, I owe everything to my family. Rhian encouraged me to write even when it was just an idea in my head and supported me even as our flat was taken over by a mountain of old rugby league magazines and newspapers. I cannot thank her enough. I'd also like to thank Jill and Robin for their support and advice throughout.

My biggest debt of all, however, is to my parents, Barry and Sue, who lived rugby league in Thatcher's Britain on the terraces. As children they taught me and my brother Chris about the importance of the game and the places in which this sport is played.

My Grandad's passing meant that I inherited a treasure trove of rugby league material that had been sitting away untouched, ready for use one day. The handwritten notes, the collection of newspaper cuttings and tickets were a window into another world. The dedication and passion to chronicle the game for future generations is what makes rugby league people unique. This book and this story is for them.

A note on sources

Hope and Glory could not have been written without the work of the people who engaged with the sport as it unfolded in the 1980s and 1990s. The work that Harry Edgar did through *Open Rugby* was essential to developing the 'battle of ideas' and his magazine forms the basis of the research for this book. Had he decided not to pack up his bags and move back to the north to pursue his aim of delivering a high-quality magazine then this book would look very different. Alongside this was the work of journalists such as Paul Fitzpatrick at *The Guardian*, Dave Hadfield at *The Independent* and Chris Irvine at *The Times*.

The *Rugby Leaguer*, which can be accessed through the British Library, remains an invaluable resource to anyone who wants to understand how the sport was changing on a week by week basis. Changes in technology have meant that historians can also access the archives of the *Daily Mirror*, *Daily Express*, *The Times*, *The Guardian* and *The Independent*, all of which covered rugby league in the period and form the basis of much of the work. I also accessed issues of *The Sun*, *The People* and the *Daily Star* through microfilm at the British Library.

In recent years historians have been able to benefit from the extensive work of history groups committed to archiving their clubs' programme collections online. The programme archives of the Oldham Heritage Trust and Featherstone Rovers helped me to understand not just what was happening at those clubs but around the game too. In terms of video content and archival match footage there are a range of sources that were available on the internet. The work of *RL Cares* in uploading their archive for public use cannot be praised highly enough. I am also indebted to all the people who have uploaded matches on YouTube for the benefit of historians.

This is not a book about what happened behind the scenes at the RFL, so the decision was taken not to access the committee minutes. There is, however, the Julia Lee archives which are essential to understanding how women were treated in the 1980s. Her work through the Life with the Lionesses is changing the way we understand this and was drawn on at various points. Another valuable resource to understand what was happening in the wider politics of the time is the Thatcher Foundation archive. This archive not only contains every speech, article or interview that Mrs Thatcher did, it also includes private papers and declassified documents which were drawn on at various points. For the Labour Party, the Neil Kinnock papers at Churchill College, Cambridge were accessed.

For those hoping to read further about this decade, there are a number of books that I drew on extensively and that tell the story of different aspects in a way that I could not. For the statistical analysis the Rothmans rugby league yearbooks are a bible for historians, followed closely by the more narrative-based 'Rugby league yearbooks'. Both differ in their style, but are integral to understanding where the sport was at the end of each season.

The work of Tony Collins has helped shaped many of the ideas in the book and his *Rugby League in Twentieth Century Britain* is the essential starting point for anyone who wants to understand the long-term social history of the sport. On the rise of the Australian influence within the game, Dave Hadfield's book *Playing Away* and Adrian McGregor's *Simply the Best* were the best-written rugby league books of the period. To understand what happened at Wigan, Paul Wilson's book *The Best Years of Our Lives* offers valuable insight into Maurice Lindsay's thinking at the beginning of the 1980s. To understand him in the 1990s, Simon Kelner's *To Jerusalem and Back* is a must-read, written just as the game was on the cusp of a bright new dawn.

Bibliography

Addison, Paul. *The Road to 1945: British Politics and the Second World War.* 2nd ed., London: Pimlico, 1994.

Beckett, Andrew. *Promised you a miracle: UK 80–82*. London: Allen Lane, 2015.

Belcher, Gary. *Kangaroo Confidential: The Inside Story of a Sensational Year.* Sydney: Pan Macmillan, 1991.

Black, Lawrence, and Pemberton, Hugh, and Thane, Pat (eds.). *Reassessing 1970s Britain*. Manchester: Manchester University Press, 2013.

Burn, Gordon. *Pocket Money.* London: Faber and Faber, 2008.

Butt, Ikram and Hannan, Tony. *Tries and Prejudice: The Autobiography of England's First Muslim Rugby International.* Leeds: Scratching Shed, 2009.

Campbell, Alastair and Hagerty, Bill (eds). *Alastair Campbell Diaries: Volume 1.* London: Hutchinson, 2010.

Carr, Richard. *Labour's Neighbours: reconceptualising the Ramsay Street boom and British politics from Thatcher to Blair.* Contemporary British History, 36:4, 516-551, 2022.

Clavane, Anthony. *A Yorkshire Tragedy; the Rise and Fall of a Sporting Powerhouse.* London: Riverun, 2017.

Clayton, Ian and Steele, Michael. *When Push Comes to Shove.* Pontefract: Yorkshire Arts Circus, 1993.

Clayton, Ian, and Daley, Ian, and Lewis, Brian (eds). *Merging on the Ridiculous*. Pontefract: Yorkshire Arts Circus, 1995.

Collins, Tony and Melling, Phil (eds). *The Glory of Their Times: Crossing the Colour Line in Rugby League*. Skipton: Vertical Editions, 2004.

Collins, Tony. *The Oval World: A Global History of Rugby*. London: Bloomsbury Sport, 2015.

Collins, Tony. *Rugby League in Twentieth-Century Britain: A Social and Cultural History*. London: Routledge, 2006.

Collins, Tony. *Rugby's Great Split*. London: Frank Cass, 1998.

Cornwell, John and Pepper, Richard. *Against the Odds: The First Decade of Sheffield Eagles RLFC, 1984–1994*. Sheffield Eagles RLFC: Sheffield, 1994.

Dennis, Norman, and Henriques, Fernando, and Slaughter, Cliff. *Coal Is Our Life*. London: Tavistock, 1969.

Dylan Jones. *The Eighties: One Day, One Decade*. London: Windmill, 2013.

Edgerton, David. *The Rise and Fall of the British Nation: A Twentieth Century History*. London: Allen Lane, 2018.

Flanagan, Mark. *The Inside Story of the 1982 Kangaroos, the Team that Changed Rugby Forever.* Chichester: Pitch Publishing, 2019.

French, Ray. *My Kind Of Rugby*. London: Faber, 1979.

Genders, Harold. *The Fulham Dream*. London: LLP, 2002.

Gormley, Joe. *Battered Cherub*. London: Hamish Hamilton, 1972.

Guscott, Jeremy. *Jeremy Guscott: the autobiography*. London: Headline, 2001.

Hadfield, Dave. *Playing Away*. London: Kingswood, 1992.

Handelman, Stephen. *Uncommon Kingdom: The British in the 1980s*. Canada: Collins, 1988.

Hannan, Tony. *Being Eddie Waring: The Life and Times of a Sporting Icon*. London: Mainstream Publishing, 2008.

Hanson, Neil. *Blood, Mud and Glory*. London: Pelham, 1991.

Hinchliffe, David. *Rugby's Class War*. London: LLP, 2000.

Hoggart, Richard. *The Uses of Literacy*. London: Chatto, 1957.

Huxley, John. *The Rugby League Challenge Cup*. London: Guinness, 1982.

Kelner, Simon. *To Jerusalem and Back*. London: Macmillan, 1996.

Lawrenson, David. *Offiah: A Blaze of Glory*. London: Methuen Publishing, 1993.

Loughlin, Paul. *From Glass to Grass*. London: London League Publications Ltd, 2011.

MacGregor, Adrian. *Simply the Best: The 1990 Kangaroos*. St Lucia: UQP, 1991.

McSmith, Andy. *No Such Thing as Society: A History of Britain in the 1980s*. London: Constable, 2010.

Moore, Charles. *Margaret Thatcher: The Authorized Biography, Volume One: Not For Turning*. London: Allen Lane, 2013.

Moorhouse, Geoffrey. *At the George*. London: Hodder, 1989.

Morley, Paul. *From Manchester with Love: The Life and Opinions of Tony Wilson*. London: Faber and Faber, 2021.

Murphy, Alex. *Saints Hit Double Top*. London: Eden Books, 1967.

Newlove, Paul. *At the Centre of Rugby League*. London: LPL, 2004.

Oddy, James. *True Professional: The Clive Sullivan Story*. Chichester: Pitch Publishing, 2017.

Orwell, George. *The Road to Wigan Pier*. Harmondsworth: Penguin, 1972.

Rickwood, J.R. *Cougarmania: The Untold Story of Rugby League's Greatest Innovators and How the Sport Nearly Destroyed Them*. Independently published, 2022.

Russell, Dave. *Looking North: Northern England and the National Imagination*. Manchester: Manchester University Press, 2004.

Sandbrook, Dominic. *State of Emergency: The Way We Were – Britain, 1970–1974*. Harmondsworth: Penguin, 2011.

Sandbrook, Dominic. *Seasons in the Sun: The Battle for Britain, 1974–1979*. Harmondsworth: Penguin, 2012.

Sandbrook, Dominic. *Who Dares Wins: Britain, 1979–1982*. London: Allen Lane, 2019.

Savage, Jon. *England's Dreaming*. London: Faber and Faber, 1991.

Seabrook, Jeremy. *What Went Wrong?* London: Gollancz, 1978.

Seymour-Ure, Colin. *The British Press and Broadcasting Since 1945*. Oxford: Blackwell, 1999.

Smith, David. *North and South: Britain's Economic, Social and Political Divide*. London: Penguin, 1989.

Spinoza, Andy. *Manchester Unspun: Pop, Property and Power in the Original Modern City*. Manchester: Manchester University Press, 2023.

Stephenson, Mike and Hemmings, Eddie. *It's Been Grand … Now It's Final*. London: Vertical, 2016.

Stewart, Graham. *Bang! A History of Britain in the 1980s*. London: Atlantic, 2013.

Storey, David. *This Sporting Life*. Harmondsworth: Penguin, 1960.

Theroux, Paul. *The Kingdom by the Sea: A Journey Around the Coast of Great Britain*. London: Penguin, 1983.

Turner, Alwyn. *Rejoice, Rejoice!: Britain in the 1980s*. London: Aurum, 2010.

Turner, Alwyn. *A Classless Society: Britain in the 1990s*. London: Aurum, 2013.

Vinen, Richard. *Thatcher's Britain: The Politics and Social Upheaval of the Thatcher Era*. London: Simon & Schuster, 2009.

Williams, Jack. *'Up and Under': Eddie Waring, Television and the Image of Rugby League. Sports Historian* 22, 115-137, 2009.

Wilson, Paul. *The Best Years of Our Lives: Wigan's Rise From Second Division to Super League.* Edinburgh: Mainstream, 1996.

Winstanley, Jack. *The Billy Boston Story.* Wigan: Independently published, 1963.

Young, Hugo. *One of Us: A Biography of Margaret Thatcher.* London: Macmillan, 1993.

Annuals, directories and yearbooks

John Player Rugby League Yearbooks

Rothmans Rugby League Yearbooks

Rugby League Review Yearbooks

Newspapers and magazines

Canberra Times

City Life

Courier Mail (Aus)

Daily Express

Daily Mail

Daily Mirror

Daily Telegraph

Evening Standard

Financial Times

Fulham Chronicle

Hull Daily Mail

Keighley News

Mail on Sunday

Manchester Evening News

Manchester Guardian

NME

Oldham Evening Chronicle
Pontefract and Castleford Express
Richmond Times
Rochdale Observer
St Helens Reporter
Sydney Morning Herald
Telegraph and Argus
Tribune
The Critic
The Independent
The Observer
The People
The Sun
The Sunday Times
The Times
Yorkshire Evening Post
Yorkshire Post

Rugby league newspapers and magazines

Big League
Rugby League Express
Rugby League Gazette
Rugby Leaguer
Rugby League Review
Rugby League Longreads
Open Rugby
The Greatest Game

Archive sources

Margaret Thatcher Papers, National Archive
Michael Foot Papers, People's History Museum

Neil Kinnock Papers, Cambridge University
Rugby Football League
Trove NSW

Programmes accessed via

Featherstone Rovers Trust
Oldham Heritage Trust

Index